MARITIME OPERATIONS LAW IN PRACTICE

The law that applies to maritime operations at sea is complex and comprises two distinct elements: treaty law (1982 United Nations Convention on the Law of the Sea), and the cases and incidents that occur at sea in both peacetime and during armed conflict which result in the creation of customary international law applicable to maritime operations at sea. Covering sovereignty and vessel status, jurisdiction and interdiction, freedom of navigation, maritime law enforcement and security, and the law of naval warfare, this edited collection brings together the most famous and influential cases and incidents at sea. Exploring the entire spectrum of maritime operations from 'high end' war-fighting to constabulary operations that are conducted by naval forces and maritime law enforcement agencies at sea to provide the factual circumstances of each case or incident; offering sophisticated analysis and insights into the case or incidents enduring importance, and their significance for the development of the law applicable to maritime operations; and offering a detailed account and evaluation of the most critical but rarely understood cases in maritime operations law, which encourages comparison between key cases, this book will be an essential reference for practitioners, scholars, teachers, and students of maritime operations law.

David Letts is the Director of the Centre for Military and Security Law, Australian National University College of Law, and an Associate Professor at the Australian National Centre for Ocean Resources and Security, University of Wollongong. He continues to serve in a part-time role in the Royal Australian Navy and has undertaken a wide range of operational, legal, and policy roles over more than four decades of navy service. David's academic research interests centre upon the application of legal regimes to military operations, and he has published academic articles and book chapters on topics including military justice, law of the sea, maritime security, the law of naval warfare, international humanitarian law, and the legal issues that arise on peacekeeping operations. He is the co-editor of *Law of the Sea in South East Asia* (Routledge 2020).

Rob McLaughlin is Professor of Law at the Australian National Centre for Ocean Resources and Security at the University of Wollongong, Senior Fellow at the Stockton Center for International Law at the U.S. Naval War College, and Honorary Professor at the Australian National University College of Law. He served for several decades in the Royal Australian Navy as a seaman and legal officer, and more recently worked in the UNODC Global Maritime Crime Programme. His research interests include the law of naval warfare, maritime security and law enforcement, the law of armed conflict, and military and security law. His most recent book is *Recognition of Belligerency and the Law of Armed Conflict* (Oxford 2020).

Routledge Research on the Law of the Sea Series

Available titles in this series include:

Freedoms of Navigation in the Asia-Pacific Region
Strategic, Political and Legal Factors
Sam Bateman

Maritime Claims and Boundary Delimitation
Tensions and Trends in the Eastern Mediterranean Sea
Nicholas A. Ioannides

Freedom of Navigation and the Law of the Sea
Warships, States and the Use of Force
Cameron Moore

Due Diligence and the High Seas
Tony Cabus

The Law of the Sea
Normative Context and Interactions with other Legal Regimes
Edited by Nele Matz-Lück, Øystein Jensen and Elise Johansen

Law of the Sea and Maritime Delimitation
State Practice and Case Law in Latin America and the Caribbean
Angel Horna

Maritime Operations Law in Practice
Key Cases and Incidents
Edited by David Letts and Rob McLaughlin

MARITIME OPERATIONS LAW IN PRACTICE

Key Cases and Incidents

Edited by David Letts and Rob McLaughlin

Routledge
Taylor & Francis Group
LONDON AND NEW YORK

Cover image: © Getty Images

First published 2023
by Routledge
4 Park Square, Milton Park, Abingdon, Oxon OX14 4RN

and by Routledge
605 Third Avenue, New York, NY 10158

Routledge is an imprint of the Taylor & Francis Group, an informa business

British Library Cataloguing-in-Publication Data
A catalogue record for this book is available from the British Library

ISBN: 978-1-032-30852-4 (hbk)
ISBN: 978-1-032-30854-8 (pbk)
ISBN: 978-1-003-30701-3 (ebk)

DOI: 10.4324/9781003307013

Typeset in Bembo
by Apex CoVantage, LLC

CONTENTS

CONTRIBUTORS

Phillip Drew is the Assistant Dean of Juris Doctor and Graduate Studies at Queen's University, and an Honorary Associate Professor at the Australian National University College of Law. A 30-year veteran of the Canadian Armed Forces, he was an intelligence officer and a military lawyer until his retirement in 2014. He earned his Dr Iuris degree from University Viadrina, and is the author of the book *The Law of Maritime Blockade* (OUP 2018). He has been a senior consultant to the United Nations Office on Drugs and Crime since 2014, working mainly in the field of maritime security law.

James Farrant is a UK Royal Navy barrister. He has served at sea all over the world, and has first-hand experience of maritime security and counter-piracy operations, non-combatant evacuation operations, and embargo enforcement operations. His areas of legal practice include public international law (with a focus on the law of the sea, the law of armed conflict, the law of neutrality, and human rights law) and English criminal and administrative law. He has published academic articles in *International Law Studies*, the *International Criminal Law Review*, and elsewhere, and he has taught military and naval students at the U.S. Naval War College, the UK Defence Academy and the Institute for International Humanitarian Law in Sanremo, Italy. Currently the UK Deputy Director Service Prosecutions, he has advocacy experience up to Appellate Court level and is an accredited advocacy trainer for new practitioners.

Martin Fink is a legal adviser in the Royal Netherlands Navy. He has held several postings as a legal adviser in the navy, ranging from the Netherlands Maritime Force (NLMARFOR), the Netherlands Defence Academy (NLDA), the administrative appeals branch, and the NATO Joint Force Command in Naples. Currently, he is Head of Legal Affairs of the Royal Netherlands Marechaussee (Dutch Constabulary Force). He has been on several operational tours, among them Iraq,

Afghanistan, Libya, South Sudan, and Israel and the Palestinian Territories. He received his LLM from the University of Leiden and holds a PhD from the University of Amsterdam. He is a senior researcher at the Amsterdam Centre of International Law at the University of Amsterdam.

Camille Goodman joined the Australian National Centre for Ocean Resources and Security (ANCORS) at the University of Wollongong as a Senior Lecturer in 2021. She is also a Visiting Fellow at the ANU College of Law, where she completed her PhD as a Sir Roland Wilson Foundation Scholar in 2019. From 2005–2020, Camille worked in the Commonwealth Attorney-General's Department, principally in the Office of International Law, providing legal and policy advice to the Australian government on a wide range of public international law issues, with a particular focus on law of the sea and international fisheries law. Her first monograph, *Coastal State Jurisdiction over Living Resources in the Exclusive Economic Zone*, was published by Oxford University Press in 2021.

Douglas Guilfoyle is Professor of International Law and Security at UNSW Canberra and an Australian Research Council Future Fellow (2022–2025). His principal areas of research are maritime security, the international law of the sea, international courts and tribunals, and the history of international law. He is the author of *Shipping Interdiction and the Law of the Sea* (CUP 2009) and *International Criminal Law* (OUP 2016). His research work is informed by his consultancy to various government and international organisations. He was previously a Professor of International Law at Monash University, and a Reader in International Law at University College London. During his graduate studies at the University of Cambridge, he was a Chevening and then a Gates scholar.

Steven Haines MA, PhD (Aberdeen), LLM (London), FRSA, FNI, is Professor of Public International Law in the University of Greenwich, where his research is focussed on international law relating to ocean governance and international security. He is a former Royal Navy officer with more than 30 years of service, which included both directing and carrying out maritime counter-terrorism and coastal security operations. He served later in the Ministry of Defence (Naval and Central Policy Staffs) from 1995–2003, during which he chaired the Editorial Board of the UK's official *Manual of the Law of Armed Conflict* (OUP 2004)

Stuart Kaye is Director and Professor of Law at the Australian National Centre for Ocean Resources and Security at the University of Wollongong. He holds degrees in arts and law from the University of Sydney, winning the Law Graduates' Association Medal, and a doctorate in law from Dalhousie University. He has written more than 120 articles, books and other publications, including *Australia's Maritime Boundaries* (CMP 2001), *The Torres Strait* (Martinus Nijhoff 1998), and *International Fisheries Management* (Kluwer Law 2001), and co-authoring *International Law: Cases and Material with Australian Perspectives* (3rd edition, CUP 2014).

David Letts is the Director of the Centre for Military and Security Law, Australian National University College of Law, and an Associate Professor at the Australian National Centre for Ocean Resources and Security, University of Wollongong. He continues to serve in a part-time role in the Royal Australian Navy and has undertaken a wide range of operational, legal, and policy roles over more than four decades of navy service. David's academic research interests centre upon the application of legal regimes to military operations, and he has published academic articles and book chapters on topics including military justice, law of the sea, maritime security, the law of naval warfare, international humanitarian law, and the legal issues that arise on peacekeeping operations. He is the co-editor of *Law of the Sea in South East Asia* (Routledge 2020).

Rob McLaughlin is Professor of Law at the Australian National Centre for Ocean Resources and Security at the University of Wollongong, Senior Fellow at the Stockton Center for International Law at the U.S. Naval War College, and Honorary Professor at the Australian National University College of Law. He served for several decades in the Royal Australian Navy as a seaman and legal officer, and more recently worked in the UNODC Global Maritime Crime Programme. His research interests include the law of naval warfare, maritime security and law enforcement, the law of armed conflict, and military and security law. His most recent book is *Recognition of Belligerency and the Law of Armed Conflict* (Oxford 2020).

Cameron Moore is the Deputy Head of the School of Law at the University of New England in Armidale, NSW. He is also an Honorary Principal Research Fellow at the Australian National Centre for Ocean Resources and Security (ANCORS) at the University of Wollongong and a visiting Associate Professor with the Centre for Military and Security Law and the Centre for Public and International Law at the Australian National University. His publications include the books *Freedom of Navigation and the Law of the Sea: Warships, States and the Use of Force* (Routledge 2021), *Crown and Sword: Executive Power and the Use of Force by the Australian Defence Force* (ANU Press 2017), and *ADF on the Beat: A Legal Analysis of Offshore Enforcement by the ADF* (University of Wollongong 2004), and other articles and chapters on the Australian Defence Force and maritime security. Between 1996 and 2003, Cameron was a Royal Australian Navy legal officer. Cameron is still an active Navy reservist, with the rank of Commander. He was also the Academic Master of Robb College at UNE in 2011 and 2012. He was made a Fellow of the Royal Geographical Society in 2015.

Tamsin Phillipa Paige is a Senior Lecturer at Deakin Law School, Melbourne, Australia, and periodically consults for the UN Office on Drugs and Crime in relation to Maritime Crime. Her work is interdisciplinary in nature, using qualitative sociological methods to analyse international law. She also does law and literature research using popular fiction to understand social perceptions of the law. Her work has examined (among other things) Somali piracy, UN Security Council decision making, and conflict based sexual violence. In a former life, she was a French trained, fine dining pâtissier.

Raul (Pete) Pedrozo (Captain, USN, Ret.) is the Howard S. Levie Chair on the Law of Armed Conflict and Professor of International Law, U.S. Naval War College, Stockton Center for International Law. Prior to assuming the Levie Chair, Capt. Pedrozo was the Principal Deputy Staff Judge Advocate, U.S. Indo-Pacific Command. Prior to his retirement from active duty after 34 years of service, he served in numerous positions advising senior military and civilian defense officials, including as Special Assistant to the Under Secretary of Defense for Policy and senior legal adviser to Commander, U.S. Pacific Command. He has lectured extensively at military and civilian academic institutions and participated in numerous multilateral and bilateral negotiations, including the International Maritime Organization (chairman of the IMO Working Group responsible for drafting the Guidelines for the Suppression of Illegal Transport of Migrants by Sea adopted by the IMO), Transnational Organized Crime Convention (lead U.S. negotiator for the maritime chapter to the Migrant Smuggling Protocol to the Convention), International Civil Aviation Organization, and US-PRC Military Maritime Consultative Agreement. Capt. Pedrozo has written extensively on maritime security and South China Sea issues and is a co-author of *International Maritime Security Law* (Brill/Martinus Nijhoff Publishers, 2013), *The Free Sea: The American Fight for Freedom of Navigation* (United States Naval Institute, 2018), and the forthcoming *Emerging Technology and the Law of the Sea* (Oxford University Press). He has an LLM (International & Comparative Law), Georgetown University Law Center and JD (Law), The Ohio State University College of Law.

FOREWORD

The variety of maritime operations defies any effort of subsuming them under an abstract all-encompassing definition. Such operations range from patrolling the seas to interference with foreign vessels, military manoeuvres, and full-scale war-fighting. Accordingly, the aims pursued by maritime operations vary considerably.

Maritime operations take place within a global common that is of importance for all states, including land-locked states. Any interference with foreign vessels has the potential of severely affecting the jurisdiction of the affected flag state, on sea trade, and on the freedom of navigation. Such interference may impede upon economic and security interests and, as a form of state practice, may be misinterpreted as precedence. It is, therefore, crucial that maritime operations are conducted in full compliance with international law.

However, the identification and correct application of the relevant rules of international law is met with various difficulties. First, there is no single all-embracing treaty. Second, treaty provisions may accord states certain rights, but they do not provide guidance as to how those rights may be enforced. Third, the interpretations of the said provisions are far from uniform. Fourth, some relevant treaties were adopted decades ago based on past technologies and may thus have to be adapted to contemporary capabilities. Fifth, maritime operations often take place in contested sea areas, which may add additional problems for the pursuit of legitimate interests at sea. Finally, in today's multipolar world, it is unlikely that states will display a general and uniform practice accompanied by *opinio juris* that could develop into new rules of customary international law filling existing gaps, or adding to legal clarity.

Despite those difficulties, there is a most helpful subsidiary source of international law – that is, case law – which operators, planners, political decision-makers, legal advisers, and academics cannot avoid consulting when it comes to the assessment of the legality of maritime operations. Unfortunately, the knowledge of many leading cases has almost vanished, or their legal relevance is no longer fully comprehended. Rob McLaughlin and David Letts, the editors and contributors to the present volume, are to be congratulated for their successful effort in inviting leading experts to report and comment on the most important cases. The readers are provided with masterly analyses of select cases that will enable them to understand the international legal framework applicable to the entire spectrum of maritime operations and of the continuing value of past and contemporary cases.

February 2022

Wolff Heintschel von Heinegg

Europa-Universität Viadrina, Germany

ACKNOWLEDGEMENTS

As practitioners, scholars, teachers, and students of maritime operations law, it is often the situation that reference to iconic incidents and cases leaves the reader or student with scant detail as to what actually occurred in each instance. This book thus began as a series of discussions amongst many of the contributors about producing a collaborative edition which brought together in one place some of the key incidents and cases that have helped to define the maritime operations law discipline. The aim of this book, consequently, is to provide a short, concise, and coherent set of case notes and studies of significant incidents in the development of this intensely practice-oriented body of law.

Upon taking up the coordination role for this endeavour in 2014, we have progressed with the speed of 1,000 nimble gazelles, or have at least attempted to. However, 'stuff' has occasionally gotten in the way, as it does, and although our collaborator/contributors have been responsive at every juncture, it has taken us until now to finalise this project. The responsibility for this glacial pace is entirely on us, and our first acknowledgement is to our very patient and tolerant contributors (one of whom progressed from lieutenant-commander to captain as he awaited publication of his chapters!) for their patience and forbearance as this volume took shape.

Second, we would like to thank our occasional research assistants who have, over the last few years, pitched in to assist us with proofing, formatting, and citation checking. Without your contribution, our delivery speed of the manuscript to the publisher would have fallen from roughly lightening to somewhere around ICC-ish pace.

Third, our colleague and friend Professor Wolff Heintschel von Heinegg agreed to write the Foreword for this book and we could not have asked a more widely respected authority on the topics covered in the book to undertake this task. We have both known Wolff for a long time, had the pleasure of working with him at different locations throughout the world, and are very grateful that he provided the Foreword for this book.

Next, we must acknowledge the guidance and assistance we have received from our Routledge editors, Siobhan and Sanjo, as the volume has taken shape: thank you.

We should also acknowledge the support for all of our academic work, over many years, which has been provided by the two academic institutions that we are both affiliated with. The Australian National University College of Law and the Australian National Centre for Ocean Resources and Security (ANCORS – University of Wollongong) have a long history of teaching and researching many different aspects of maritime operations law, and being affiliated with these two institutions has been a tremendous benefit for us.

Finally, we both owe a continuing debt of gratitude to our respective spouses, Shakira and Sally, and our families, who have put up with our absences and obsession with maritime operations law over many long years. We have occasionally had the pleasure of our spouses and families being able to accompany us on some of the research activities we have undertaken, but all too often, we have left them at home while we have individually and collaboratively travelled the world in search of research material.

We hope that this volume proves a useful addition to the academic literature, as well as being an enjoyable read for all of you.

Rob McLaughlin and David Letts
Canberra, February 2022

TREATIES, LAWS, AND CASES CITED

Treaties and international arrangements

Convention Regulating the Fisheries Outside Territorial Waters in the Ocean Surrounding the Faroe Islands and Iceland, signed at London on 24 June 1901 UKTS 005/1903: Cd 1530

Convention Relating to the Conversion of Merchant Ships into Warships (VII Convention) (1907) UKTS 11 (1910), Cd. 5115

Convention (VIII) Relative to the Laying of Automatic Submarine Contact Mines (VIII Convention) (1907) 36 Stat. 2332

Convention Relative to Certain Restrictions with Regard to the Exercise of the Right of Capture in Naval Warfare (XI Convention) (1907) 36 Stat. 2396

Convention Concerning the Rights and Duties of Neutral Powers in Case of Naval Warfare (XIII Convention) (1907) 36 Stat. 2415

Convention of Lausanne of July 24th 1923 Respecting Conditions of Residence and Business and Jurisdiction (1923) 28 LNTS 151

Hague Regulations on Aerial Warfare (1923) UK Misc. 14 (1924), Cmd. 2201

Convention between the United States of America and Great Britain to Aid in the Prevention of the Smuggling of Intoxicating Liquors into the United States (1924), signed at Washington 23 January 1924, 27 LNTS 182, US Treaty Series No. 685

International Convention for the Unification of Certain Rules Concerning the Immunity of State Owned Ships (1926) 176 LNTS 199

Convention on Maritime Neutrality, Havana, 20 February 1928, 135 LNTS 187

1936 London Procès-Verbal Relating to the Rules of Submarine Warfare Set Forth in Part IV of the Treaty of London of 22 April 1930 UKTS 29 (1936) Cmd 5302

Denmark-Finland-Iceland-Norway-Sweden Declaration Regarding Similar Rules of Neutrality (1938) 188 LNTS 293

Geneva Convention II for the Amelioration of the Condition of Wounded, Sick and Shipwrecked Members of Armed Forces at Sea (1949) 75 UNTS 85

Geneva Convention III relating to the Treatment of Prisoners of War (1949) 75 UNTS 135

European Convention for the Protection of Human Rights and Fundamental Freedoms (1950) 213 UNTS 221

Brussels International Convention for the Unification of Certain Rules Relating to Penal Jurisdiction in Matters of Collision and Other Incidents of Navigation (1952) 439 UNTS 233

Exchange of Notes amending the Convention between the United Kingdom and Denmark for regulating the fisheries outside territorial waters in the ocean surrounding the Faroe Islands of 24 June 1901, London, 23 July 1954 and 22 April 1955 UKTS 029/1955: Cmd 9452

Convention for the High Seas (1958) 450 UNTS 11

Convention on the Continental Shelf (1958) 499 UNTS 312

Convention on the Territorial Sea and Contiguous Zone (1958) 516 UNTS 206

Convention on Fishing and Conservation of the Living Resources of the High Seas (1958) 559 UNTS 286

Exchange of Notes modifying the Convention of June 24, 1901, as later amended, concerning the Regulation of Fishing around the Faroe Islands, Copenhagen 27 April 1959, UKTS 055/1959: Cmnd 776

Exchange of Notes constituting an agreement establishing a Commission of Enquiry to investigate certain incidents affecting the British trawler Red Crusader, London 15 November 1961, (1962) 420 UNTS 6041

International Covenant on Civil and Political Rights (ICCPR) 999 UNTS 171

Vienna Convention on the Law of Treaties (1969) 1155 UNTS 331

Hague Convention for the Suppression of the Unlawful Seizure of Aircraft (1970) 860 UNTS 105

Agreement Between the Government of The United States of America and the Government of The Union of Soviet Socialist Republics on the Prevention of Incidents On and Over the High Seas, 1972, 23 UST 1168

Protocol to the Agreement on the Prevention of Incidents On and Over the High Seas (1973) 24 UST 1063

Protocol Additional to the Geneva Conventions of 12 August 1949 and Relating to the Protection of Victims of International Armed Conflicts (Additional Protocol I) (1977) 1125 UNTS 3

Protocol Additional to the Geneva Conventions of 12 August 1949, and relating to the Protection of Victims of Non-International Armed Conflicts (Additional Protocol II) (1977) 1125 UNTS 609

United Nations Convention on the Law of the Sea (1982) 1833 UNTS 3

Convention for the Suppression of Unlawful Acts Against the Safety of Maritime Navigation and its Protocol for the Suppression of Unlawful Acts Against the Safety of Fixed Platforms Located on the Continental Shelf (1988/2005) 1678 UNTS 221

1988 United Nations Convention against Illicit Traffic in Narcotic Drugs and Psychotropic Substances 1582 UNTS 165

United States of America-Union of Soviet Socialist Republics: Joint Statement with attached Uniform Interpretation of Rules of International Law Governing Innocent Passage, done at Jackson Hole, Wyoming, 23 September 1989, 28 ILM 1444

Agreement between the Government of the United States of America and the Government of the Union of Soviet Socialist Republic on the Prevention of Dangerous Military Activities (1989), 28 ILM 977

Agreement relating to the Maritime Delimitation in the area between the United Kingdom and the Faroe Islands 21 July 1999, UKTS No. 76 (1999)

Underwater Cultural Heritage Convention (2001) 2562 UNTS 3

Agreement between the US and the Republic of Liberia concerning Cooperation to Suppress the Proliferation of Weapons of Mass Destruction, Their Delivery Systems, and Related Materials by Sea (2004)

Agreement between the US and the Republic of the Marshall Islands concerning Cooperation to Suppress the Proliferation of Weapons of Mass Destruction, Their Delivery Systems, and Related Materials by Sea (2004)

Protocol of 2005 to the Convention for the Suppression of Unlawful Acts Against the Safety of Maritime Navigation (2005)

International cases, inquiries, and reports

Costa Rica Packet award (UK v Netherlands) Stuyt (1897) No 188

Report of the Wreck Commissioner's Investigation into the Loss of Lusitania ('Wreck Commissioner's Investigation') 17 July 1915 (Lord Mersey, Wreck Commissioner)

Opinion in the Lusitania Cases, 1 November 1923, 7 RIAA 32

Maud Thompson de Gennes (United States) v Germany, 11 March 1925, 7 RIAA 166

Lotus Case (France v Turkey), Judgment (1927) Series A PCIJ Reports 10

S.S. "I'm Alone" Case (Canada/United States, 1935) 3 RIAA 1609

The Trial of German Major War Criminals: Doenitz, Proceedings of the International Military Tribunal sitting at Nuremberg, Germany, Part 22 (22 August 1946 to 1 October 1946) 508

Corfu Channel case (UK v Albania), Merits (Judgment of 9 April 1949) ICJ Reports 4

Report of 23 March 1962 of the Commission of Enquiry established by the Government of the United Kingdom of Great Britain and Northern Ireland and the Government of the Kingdom of Denmark on 15 November 1961, 29 RIAA 521

Barcelona Traction (Belgium v Spain) (1970) ICJ Reports 3

Fisheries Jurisdiction (U.K. v. Iceland), Merits (1974) ICJ Reports 3

Advisory Opinion on the Legality of the Threat or Use of Nuclear Weapons [1996] ICJ Reports 226

MV Saiga (No. 2) (Saint Vincent and the Grenadines v Guinea), Judgment (1999) ITLOS Case No. 2

Responsibility of States for Internationally Wrongful Acts 2001, General Assembly resolution 56/83 of 12 December 2001, and corrected by document A/56/49(Vol. I)/Corr.4.

Arrest Warrant of 11 April 2000 (Democratic Republic of the Congo v. Belgium), Judgment, (2002) ICJ Reports 3

Oil Platforms (Islamic Republic of Iran v United States of America), Judgment, (2003) ICJ Reports 161

Legal Consequences of the Construction of a Wall in the Occupied Territory, Advisory Opinion, (2004) ICJ Reports 136

Guyana v Suriname (2008) 47 ILM 166 at 231

Report of the international fact-finding mission to investigate violations of international law, including international humanitarian and human rights law, resulting from the Israeli attacks on the flotilla of ships carrying humanitarian assistance, Human Rights Council, 27 September 2010, UN Doc. A/HRC/15/21

The Public Commission to Examine the Maritime Incident of 31 May 2010, 'Report: Part One' (23 January 2011)

Report of the Secretary-General's Panel of Inquiry on the 31 May 2010 Flotilla Incident (September 2011) (Palmer Report)

Hirsi Jamaa and Others v Italy App no 27765/09 (ECtHR 23 February 2012)

The 'ARA Libertad' Case (Argentina v. Ghana), 15 December 2012 ITLOS, Case No. 20

Office of the Prosecutor (International Criminal Court), *Situation on Registered Vessels of Comoros, Greece and Cambodia: Article 53(1) Report*, 6 November 2014

The Arctic Sunrise Arbitration (Kingdom of the Netherlands and the Russian Federation), 14 August 2015 (PCA Case No. 2014–02)

M/V 'Norstar' (Panama v Italy) (Judgment) [2018–2019] ITLOS Rep 7

The 'Enrica Lexie' Incident (Italy v India) [2020] PCA Case 2015–28

National legislation

Australia

Maritime Powers Act (2013) (Commonwealth)

Denmark

Act No. 597 of 17 December 1976 on the Fishing Territory of the Kingdom of Denmark

Decree No.598 of 21 December 1976: the Fishing territory of the Faroe Islands

Ordinance No. 599 of 21 December 1976 on the Delimitation of the Territorial Sea around the Faroe Islands

Act No. 200 of 7 April 1999 on the delimitation of the territorial sea

Decree No.240 of 30 April 2002 on the Coming into Force of the Act on the Delimitation of the Territorial Sea for the Faroe Islands

Decree No. 241 of 30 April 2002 to Amend the Decree on the Fishing Territory of the Faroe Islands

Decree of 17 September 2009 amending the Decree on the fishing territory off the Faroe Islands

Guinea

Law L/94/007

The Customs Code of Guinea

Sweden

Act Concerning the Territorial Waters of Sweden of 3 June 1966 (with amendments No 959 enacted on 18 December 1978, and No 1140, on 20 December 1979).

Turkey

Law No. 765 of March 1st, 1926 (Officia1 Gazette No. 320 of March 13th, 1926)

United Kingdom

Aviation and Maritime Security Act 1990

Merchant Shipping and Maritime Security Act 1997

United States

U.S. Presidential Proclamation No. 2667 of 28 September 1945, Policy of the United States with Respect to the Natural Resources of the Subsoil and Sea Bed of Continental Shelf

U.S. Presidential Proclamation No. 2668 of 28 September 1945, Policy of the United States with Respect to Coastal Fisheries in certain areas of the High Seas

U.S. Code Title 18 section 371

U.S. Code Title 18 section 1651

U.S. Code Title 18 section 2280

USSR

Law of the Union of Soviet Socialist Republics on the State frontier of the USSR (24 November 1982)

Rules for Navigation and Sojourn of Foreign Warships in the Territorial Waters and Internal Waters and Ports of the USSR, ratified by the Council of Ministers Decree No. 384 of 25 April 1983

The Instruction for the Navigation of Vessels in Coastal Waters within Artillery Range of Shore Batteries in Peacetime (5 July 1924)

National cases

Belgium

Ekbatana/West-Hinder, Clunet (1914) 1327
Mohamed Abdi Hassan [2017] Hof van Cassatie van België P. 17.0727.N

France

Ortigia/Oncle-Joseph, Clunet (1885) 286

Italy

Ortigia/Oncle-Joseph, Clunet (1885) 287

Kenya

Hassan M Ahmed v Republic [2009] eKLR (High Court of Kenya at Mombassa)

Seychelles

Shire v R [2015] SCCA 25

United Kingdom

The Felicity (1819) 2 Dodson 386
R v Keyn (1876) 2 Ex D 63
R v Nillins (1884) 53 LJ 157
R v Godfrey (1923) 1 KB 24
Pierce v Bemis; The Lusitania [1986] QB 384
Al Jedda v United Kingdom (2011) 53 BHRR 23
Hassan v United Kingdom (2014) 38 BHRC 358
Al-Waheed v Ministry of Defence [2017] UKSC 2

United States

The Schooner Exchange v McFadden 11 U.S. 7 Cranch 116 (1812)
United States v Smith, 5 Wheat. 153, 18 US 153, 161, 5 L.Ed. 57 (1820)
Ker v Illinios, 119 U.S. 436, 7 S.Ct. 225, 30 L.Ed. 421 (1886)
The Lusitania 251 F 715 (SDNY 1918)
Cunard Steamship Co v Mellon (1923) 262 US 100
Cook v United States (1933) 288 US 102
Frisbie v Collins, 342 U.S. 519, 522, 72 S.Ct. 509, 96 L.Ed. 541 (1952)
Bemis v Lusitania (1998) 523 US 1093, 140 L Ed 2d 791
Hamdi v. Rumsfeld, 542 U.S. 507 (2004)

Hamdan v Rumsfeld, 548 US 557, 630 (2006)
Boumediene v Bush 553 US 723 (2008)
Shi v United States, 129 S Ct 324 (2008), 6 October 2008
United States v Lei Shi, 525 F.3d 709 (9th Cir. 2008)
United States v Muse, US District Court for the Southern District of New York (Manhattan) (2011) Case 1:09-cr-00512-LAP
United States of America v Ali Mohamed Ali, also known as Ahmed Ali Adan, also known as Ismail Ali [2013] Unreported
United States of America v Ali Mohamed Ali – Memorandum Opinion [2013] Unreported
United States of America v Mohammad Saaili Shibin, a/k/a Khalif Ahmed Shibin, a/k/a Mohammad Ali, a/k/a Ali Jama [2013] Unreported
Kiobel v. Royal Dutch Petroleum Co. (17 April 2013) 569 US (USSC, No. 10–1491)

1

INTRODUCTION

David Letts and Rob McLaughlin

I. Introduction

The law that applies to maritime operations at sea is of diverse provenance, but can be conveniently understood – as with most international law matters – by reference to the two distinct (albeit interlinked) rule-sets that constitute its main corpus. The first body of relevant law is, of course, treaty law with application to maritime concerns, made up of a number of instruments that deal with both general norms as well as discrete components of the law that applies at sea. The most prominent among these instruments is the 1982 UN Convention on the Law of the Sea,[1] which has been described by Ambassador Tommy Koh, President of the Third UN Conference on the Law of the Sea, as a 'constitution for the oceans'.[2] Key aspects of this fundamental component of maritime operations law have been the subject of extensive analysis and incorporation into national doctrines over many years.[3]

1 1833 UNTS 3 (hereafter LOSC). Citations for the 1982 UN Convention on the Law of the Sea vary, with some authors in this volume preferring to use 1833 UNTS 397, the page number where the English language version of the Convention commences in UNTS Volume 1833. Similarly, some authors refer to the Convention as 'LOSC' while others prefer 'UNCLOS' as a matter of personal choice.

2 The UN Division for Ocean Affairs and the Law of the Sea's website contains numerous links to key law of the sea documents including 'A Constitution for the Oceans' which is a document that is 'Adapted from statements of the President on 6 and 11 December 1982 at the final session of the Conference at Montego Bay' <www.un.org/depts/los/convention_agreements/texts/koh_english.pdf>.

3 Including, indicatively: Canada, Law of Armed Conflict at the Operational and Tactical Levels (2001), ch8; Denmark, Military Manual on International Law Relevant to Danish Armed Forces in International Operations (2016 en edn), ch14; Germany, Commander's Handbook Legal Bases for the Operations of Naval Forces (2002); New Zealand, Manual of Armed Forces Law: Vol 4 – Law of Armed Conflict (2017), ch 10; Norway, Manual of the Law of Armed Conflict (2013 en

DOI: 10.4324/9781003307013-1

A second set of treaties relevant to maritime operations are those that concern the conduct of armed conflict at sea.[4] These rule-sets apply, of course, only during situations of armed conflict, but in the maritime domain, their reach and scope across both 'the commons' and neutrals is extensive. A third set of important maritime operations law treaties are those that define and confer powers in respect of specific maritime law enforcement and security matters. Examples of these treaties include the 'SUA Convention'[5] and the 1988 Vienna Convention.[6]

The second key body of rules relevant to maritime operations law is customary international law (CIL).[7] Indeed, as has been noted of (for example) the law applicable to armed conflict at sea, this body of relevant international law

> is to be found mainly in rules of customary law derived from state practice. It has not been codified or developed in treaty form to anything like the same extent as the law of armed conflict on land, although there are various treaties, mostly dating from the early twentieth century, which may continue to be of some importance.[8]

---

edn), ch 10; UK, Manual on the Law of Armed Conflict (2004), ch 13; US, Naval Commander's Handbook on the Law of Naval Operations (2017); a range of relevant national manuals and doctrine publications is available on the U.S. Naval War College's 'Stockton Portal' <https://usnwc.libguides.com/c.php?g=86619&p=557511>. In relation to analysis and commentary, see indicatively: D.P. O'Connell, *The Influence of Law on Sea Power* (Manchester University Press, 1975); Rob McLaughlin, *United Nations Naval Peace Operations in the Territorial Sea* (Brill, 2009); Douglas Guilfoyle, *Shipping Interdiction and the Law of the Sea* (CUP, 2009); Donald Rothwell and Tim Stephens, *The International Law of the Sea* (Hart, 2010), chs 10, 12, 17; Natalie Klein, *Maritime Security and the Law of the Sea* (OUP, 2011); James Kraska and Raul Pedrozo, *Maritime Security Law* (Martinus Nijhof, 2013); Efthymios Papastravridis, *The Interception of Vessels on the High Seas* (Hart, 2014); Martin Fink, *Maritime Interception and the Law of Naval Operations* (Springer, 2018); Cameron Moore, *Freedom of Navigation and the Law of the Sea* (Routledge, 2021); and the extensive writings of, amongst others, Wolff Heintschel von Heinegg, and many of the chapter authors in this volume.

4 In particular, the 1907 Hague Conventions VI-XIII, 1949 Geneva Convention II for the Amelioration of the Condition of Wounded, Sick and Shipwrecked Members of Armed Forces at Sea, and the ICRC Commentary on 1949 Geneva Convention II (2017). On commentary and distillation, see indicatively: Louise Doswald-Beck (ed), *San Remo Manual on International Law Applicable to Armed Conflicts at Sea* (CUP/IIHL, 1995); George Politakis, *Modern Aspects of the Laws of Naval Warfare and Maritime Neutrality* (Kegan Paul, 1998); Phillip Drew, *The Law of Maritime Blockade* (OUP, 2017); Dale Stephens and Matthew Stubbs (eds), *The Law of Naval Warfare* (LexisNexis, 2019).

5 This convention comprises the 1988 Convention for the Suppression of Unlawful Acts Against the Safety of Maritime Navigation and its Protocol for the Suppression of Unlawful Acts Against the Safety of Fixed Platforms Located on the Continental Shelf 1678 UNTS 221, and are together commonly referred to as the 'SUA Convention'.

6 1988 United Nations Convention against Illicit Traffic in Narcotic Drugs and Psychotropic Substances 1582 UNTS 165.

7 ICJ Statute Article 38 (1). See, inter alia, UNODC, *Maritime Crime: A Manual for Criminal Justice Practitioners* (Third edn, 2020), section 1.2. <www.unodc.org/documents/Maritime_crime/GMCP_Maritime_3rd_edition_Ebook.pdf>.

8 UK, Manual of the Law of Armed Conflict, above n 3, para 13.2.

Within the discipline of maritime operations law, this highly diverse body of applicable CIL includes a wide range of non-treaty level instruments. Examples include the 1945 proclamations by U.S. President Harry S. Truman relating to the continental shelf and to fisheries[9] (which had significant influence on the 1958 Geneva Conventions and the 1982 LOSC), and general rule-sets applied at sea as equally as ashore (such as the rules on state responsibility[10]). However, these sources provide only part of the maritime operations CIL narrative; equally important as a source of interpretive and contextual guidance are those cases and incidents that tend to be analysed, cited, and compared as indicia of the practice of maritime operations law.

A. Why these cases and incidents matter

As previously noted, the law applicable to maritime operations references a wide range of orthodox and readily available CIL sources, such as proclamations and institutional declarations, as well as reflective and authoritative expert rule distillations. Nevertheless, the law applicable to maritime operations is often invisible in execution to those not engaged directly in conducting, advising upon, observing, or researching such operations. Further, this body of law is often considered to be laggard in responding to advances in technology and operational practice. These and other factors have contributed to the law sometimes being considered somewhat opaque.[11] In part, this is precisely because an important component of maritime operations law is comprised of cases and incidents, such as those discussed in this book, that require some specialised contextual and background knowledge in order for their legal implications to be fully appreciated. The importance and influence of cases and incidents that occur at sea – both in peacetime, and during armed conflict – and which exert a fundamental influence over state practice at sea, is therefore perhaps especially notable; some key examples are the rules around best practice at sea when conducting hot pursuit[12] and the evolution of Cold War incidents at sea management arrangements.[13] Many of these cases and incidents have ultimately resulted in the creation of customary international law applicable

9 US Presidential Proclamation No. 2667 of 28 September 1945, Policy of the United States with Respect to the Natural Resources of the Subsoil and Sea Bed of Continental Shelf <www.gc.noaa.gov/documents/gcil_proc_2667.pdf>; US Presidential Proclamation No. 2668 of 28 September 1945, Policy of the United States with Respect to Coastal Fisheries in certain areas of the High Seas <www.archives.gov/federal-register/codification/proclamations/02668.html>.

10 Responsibility of States for Internationally Wrongful Acts 2001, General Assembly resolution 56/83 of 12 December 2001, and corrected by document A/56/49(Vol. I)/Corr.4. <https://legal.un.org/ilc/texts/instruments/english/draft_articles/9_6_2001.pdf>.

11 O'Connell, *The Influence of Law on Sea Power*, above n 3, xiii, 16; Politakis, *Modern Aspects of the Laws of Naval Warfare and Maritime Neutrality*, above n 4, 23, 639.

12 Chapter 9, Chapter 10, Chapter 11; see, inter alia, Rob McLaughlin, 'Authorizations for maritime law enforcement operations' (2016) 98:2 *International Review of the Red Cross* 465, 469–470.

13 Chapter 8; see inter alia, James Doyle, 'International Law and Naval Operations' (1998) 72 *International Law Studies* 17–20.

to maritime operations at sea (such as, in some respects, the *Lotus* case[14]). Others have played a significant role in the development of subsequent treaty law (such as the *Achille Lauro* hijacking and the *So San* incident,[15] which played roles in the development of the 1988 SUA Convention[16] and the two 2005 SUA Protocols,[17] respectively). Another set of cases and incidents have served more to illustrate the application of customary or treaty rules, rather than to establish these rules (such as the *Altmark* incident in respect of maritime neutrality,[18] and the 'Whiskey on the Rocks' incident in respect of submerged submarines detected in the territorial sea[19]). Yet, while understanding and contextualising such cases and incidents is thus essential to the practice of maritime operations law, integrated analysis of this component of the discipline's source material has on the whole been much less extensive than parallel analyses of both the applicable treaty law and general CIL rule-sets. Indeed, locating accurate, concise, and easily accessible distillations and analyses of these cases and incidents has often proved both time consuming and challenging.

In partial response to this shortfall in the academic literature, this edited collection brings together – for the first time in a single publication – a convenient and concise set of assessments concerning some of the more famous and influential maritime operations law cases and incidents. Noting both the scope and inter-connectedness of treaty and customary international law relevant to maritime operations across the passage and presence, enforcement, and armed conflict contexts, the cases and incidents collated in this book therefore cover the full spectrum of maritime operations: from 'high end' war-fighting to constabulary and presence operations conducted by naval forces and maritime law enforcement agencies at sea. This naturally leads to the question of why these cases and incidents have been chosen and not some others. In any 'anthology' or 'cases and materials' volume, this is an important point – and is to some extent a 'six of one, half a dozen of the other' issue; nevertheless, it is important to explain the approach adopted.

B. The selection of cases and incidents for this book: what was included and what was not

When first developing the idea of this book, the editors gave the selected authors significant leeway in suggesting the cases they thought, from their experience, to

14 Chapter 2.

15 Chapter 4 and Chapter 5; see inter alia, Rob McLaughlin, '"Terrorism" as a Central Theme in the Evolution of Maritime Operations Law Since 11 September 2001' (2011) 14 *Yearbook of International Humanitarian Law* 391.

16 Above, n 5

17 IMO Doc. LEG/CONF. 15/21, 1 November 2005 and IMO Doc. LEG/CONF. 15/21, 1 November 2005

18 Chapter 15.

19 Chapter 12.

be most relevant or representative for an initial volume of this type, and the book was constructed around these individual and collective decisions. This said, it must nevertheless be acknowledged that there are many other cases and incidents that could equally have been included. For example, the *Corfu Channel* case[20] and *Oil Platforms* case[21] are as important to understanding the seams in maritime operations law as the *So San* incident[22]; the *USNS Impeccable*[23] and the *USS Pueblo*[24] incidents are rightly as studied and analysed as the Black Sea bumping incident;[25] and *The Schooner Exchange v McFadden*[26] is as fundamental to understanding sovereign immunity as is the *ARA Libertad* case.[27] Additionally, one example of a 'missing' issue in this volume is maritime operations and the application of environmental law at sea – potentially represented by, for example, the *Torrey Canyon* incident and its consequences and legacies.[28] These inclusions and exclusions are simply editorial choices, not comments upon the relative importance or otherwise of one case or incident in relation to others; indeed, we hope to address many of these 'missing' cases and issues in a follow-on volume (or volumes).

II. The structure of this book

In order to achieve the aim envisaged by the editors, an international group of subject matter expert scholars and practitioners have each provided one or more case study chapters. Each chapter employs a template structure in order to make the case studies readily comparable. To this end, each chapter follows a roughly similar format, beginning with the necessary background to the case or incident, what happened during the incident, and – where relevant – a note on the legal or inquiry process(es) adopted in any contemporaneous assessment of the incident. This is followed by a concise distillation of the key maritime operations law–related outcomes and issues illustrated by the incident or case. Each chapter then concludes with a short assessment as to whether, and how or why, that case or incident is of enduring significance for the practice and analysis of maritime operations law.

20 *Corfu Channel case (UK v Albania)*, Judgment of 09 April 1949 (1949) ICJ Reps 4.
21 *Oil Platforms (Islamic Republic of Iran v United States of America)*, Judgment of 06 November 2003, (2003) ICJ Reps 161.
22 Chapter 5.
23 See, e.g., Raul Pedrozo, 'Close Encounters at Sea: The USNS Impeccable Incident' (2009) 62:3 *Naval War College Review* 101.
24 See, for example, George Aldrich, 'Questions of International Law Raised by the Seizure of the U.S.S. *Pueblo*' (1969) 63 *Proceedings of the American Society of International Law at its Annual Meeting* 1.
25 Chapter 8.
26 11 U.S. 7 Cranch 116 (1812) < https://supreme.justia.com/cases/federal/us/11/116/>.
27 Chapter 3.
28 See, e.g., the entry by Julia Pfeil, 'The Torrey Canyon', in *Max Planck Encyclopedia of Public International Law* (MPEPIL).

A. A brief outline of the chapters

Following this introductory chapter, Part I of the book deals with the fundamental issues of sovereignty over vessels and vessel status. Commencing this analysis is Chapter 2, by Camille Goodman, which reviews the iconic *Lotus* case – an essential (and often misunderstood) foundational case on jurisdiction in international law, and in relation to vessels, which had significantly wider implications for international law than for just maritime operations law. With this general baseline explored, Chapter 3 by Martin Fink examines the narrower issue of sovereign immunity of warships through an analysis of the *ARA Libertad* case – a significant International Tribunal for the Law of the Sea decision dealing with the definition of 'warship' and the application of associated sovereign immunity within third state internal waters and territorial seas.

Part II of the book seeks to provide a more specialised assessment of issues of jurisdiction in the context of maritime interdiction operations. Chapter 4 concerns the *MS Achille Lauro* hijacking incident, analysed by Steven Haines. The *Achille Lauro* hijacking had significant implications for maritime operations law in relation to dealing with instances of terrorism at sea and – separately – the inapplicability of the international law offence of piracy in certain circumstances; it subsequently contributed to the impetus for, and negotiation of, the 1988 Suppression of Unlawful Activities at Sea Convention. Chapter 5, by Douglas Guilfoyle, then brings this interdiction jurisdiction narrative into the post-11 September 2001 milieu, with an assessment of the *So San* incident. This incident clearly highlighted perceived gaps in – but also the orthodox operation of – the scheme of flag state primacy in respect of jurisdiction over weapons of mass destruction at sea, and was a foundational component in the development of the Proliferation Security Initiative. Further, just as the *Achille Lauro* incident played an important role in contextualising and shaping the subsequent 1988 SUA Convention, the *So San* incident's operational exposure of the edges of enforcement jurisdictions available in maritime interdiction situations similarly cast a shadow across the negotiations for the 2005 Protocols to the SUA Convention.

Chapters 6–7 then turn to the domestic implementation of certain maritime operations law jurisdictions, and subsequent legal processes, in relation to interdiction operations. Chapter 6, by David Letts, deals with the case of *United States of America v Lei Shi*. Quite apart from being an important U.S. case on the application of the 'prosecute or extradite' provisions of the 1988 SUA Convention, *US v Lei Shi* is also illustrative of the domestic implementation requirements presaged by these obligations, as well as the application by a national court, and operationalisation by a maritime law enforcement agency, of this specific jurisdictional grant. In Chapter 7, Tamsin Phillipa Paige and Rob McLaughlin assess the implications of the U.S. piracy-focussed *Ali* and *Shibin* cases. These cases were selected because although there has been much recent analysis of (mostly Somali) piracy cases, these have often focussed upon the 'on-water' aspects of the offence. The *Ali* and *Shibin* cases, by contrast, are significant because they deal with the much less analysed issue of LOSC Article 101(c) facilitation of piracy – an offence-set that is often required to focus upon 'on-shore' aspects of piracy. Because of this, the issue of jurisdictional boundaries is perhaps more sharply presented by the *Ali* and *Shibin* cases than in the wider array of recent 'on-water' focussed piracy prosecutions that have manifested over the last two decades.

In Part III, the book turns to issues of use of force in respect of freedom of navigation, and in relation to maritime law enforcement and maritime security powers. The Black Sea bumping incident, analysed in Chapter 8 by Raul (Pete) Pedrozo, is an iconic incident concerning U.S. and USSR differences in interpretation and application of the territorial sea and warship innocent passage regimes. Amongst its many antecedents is the Jackson Hole Declaration of 1989,[29] which asserted a jointly agreed U.S.–USSR approach to interpreting a range of law of the sea obligations and authorisations. Following this, in Chapters 9–11, the book engages with the iconic 'triptych' of cases that trace the evolution of maritime law enforcement appreciations of hot pursuit and use of force. The first of this series is the *I'm Alone*, explored by Stuart Kaye in Chapter 9. This case is one of the more widely referenced cases in maritime operations law, especially in relation to rules regarding the use of force in hot pursuit. The second in this often-cited 'trinity' of foundational cases on use of force in hot pursuit and maritime law enforcement is the *Red Crusader*, analysed in Chapter 10 by Rob McLaughlin. This case study is informative in that where the *I'm Alone* case might be said to represent the 'right of arc' in terms of an appreciation of maritime law enforcement powers, the *Red Crusader* incident in many respects reflects a more restrictive 'left of arc', evidencing both continuities and discontinuities with *I'm Alone*. The third of the 'trinity' – analysed in Chapter 11 by Phillip Drew – is the seminal International Tribunal for the Law of the Sea (ITLOS) case of *MV Saiga (No. 2)*. This case significantly updated (and, in some respects, diverged from) the findings in the earlier two cases and is – in many ways – the case study that most accurately elaborates modern maritime law enforcement best practice in respect to hot pursuit. Finally, in Chapter 12, Cameron Moore examines the 'Whiskey on the Rocks', a fascinating Cold War incident. Highlighting the legal issues associated with dived submarines inside foreign territorial seas and internal waters, sovereign immunity, and the use of force against submerged contacts, this incident is as relevant to informing the practice of maritime operations law today as it was at the height of the Cold War.

Finally, in Part IV, the book examines a series of important or representative law of naval warfare cases and incidents. The first, in Chapter 13, is the sinking of *RMS Lusitania*. This is, as Cameron Moore observes, an intensely significant and still relevant incident from the First World War that invoked issues of targeting and neutrality under the law of naval warfare. Following this, in Chapters 14–15, James Farrant examines two interlinked incidents from the Second World War. The first is the consequences of the German pocket battleship *Admiral Graf Spee*'s stay

29 14 LOSB 13

in (neutral) Montevideo harbour after the Battle of the River Plate. This famous incident raised important issues as to regulating the presence of – and limitations on – belligerent warships in neutral ports, and the internment of belligerent crews by neutral powers. Similarly, the *Altmark* incident, which James Farrant assesses in Chapter 15, provides an important case study regarding legal characterisations of 'un-neutral service' in relation to British operations against a German prisoner-of-war holding ship in Norwegian internal waters and territorial sea. Coming forward to the 1982 Falklands/Malvinas War, in Chapter 16, David Letts then explores the sinking of the Argentine cruiser *ARA General Belgrano* by *HMS Conqueror*. This was an incident of almost unparalleled political significance during that war, but it is also of significance to our understanding of the application of the law of naval warfare in terms of the legal implications and operation of exclusion zones, and targeting, during armed conflict at sea. Finally, Douglas Guilfoyle analyses the *Mavi Marmara* incident in Chapter 17. This incident in 2010 was subject to several international and national inquiry processes and involved myriad questions as to conflict characterisation at sea, use of force in boarding operations, and the modern application of the law of blockade. In this regard, it repays close attention as an important recent crystallising incident which has lessons for maritime operations law on many levels – from granular rules of engagement, through to the contextual validity and availability of blockade as a method of naval warfare.

III. Conclusion

The cases and incidents examined in this book have been selected because of their prominence or representative value in illustrating and explaining the law applicable to maritime operations. In the hope of making this intensely domain-nuanced body of law more accessible, each chapter has been designed to accommodate readers who do not necessarily have a detailed understanding of the nuances and peculiarities that commonly accompany maritime matters. To this end, each case and incident analysis in this book follows a format that is intended to facilitate ready engagement with that case or incident, and the maritime operations law issues it raises. Accordingly, the reader does not need to start at Chapter 2, and then meticulously and iteratively read each chapter in sequential order. Rather, the reader may find the best approach to engaging with this book is to simply select a chapter that immediately appeals, and to read that chapter followed by others as they likewise appeal. Whatever approach is employed, the style and format adopted in this book seek to ensure that these case studies are presented in a manner accessible to all – whether maritime operations law practitioner, scholar, or interested observer. It is the hope of the editors and contributors that those who read this book will continue to be fascinated by the diversity of, and nuance in, the legal issues that arise from interactions and incidents that occur between ships, aircraft, people, and the law applicable at sea.

PART I

Sovereignty and vessel status

2

THE *LOTUS* CASE (FRANCE V TURKEY)

Camille Goodman

I. Introduction

The *Lotus* case arose out of a collision between a French vessel (the *Lotus*) and a Turkish vessel (the *Boz-Court*) on the high seas, during which the *Boz-Court* sank and eight Turkish nationals perished. After rescuing the survivors, the *Lotus* sailed on to the Turkish port of Constantinople, where the captain of the *Boz-Court* and the first officer of the *Lotus* were arrested, prosecuted in the Turkish courts, and found guilty of manslaughter. The French government protested, demanding that the first officer of the *Lotus* be released or the case transferred to the French courts. The parties referred the matter to the Permanent Court of International Justice, which found (in a narrowly decided majority judgement) that there was no principle of international law prohibiting Turkey from exercising jurisdiction in the circumstances of the case. This chapter will examine the specific maritime law issues that arose in the *Lotus* case (and the way in which many of them have since been conclusively overtaken by developments in the law of the sea), as well as the broader and ongoing questions that the case raises about the nature of jurisdiction under international law.

II. Background

Just before midnight on 2 August 1926, a collision occurred in the Aegean sea between the French mail steamer *Lotus*, proceeding to the Turkish port of Constantinople (now Istanbul), and the Turkish collier *Boz-Court*. The collision took place on the high seas, between 5 and 6 nautical miles (nm) to the north of Cape Sigri, on the western side of the Greek island of Lesbos (also known as Mitylene). The *Boz-Court* was cut in two and sank, and eight Turkish nationals who were on board perished. After rendering assistance and rescuing ten people, the *Lotus*

DOI: 10.4324/9781003307013-3

continued on its course to Constantinople, where it arrived on 3 August 1926. At the time of the collision, the officer of the watch on board the *Lotus* was Monsieur Demons, a French citizen, lieutenant in the merchant service and first officer of the ship, whilst the movements of the *Boz-Court* were directed by Captain Hassan Bey, who was one of those saved from the wreck.[1]

The Turkish police commenced their enquiry into the collision as soon as the *Lotus* arrived in port on 3 August 1926, interviewing the personnel of the *Lotus* as well as those rescued from the wreck of the *Boz-Court*.[2] On the following day, 4 August, the captain of the *Lotus* handed in his master's report at the French Consulate-General, transmitting a copy to the harbour master.[3] On 5 August, just as the *Lotus* was preparing to depart, the Turkish authorities requested Lieutenant Demons to go ashore and give evidence. Following this examination (the length of which delayed the departure of the *Lotus*), the authorities arrested Lieutenant Demons, along with two sailors from the *Lotus* and Captain Hassan Bey of the *Boz-Court*. While the sailors were released the following day, the arrests of Lieutenant Demons and Hassan Bey were maintained.[4]

On his first appearance before the Criminal Court of Constantinople on 28 August 1926, Lieutenant Demons submitted (through a written note translated by an interpreter) that the Turkish courts had no jurisdiction, but the Criminal Court overruled his objection and declared itself competent in the matter. When the proceedings resumed on 11 September, Lieutenant Demons sought release on bail, which was granted on 13 September, the bail being fixed at 6,000 Turkish pounds. The Criminal Court delivered its judgement on 15 September, sentencing Lieutenant Demons to two months and 20 days' imprisonment and a fine of £22. Hassan Bey received four months' imprisonment and a fine of £33. The owners of the *Lotus* and the *Boz-Court* were each fined £5000, to be shared between the families of the victims.[5]

The French government reacted swiftly to Turkey's arrest and prosecution of Lieutenant Demons, arguing that Turkey had no right to exercise criminal jurisdiction over personnel of a French vessel in relation to an incident that had taken place on the high seas. France requested that Lieutenant Demons be released from custody, or that the case be transferred to the French courts. The Turkish government maintained that its courts had competence over the matter under both domestic and international law, but noted that it would have no objection to submitting the

1 *Lotus Case (France v Turkey), Judgment* (1927) Series A PCIJ Reports 10.
2 Memorial of the Government of France, *Lotus Case (France v Turkey), Other Documents* (1927) Series C PCIJ Reports 173, 173.
3 *Lotus Case* above n 1
4 Memorial of the Government of France, *Lotus Case (France v Turkey), Other Documents* (1927) Series C PCIJ Reports 173, 174.
5 Ibid 175–176.

question of jurisdiction to the Permanent Court of International Justice (PCIJ or 'the Court') in The Hague for resolution.[6]

III. The legal process

Since Turkey was not a member of the League of Nations, it was not eligible to recognise the compulsory jurisdiction of the PCIJ.[7] Accordingly, the case had to be brought before the Court by means of a special agreement between the parties,[8] which asked the Court to determine:

> Has Turkey, contrary to Article 15 of the Convention of Lausanne of July 24th, 1923, respecting conditions of residence and business and jurisdiction, acted in conflict with the principles of international law – and if so, what principles – by instituting, following the collision which occurred on August 2nd, 1926, on the high seas between the French steamer *Lotus* and the Turkish steamer *Boz-Kourt* and upon the arrival of the French steamer at Constantinople – as well as against the captain of the Turkish steamship – joint criminal proceedings in pursuance of Turkish law against M. Demons, officer of the watch on board the *Lotus* at the time of the collision, in consequence of the loss of the *Boz-Kourt* having involved the death of eight Turkish sailors and passengers?[9]

While the special agreement did not refer to the domestic legislative basis for the prosecution (and no evidence was specifically put before the Court in this regard), it was common ground that the relevant provision was Article 6 of the Turkish Penal Code,[10] which provided:

6 *Lotus Case*, above n 1, 11.

7 Pursuant to Article 36 of the Statute of the Court, only members of the League of Nations and states listed in the Annex to the Covenant of the League of Nations could recognise the compulsory jurisdiction of the Court; the Court would be open to other states under conditions to be fixed by the Council. In accordance with the Council's resolution of 17 May 1922, Turkey was required to file a declaration accepting the Court's jurisdiction in respect of the case. Turkey also availed itself of its right under Article 31 of the Statute to appoint an *ad hoc* judge of Turkish nationality, by appointing Judge Feïzi-Daïm Bey. As there was already a judge of French nationality on the Court (Vice President Weiss), there was no need for France to appoint a judge *ad hoc*.

8 Article 40 of the Statute of the Court.

9 *Lotus Case* above n 1, 5. The *Convention of Lausanne of July 24th 1923 Respecting Conditions of Residence and Business and Jurisdiction* was a companion to the Treaty of Peace which formally concluded hostilities between Turkey and the Allied Powers following the First World War, and provided in Article 15 that 'all questions of jurisdiction shall, as between Turkey and the other contracting Powers, be decided in accordance with the principles of international law'.

10 In the course of the proceedings, France stated that the Turkish court claimed jurisdiction under Article 6 of the Turkish Penal Code. Turkey did not deny this statement, and contended that the provision was in conformity with international law. However, it is not clear from the proceedings before the Permanent Court of International Justice whether or not the prosecution of Lieutenant Demons was instituted solely on the basis of this provision.

> Any foreigner who, apart from the cases contemplated by Article 4, commits an offence abroad to the prejudice of Turkey or of a Turkish subject, for which offence Turkish law prescribes a penalty involving loss of freedom for a minimum period of not less than one year, shall be punished in accordance with the Turkish Penal Code provided that he is arrested in Turkey. The penalty shall however be reduced by one third and instead of the death penalty, twenty years of penal servitude shall be awarded. Nevertheless, in such cases, the prosecution will only be instituted at the request of the Minister of Justice or on the complaint of the injured Party.[11]

The French case was that jurisdiction over Lieutenant Demons inhered exclusively in the French courts, pursuant to the Convention of Lausanne and the principles of international law, which do not permit states to exercise jurisdiction over crimes committed abroad solely on the basis of the nationality of the victim. Moreover, France submitted, international law provides for exclusive flag state jurisdiction in relation to crimes committed on the high seas – particularly in relation to collision cases, which must be decided by the relevant national authority on the basis of the national laws governing the operation of the vessel. Accordingly, France argued that the arrest, conviction, and imprisonment of Lieutenant Demons constituted an unlawful exercise of jurisdiction on the part of Turkey, and sought an order for £6,000 in reparation.[12]

The Turkish government argued that the obligation under the Convention of Lausanne was simply to refrain from exercising jurisdiction contrary to the principles of international law. In this regard, Turkey submitted that Article 6 of the Turkish Penal Code was consistent with international law. Moreover, Turkey argued, since vessels on the high seas are considered to be part of the territory of the nation whose flag they fly, the *Boz-Court* should be considered to be analogous to Turkish territory, and Turkey's jurisdiction over the offence was as clear as if it had been committed within the national territory of Turkey itself. Finally, Turkey submitted that there was no principle of international law to bar the exercise of Turkey's jurisdiction in relation to a collision case – whether in civil proceedings for damages or through the institution of criminal proceedings. Accordingly, Turkey sought the Court's recognition of the validity of the jurisdiction of the Turkish courts in the proceedings.[13]

The Court delivered its judgement on 7 September 1927. Since the 12 judges were evenly divided, the judgement was adopted by the deciding vote of President Max Huber. The majority found that Turkey had *not* acted in conflict with the principles of international law, on the basis that the *Boz-Court* was in the

11 Law No. 765 of March 1st, 1926 (Official Gazette No. 320 of March 13th, 1926), as translated and cited in the majority judgement at 14.

12 *Lotus Case*, above n 1, 6–8.

13 Ibid, 9.

same position as Turkish territory, and that there was no rule of international law restricting criminal proceedings in collision cases to the jurisdiction of the flag state. Separate opinions were rendered by five dissenting judges (Judges Loder, Weiss, Finlay, Nyholm, and Altamira) and by Judge Moore, who dissented from the majority only in regard to the connection between the criminal proceedings and Article 6 of the Turkish Penal Code.

IV. Analysis and outcomes

At its heart, the question before the Court was whether or not the taking of criminal proceedings by Turkey against Lieutenant Demons violated any principle of international law. Accordingly, it was not necessary for the Court to consider the validity of any particular step in those proceedings (such as the arrest, detention, trial, or judgement), or whether the Turkish legislation relied upon was consistent with international law – the only relevant question was whether or not criminal jurisdiction existed.[14] However, this was not a simple question – it involved consideration of how to allocate jurisdiction in circumstances where the act and its consequences were not restricted to the territory of a single state. It also raised fundamental questions about exclusive and concurrent jurisdiction, and how the sovereignty of one state can be balanced with the sovereignty of another in serious cases involving criminal jurisdiction and loss of life.[15] In addition to these issues of jurisdiction under general international law, the factual circumstances of the case necessarily gave rise to significant questions regarding the laws governing the exercise of jurisdiction at sea

A. Jurisdiction under general international law

The way in which the dispute was framed in the special agreement gave rise to a question of principle that was fundamental to the Court's approach: did Turkey have to prove a positive right under international law in order to exercise jurisdiction (as contended by France), or was Turkey free to exercise jurisdiction provided it was not 'in conflict with the principles of international law' (as contended by Turkey)?[16] For the majority, the answer to this question flowed automatically from the nature of the international legal system itself. The majority judgement commenced with a general observation that:

> International law governs relations between independent States. The rules of law binding upon States therefore emanate from their own free will as

14 Ibid, 15.

15 An Hertogen, 'Letting Lotus Bloom' (2015) 26 *European Journal of International Law* 901–905.

16 *Lotus Case*, above n 1, 18. The wording of the special agreement directed the Court to apply a test of non-conflict with the principles of international law (rather than seeking to identify whether there was a positive right). This likely had a significant effect on the outcome of the case, particularly given the narrow majority.

> expressed in conventions or by usages generally accepted as expressing principles of law and established in order to regulate the relations between these co-existing independent communities or with a view to the achievement of common aims. Restrictions upon the independence of States cannot therefore be presumed.[17]

However, the Court went on to immediately qualify this general statement with a number of restrictions, distinguishing clearly between *extraterritorial* jurisdiction (which the Court found was generally prohibited in the absence of a specific permissive rule), and *territorial* jurisdiction (which the Court found was generally permitted unless limited by prohibitive rules). Importantly, the Court found that states may exercise *prescriptive* jurisdiction extraterritorially unless there is a prohibition, but may not exercise *enforcement* jurisdiction outside their territory without some form of specific permission. Having drawn this distinction between the extent of prescriptive and enforcement jurisdiction on the basis of territoriality, the Court concluded that '[a]ll that can be required of a State is that it should not overstep the limits which international law places upon its jurisdiction; within these limits, its title to exercise jurisdiction rests in its sovereignty'.[18]

The majority then went on to consider whether this rule applied equally in the situation of civil and criminal jurisdiction, and observed that the territoriality of criminal law does not coincide with territorial jurisdiction, and that almost all states extend the application of their criminal laws beyond their borders, albeit in different ways and for different offences. Under these circumstances, the Court concluded that there was insufficient evidence of a customary prohibition on the extraterritorial extension of criminal jurisdiction in the absence of a special permissive rule. Rather, consistent with its earlier statement of general principle, the Court found in favour of a freedom for states to extend the application of their criminal jurisdiction at their discretion, provided such discretion does not conflict with a restriction posed by international law.[19]

It thus remained for the Court to consider whether there was a principle of international law prohibiting Turkey's exercise of jurisdiction in this case. Given the circumstances of the case, this necessarily involved consideration of the principles of international law governing jurisdiction in relation to activities at sea.

B. Jurisdiction under the law of the sea

The Court turned first to the French argument that international law prohibits a state from punishing a foreigner for offences committed abroad simply by reason of the nationality of the victim – or as we would now describe it, passive personality

17 Ibid, 18.
18 Ibid, 18–19.
19 Ibid, 20–21.

jurisdiction. In this regard, the Court concluded that since the offence had produced its effects on a Turkish vessel, which could be assimilated to Turkish territory, Turkey's exercise of jurisdiction could be justified on the basis of territoriality.[20] Accordingly, the Court found it unnecessary to consider the lawfulness of passive personality jurisdiction, and declined to express a view on the legality of Article 6 of the Turkish Penal Code (which potentially had this effect, if relied on as the sole basis for jurisdiction).[21]

The second argument put by France was that a flag state has exclusive jurisdiction over everything that occurs on board a merchant ship on the high seas. In this regard, the Court acknowledged:

> [i]t is certainly true that vessels on the high seas are subject to no authority except that of the State whose flag they fly. In virtue of the principle of the freedom of the seas, that is to say, the absence of any territorial sovereignty upon the high seas, no State may exercise any kind of jurisdiction over foreign vessels upon them.[22]

However, the Court went on to observe that:

> it by no means follows that a State can never in its own territory exercise jurisdiction over acts which have occurred on board a foreign ship on the high seas. A corollary of the principle of the freedom of the seas is that a ship on the high seas is assimilated to the territory of the State the flag of which it flies, for, just as in its own territory, that State exercises its authority upon it, and no other State may do so. All that can be said is that by virtue of the principle of the freedom of the seas, a ship is placed in the same position as national territory; but there is nothing to support the claim according to which the rights of the State under whose flag the vessel sails may go farther than the rights which it exercises within its territory properly so called. It follows that what occurs on board a vessel on the high seas must be regarded as if it occurred on the territory of the State whose flag the ship flies. If, therefore, a guilty act committed on the high seas produces its effects on a vessel flying another flag or in foreign territory, the same principles must be applied as if the territories of two different States were concerned, and the

20 Ibid, 23. Turkey's exercise of jurisdiction in these proceedings is generally described by commentators as being based on the 'objective' territorial principle (which requires that a constituent element of the offence be consummated on the territory of the State exercising jurisdiction), see, e.g., James R. Crawford, *Brownlie's Principles of Public International Law* (Oxford University Press, 8th ed, 2012), 459.

21 *Lotus Case*, above n 1, 18 and 26. Passive personality jurisdiction is now more or less generally accepted under international law (at least in relation to certain crimes). See *Arrest Warrant of 11 April 2000 (Democratic Republic of the Congo* v. *Belgium), Separate Opinion of Judges Higgins, Kooijmans and Buergenthal [2002] ICJ Reports 63, [48].*

22 *Lotus Case*, above n 1, 25.

> conclusion must therefore be drawn that there is no rule of international law prohibiting the State to which the ship on which the effects of the offence have taken place belongs, from regarding the offence as having been committed in its territory and prosecuting, accordingly, the delinquent.[23]

The Court acknowledged that this conclusion could be overcome by a customary international law rule establishing the exclusive jurisdiction of the flag state, but (notwithstanding the authorities relied upon by France)[24] considered that such a rule had not been proved.

Finally, the Court considered France's third argument that a special rule of customary international law applied with respect to collision cases. There were no relevant decisions of international tribunals on this question, and the municipal court decisions put forward by the parties were divided on the issue.[25] Accordingly, the Court found that there was 'no rule of international law in regard to collision cases to the effect that criminal proceedings are exclusively within the jurisdiction of the State whose flag is flown'. Instead, the Court described this as a case of concurrent jurisdiction on the basis that:

> [t]he offence for which Lieutenant Demons appears to have been prosecuted was an act – of negligence or imprudence – having its origin on board the *Lotus*, whilst its effects made themselves felt on board the *Boz-Kourt*. These two elements are, legally, entirely inseparable, so much so that their separation renders the offence non-existent. Neither the exclusive jurisdiction of either State, nor the limitations of the jurisdiction of each to the occurrences which took place on the respective ships would appear calculated to satisfy

23 Ibid, 25.

24 In this regard, the Court noted that none of the precedents relied on by France (including the 1897 *Costa Rica Packet award (UK v Netherlands)*, Stuyt [1897] No 188) related to offences affecting two ships flying the flags of different countries; however, there were many cases in which a state had claimed the right to prosecute an offence committed on a foreign ship which it regarded as punishable under its legislation.

25 To support its contention regarding the exclusive jurisdiction of the flag state, France relied on *Ortigia/Oncle-Joseph, Clunet (1885) 286,* in which the Court of Appeal of Aix (France) refused to recognise the jurisdiction of an Italian court over the French captain of a French vessel involved in a collision with an Italian vessel on the high seas, and *R v Keyn* (1876) 2 Ex D 63, in which a majority of the Central Criminal Court (UK) found that the UK had no jurisdiction to try offences by foreigners on board foreign ships, whether within or without the 3-nautical-mile limit. However, in support of the opposite contention, Turkey was able to rely on *Ortigia/Oncle-Joseph*, Clunet (1885) 287, in which the Court of Appeal of Florence (Italy) confirmed the jurisdiction of the Italian courts over the French captain of a French vessel involved in a collision with an Italian vessel on the high seas (in respect of the same incident as the judgement of the French courts referred to previously), and *Ekbatana/West-Hinder*, Clunet (1914) 1327, in which the Belgian courts confirmed the jurisdiction of Belgium over the German captain of a German vessel involved in a collision with a Belgian vessel on the high seas. Moreover, as the Court noted, the decision in *R v Keyn* regarding the locality of the offence was abandoned in subsequent decisions of the UK courts, including *R v Nillins* (1884) 53 LJ 157 and *R v Godfrey* (1923) 1 KB 24.

> the requirements of justice and effectively to protect the interests of the two States. It is only natural that each should be able to exercise jurisdiction and to do so in respect of the incident as a whole. It is therefore a case of concurrent jurisdiction.[26]

Having failed to identify any principle of international law prohibiting the exercise of jurisdiction by Turkey in the circumstances of the case, the Court found that Turkey had not acted unlawfully in instituting proceedings against Lieutenant Demons.

V. Ongoing significance

Somewhat ironically, the issue on which the Court actually made its decision – the application of the territorial principle to vessels – has never really been part of the debate on the meaning and applicability of the *Lotus* case.[27] Rather, it is the Court's *obiter* statements that '[r]estrictions upon the independence of States cannot therefore be presumed' and that international law leaves to states 'a wide measure of discretion which is only limited in certain cases by prohibitive rules' that have formed the basis of the 'tiresome and oddly persistent fallacy'[28] generally described as the '*Lotus* principle'.[29] The *Lotus* principle is cited as authority for the position that, by virtue of their sovereignty, states can take whatever action they please provided it is not prohibited by international law.[30] On this basis, the *Lotus* case has been widely criticised as outdated,[31] overly positivist,[32] and 'a most unfortunate and retrograde theory'.[33] However, for others (including this author), this understanding of the *Lotus* principle reflects an incomplete reading of the judgement, and fails to take account of its full content or context.[34] The final section of this chapter will seek

26 *Lotus Case*, above n 1, 30–31.
27 This Section draws heavily on the discussion of the *Lotus* case in Camille Goodman, *Coastal State Jurisdiction Over Living Resources in the Exclusive Economic Zone* (Oxford University Press, 2021), 4–6.
28 Christopher Staker, 'Jurisdiction' in Malcolm D Evans (ed), *International Law* (Oxford University Press, 4th ed, 2014), 309–313.
29 Ole Spierman, '"Lotus" and the Double Structure of International Legal Argument' in Laurence Boisson de Chazournes and Philippe Sands (eds), *The International Court of Justice and Nuclear Weapons* (Cambridge University Press, 1999) 131, 132.
30 Gerald Fitzmaurice, 'The Law and Procedure of the International Court of Justice, 1951–54: General Principles and Sources of Law' (1953) 30 *British Year Book of International Law* 1, 16–17.
31 Rosalyn Higgins, 'International Trade Law and the Avoidance, Containment and Resolution of Disputes' (1991) 230 *Recueil des Cours* 9, 114. See also *Advisory Opinion on the Legality of the Threat or Use of Nuclear Weapons, Declaration of President Bedjaoui* [1996] ICJ Reports 268, 270.
32 JL Brierly, 'The "Lotus" Case' (1928) 44 *Law Quarterly Review* 154–155; Charles de Visscher, 'Justice et Mediation Internationales' (1928) 9 *Revue de droit international et de legislation comparee* 33, 157.
33 FA Mann, 'The Doctrine of Jurisdiction in International Law' (1964) III *Recueil des Cours* 1, 35.
34 See, e.g., Staker, 'Jurisdiction', above n 28, 313–314; Spierman, '"Lotus" and the Double Structure of International Legal Argument', above n 29, 141–142; Hugh Handeyside, 'The Lotus Principle in ICJ Jurisprudence: Was the Ship Ever Afloat?' (2007) 1 *Michigan Journal of International Law* 71–76;

to accurately place the key conclusions of the *Lotus* case in their contemporary context, addressing first the important and ongoing questions that the case raises about the nature of jurisdiction under general international law, and second the specific issue of the exercise of non-flag state jurisdiction at sea, which remains a controversial question in the law of the sea.

A. Jurisdiction under general international law

The *Lotus* case is commonly understood to represent the proposition that 'under international law, everything which is not prohibited is permitted'.[35] However, a careful reading of the Court's judgement reveals this to be an overly broad interpretation, reflecting an incomplete reading of the judgement. As described previously, the majority judgement clearly distinguished between territorial and extraterritorial exercises of jurisdiction, and between prescriptive and enforcement jurisdiction. Accordingly, the Court's dictum in *Lotus* cannot reasonably be read any higher than indicating that, once it has been determined that there is no express prohibition, a state may exercise prescriptive jurisdiction with respect to persons, property, and acts outside its territory, provided that it does not *enforce* such jurisdiction extraterritorially.[36] Even on this reading, however, the '*Lotus* principle' has remained contentious – how can such a 'permissive' approach, based on freedom of action in the absence of prohibition, effectively regulate the relationships between independent sovereign states?

At the heart of this controversy is the characterisation of the relationship between sovereignty and jurisdiction. The starting point for both sovereignty and jurisdiction is territoriality: since states have sovereignty over their territory, they have the right to prescribe the laws for public order, which apply to everyone within that territory.[37] However, this does not equate to unrestrained freedom: in a system of multiple co-existent sovereigns, there are inherent limits on the freedom of action of each state. This was addressed by Judge Shahabudeen in his dissenting opinion in the *Nuclear Weapons* Advisory Opinion:

> The existence of a number of sovereignties side by side places limits on the freedom of each State to act as if the others did not exist. These limits define an objective structural framework within which sovereignty must necessarily exist; the framework, and its defining limits, are implicit in the reference in 'Lotus' to 'co-existing independent communities' . . . . Thus, however

Hertogen, 'Letting Lotus Bloom', above n 15, 903, Douglas Guilfoyle, 'SS Lotus' in Eirik Bjorge and Cameron Miles (eds), *Landmark Cases in Public International Law* (Hart 2017) 107.

35 *Lotus Case (France v Turkey), Dissenting Opinion of Judge Loder* (1927) Series A PCIJ Reports 34.

36 See *Arrest Warrants Case*, above n 21, *Dissenting Opinion of Judge van den Wyngaert* [2002] ICJ Reports 137, 168; Cedric Ryngaert, *Jurisdiction in International Law* (Oxford University Press, 2nd ed, 2016), 31–32.

37 Staker, 'Jurisdiction', above n 28, 316.

> far-reaching may be the rights conferred by sovereignty, those rights cannot extend beyond the framework within which sovereignty itself exists.'[38]

As Hertogen points out, the understanding of territorial sovereignty was the real point of difference between the majority and the minority in *Lotus*: for the minority, the effect of territorial sovereignty was to restrict the exercise of extraterritorial jurisdiction to circumstances in which specific permissive rules apply, whereas for the majority, territorial sovereignty was the basis for the state's right to exercise jurisdiction, but was inherently limited by the sovereignty of other states.[39] Unfortunately, the majority judgement in *Lotus* did not *explicitly* set out this notion of limitation or restraint – but it is *implicit* in the Court's general observation regarding the nature of the international system, and its statement that rules of international law are established in order to 'regulate the relations between co-existing independent communities' and achieve common aims.[40]

Accordingly, the *Lotus* principle can properly be understood to mean that states have a wide *discretion* – not an unlimited freedom – to exercise jurisdiction within their territory in respect of events occurring outside it, provided there is no prohibition under international law (whether constituted by an explicit rule prohibiting the exercise of jurisdiction in a specific instance, or the inherent limitation on exercising jurisdiction in a way which would infringe the sovereignty of another state). This is consistent with the statement of Judge Fitzmaurice in the *Barcelona Traction* case that although public international law does not prescribe hard and fast limits on the exercise of jurisdiction, it does 'postulate the existence of limits' and 'involve for every State an obligation to exercise moderation and restraint . . . and to avoid undue encroachment on a jurisdiction more properly appertaining to, or more appropriately exercisable by, another State'.[41]

Of course, this may still give rise – as it did in the *Lotus* case – to situations of concurrent jurisdiction, in which two or more states have a legitimate right to exercise jurisdiction in respect of the same set of circumstances.[42] As the Court noted,

> This discretion left to States by international law explains the great variety of rules which they have been able to adopt without objections or complaints on the part of other States; it is in order to remedy the difficulties resulting from such variety that efforts have been made for many years past, both in

38 *Advisory Opinion on the Legality of the Threat or Use of Nuclear Weapons, Dissenting Opinion of Judge Shahabuddeen* [1996] ICJ Reports 375, 393.

39 Hertogen, 'Letting Lotus Bloom', above n 15, 910.

40 *Lotus Case*, above n 1, 18. See in this regard: *Advisory Opinion on the Legality of the Threat or Use of Nuclear Weapons, Dissenting Opinion of Judge Shahabuddeen* [1996] ICJ Reports 375, 393; Hertogen, 'Letting Lotus Bloom', above n 15, 903; Staker, 'Jurisdiction', above n 28, 314–315.

41 *Barcelona Traction (Belgium v Spain), Separate Opinion of Judge Sir Gerald Fitzmaurice* (1970) 1 ICJ Reports 64 [70].

42 *Lotus Case*, above n 1, 30.

> Europe and America, to prepare conventions the effect of which would be precisely to limit the discretion at present left to States in this respect by international law, thus making good the existing lacunae in respect of jurisdiction or removing the conflicting jurisdictions arising from the diversity of the principles adopted by the various States.[43]

In this regard, concurrent jurisdiction actually 'serves an important signalling function in international law',[44] since concurrent exercises of jurisdiction can reveal competing interests and tensions between states in relation to particular issues, which may then be addressed through the development of treaties or customary international law. This was exactly what occurred in the *Lotus* case, in which the Court's technical findings regarding the exercise of jurisdiction at sea led to the development of new conventional and customary law rules governing the status of vessels, jurisdiction over collisions at sea, and the nature of flag state jurisdiction.

B. Jurisdiction at sea

At first glance, the *Lotus* case may seem to have little relevance to contemporary maritime operations law. On closer inspection, however, the threads of the *Lotus* judgement are reflected in a range of issues relating to the nature and extent of flag state jurisdiction, both in conventional and customary international law, and in cases before courts and tribunals. In some cases, this is because the technical findings of the Court were conclusively rejected by states and stimulated the development of new law; in other cases, it is because the judgement raised complex and important issues that are of ongoing relevance in the law of the sea.

The issue which was most quickly superseded by the development of new international law is also the issue upon which the Court based its ruling in favour of Turkey – the assimilation of a vessel to the territory of a state. While this concept had received some support in the 19th and early 20th centuries as a justification for the exclusive jurisdiction of the flag state, on the basis that a ship constituted a part of national territory (or 'floating island'),[45] it was by no means a universally accepted idea.[46] Moreover, the application of this concept to justify the exercise of objective territorial jurisdiction over a criminal offence committed on the high seas was, as described in Lord Finlay's dissent, a 'new and startling application' of

43 Ibid, 30, 19.

44 Hertogen, 'Letting Lotus Bloom', above n 15, 909.

45 D.P. O'Connell, *The International Law of the Sea* (Oxford University Press, 1982), 735; Rosemary Rayfuse, *Non-Flag State Enforcement in High Seas Fisheries* (Brill, 2004), 21.

46 See, e.g., Philip C Jessup, *The Law of Territorial Waters and Maritime Jurisdiction* (Kraus Reprint Co, 1927), 122; *Cunard Steamship Co v Mellon* (1923) 262 US 100 (in which the United States Supreme Court described the concept of territoriality of ships as 'a figure of speech, a metaphor') at 123.

the metaphor.[47] This aspect of the judgement was clearly repudiated by the Privy Council in the 1939 case of *Chung Chi Cheung v R*, in which Lord Atkin stated:

> However the doctrine of extraterritoriality is expressed, it is a fiction, and legal fictions have a tendency to pass beyond their appointed bounds and to harden into dangerous facts. The truth is that the enunciators of the floating island theory have failed to face very obvious possibilities that make the doctrine quite impracticable when tested by the actualities of life on board ship and ashore.[48]

The idea that a vessel is part of the territory of the state has been conclusively overtaken by subsequent developments;[49] under contemporary international law, flag state jurisdiction is understood in terms of nationality, not territoriality. As set out in Article 91(1) of the 1982 United Nations Convention on the Law of the Sea (LOSC),[50] 'Ships have the nationality of the state whose flag they are entitled to fly',[51] and the terms 'nationality' and 'flag' are generally considered as synonymous as they relate to vessels in the law of the sea.[52]

A second key aspect of *Lotus* that has been superseded is the Court's conclusion that international law did not provide for exclusive flag state jurisdiction in criminal proceedings relating to collision at sea. This aspect of the judgement 'was strongly criticised and caused serious disquiet in international maritime circles',[53] and was specifically reversed by the Brussels International Convention for the Unification of Certain Rules Relating to Penal Jurisdiction in Matters of Collision and Other Incidents of Navigation,[54] which limited criminal jurisdiction over collisions on the high seas to the flag state and the state of nationality of the crew. This rule is now embodied in Article 97 of the LOSC, which provides:

> In the event of a collision or any other incident of navigation concerning a ship on the high seas, involving the penal or disciplinary responsibility of the

47 *Lotus Case*, above n 1, *Dissenting Opinion of Lord Finlay* (1927) Series A PCIJ Reports 52.

48 [1939] AC 160, 174.

49 Higgins, 'International Trade Law and the Avoidance, Containment and Resolution of Disputes', above n 31, 100; Crawford, *Brownlie's Principles of Public International Law*, above n 20, 459.

50 Opened for signature 10 December 1982, 1833 UNTS 3 (entered into force 16 November 1994). This provision is modelled on Article 6(1) of the 1958 *Convention for the High Seas*, opened for signature 29 April 1958, 450 UNTS 11 (entered into force 30 September 1962) ('High Seas Convention').

51 This provision is modelled on Article 5(1) of the High Seas Convention, and 'codifies a well-accepted rule of general international law' (*M/V Saiga [No 2] (Saint Vincent and the Grenadines v Guinea), Judgment* [1999] ITLOS Case No 2 [63]).

52 Rosemary Rayfuse, 'Countermeasures and High Seas Fisheries Enforcement' (2004) 51 *Netherlands International Law Review* 41, 22–23.

53 International Law Commission, 'Articles Concerning the Law of the Sea with Commentaries' (1956) II *Yearbook of the International Law Commission* 265, 281.

54 Opened for signature 10 May 1952, 439 UNTS 233 (entered into force 20 November 1955).

> master or of any other person in the service of the ship, no penal or disciplinary proceedings may be instituted against such person except before the judicial or administrative authorities either of the flag State or of the State of which such person is a national.[55]

Accordingly, unlike Turkey in the *Lotus* case, a state whose nationals are injured during a collision at sea is now effectively prohibited from instituting criminal proceedings against the responsible parties.[56]

There is one aspect of the *Lotus* judgement relating to the law of the sea that remains both accurate and highly relevant. This is the concept of exclusive flag state jurisdiction on the high seas, which was endorsed by all six dissenting judges[57] as well as the majority[58] in *Lotus*, and has become one of the fundamental tenets of the law of the sea. As the *Lotus* judgement noted:

> vessels on the high seas are subject to no authority except that of the State whose flag they fly. In virtue of the principle of the freedom of the seas, that is to say the absence of any territorial sovereignty upon the high seas, no state may exercise any kind of jurisdiction over foreign vessels upon them.[59]

This principle is now codified in Article 92(1) of the LOSC which states: 'Ships shall sail under the flag of one State only and, save in exceptional cases expressly provided for in international treaties or in this Convention, shall be subject to its exclusive jurisdiction on the high seas'. Pursuant to this rule, which reflects customary international law,[60] one state may not exercise jurisdiction over the vessel of another state on the high seas without that state's consent, except in relation to certain 'exceptional cases' explicitly provided for in the LOSC[61] or in other international treaties. However, the rule of exclusive flag state jurisdiction applies with respect to *enforcement* at sea, and is to be distinguished from the exercise of prescriptive jurisdiction, which is governed by general international law – and thus by the *Lotus* principle.[62]

55 This provision was reproduced without alteration from Article 11 of the High Seas Convention.
56 Donald R Rothwell and Tim Stephens, *The International Law of the Sea* (Hart Publishing, 2nd ed, 2016), 70.
57 *Lotus Case*, above n 1, Dissenting Opinions of: Lord Finlay, 7; Judge Loder, 38; Judge Weiss, 45–46; Judge Nyholm, 62–63; Judge Moore, 69; Judge Altamira, 97.
58 Ibid, 25.
59 Ibid.
60 Crawford, a *Brownlie's Principles of Public International Law*, above n 20, 301; J Ashley Roach, 'Today's Customary International Law of the Sea' (2014) 45 *Ocean Development & International Law* 239, 248–249.
61 These exceptions include: art 99 (Prohibition of the transport of slaves); art 105 (Seizure of a pirate ship or aircraft); art 109 (Unauthorized broadcasting from the high seas); art 110 (Right of visit); and art 111 (Right of hot pursuit).
62 Crawford, *Brownlie's Principles of Public International Law*, above n 20, 301; Douglas Guilfoyle, *Shipping Interdiction and the Law of the Sea* (Cambridge University Press, 2009), 7–8.

In this regard, there is still significant uncertainty about the extent to which states may exercise prescriptive jurisdiction with respect to criminal offences committed at sea. This is highlighted by a 2019 case involving the Panamanian-flagged fuel tanker *Norstar*. The *Norstar* was alleged to have been engaged in a smuggling and tax evasion scheme involving the purchase of tax-exempt fuel in Italy in order to sell it to 'mega yachts' on the high seas just outside the territorial waters of Italy, Spain, and France. Pursuant to a mutual assistance request from Italy, the *Norstar* was arrested by Spanish authorities while at anchor in Spain's internal waters. Panama instituted proceedings in the International Tribunal for the Law of the Sea (ITLOS), in which it alleged that by asserting prescriptive jurisdiction in relation to the *Norstar's* bunkering activities on the high seas, Italy had violated the right to freedom of navigation under Article 87 of the LOSC – even though the enforcement of this jurisdiction had taken place in internal waters.

ITLOS agreed with Panama's assertion, issuing a majority decision which found that the principle of exclusive flag state jurisdiction under Article 92 of the LOSC is an 'inherent component' of the freedom of navigation under Article 87, and prohibits the exercise of both enforcement *and* prescriptive jurisdiction over the 'lawful activities' of foreign-flagged vessels on the high seas.[63] In other words, if a non-flag state were to apply its legislation to the activities of foreign ships on the high seas in a situation not specifically 'justified by the [LOSC] or other international treaties', this may result in a breach of the freedom of navigation – even if the *enforcement* of such laws was only carried out in internal waters.[64] This finding was opposed by a minority of seven judges, who issued a strongly worded dissent arguing that nothing in the LOSC, its *travaux préparatoires*, other international treaties, customary international law, or state practice suggests that Article 87 altogether excludes the right of non-flag states to exercise prescriptive criminal jurisdiction with respect to activities on the high seas, and specifically cited the *Lotus* principle.[65]

While this aspect of the *Norstar* decision was subsequently noted with approval (although not actually applied) by an Arbitral Tribunal in the 2020 *Enrica Lexie* decision,[66] its ongoing effect is yet to be seen, and is difficult to predict.[67] Given the questions raised by this expansive approach to the interpretation of exclusive flag state jurisdiction – and its potential effects on the application of prescriptive jurisdiction to the activities of foreign-flagged vessels on the high seas – it seems reasonable to conclude that even though more than 95 years has passed since the sinking of the *Boz-Court*, this aspect of the *Lotus* case is not yet completely closed.

63 *M/V "Norstar" (Panama v Italy)* (Judgment) [2018–2019] ITLOS Rep 7 [225].

64 Ibid, [225]-[226].

65 Ibid, Joint Dissenting Opinion of Judges Cot, Pawlak, Yanai, Hoffmann, Kolodkin, Lijnzaad and Treves, [19] and [36].

66 The *"Enrica Lexie"* Incident (Italy v India) [2020] PCA Case 2015–28 [527].

67 No reasoning was given in either case to support or explain this new and expansive approach to the interpretation of Article 92, making its application difficult to justify in other cases; this approach is contrary to existing law and practice, and in particular the *Lotus* principle; and it produced significant disagreement amongst the members of ITLOS.

3

ARA LIBERTAD

Refining the legal grounds for warship-immunity in foreign ports

Martin Fink

I. Introduction

The case of the Argentine warship *ARA Libertad* deals in essence with immunity enjoyed by warships. One would think that today this subject is left without dark corners. There is neither any real controversy on the principle that warships enjoy sovereign immunity, nor is there any real debate on the definition of warships.[1] As one commentator on this subject put it, 'There is little public evidence of question or disputes arising in recent years respecting sovereign immune vessels'.[2] Some attention to the immunity relating to warships came to the fore in light of the issue of sunken warships, addressed in the Underwater Cultural Heritage Convention (2001),[3] a discussion that re-emerged in 2017 when three Dutch warships sunk during the Battle of the Java Sea (1942) were discovered to be missing from the bottom of the ocean.[4] But other than this particular subject, it is widely accepted that the immunity of warships is a well-established rule in international law. In that sense, it has been somewhat surprising that the *ARA Libertad* case surfaced as

1 See also B. Spielman, '"Warships" in the North Sea Continental Shelf cases: why the definition of 'warships' for determining sovereign immunity settled 25 years ago' (2009) 15 *Journal of International Maritime Law* 322–339.

2 T.L. McDorman, 'Sovereign Immune Vessels: Immunities, Responsibilities and Exemptions' in H. Ringbom (ed), *Jurisdiction over Ships* (Brill, 2015), 82–102, 82.

3 See e.g. D.J. Bederman, 'Rethinking the Legal Status of Sunken Warships' (2000) 31:1–2 *Ocean Development and International Law* 97–125; N. Ronzitti, 'The Legal Regime of Wrecks of Warships and Other State-owned Ships in International Law: Report' (2011) 74 *Yearbook of Institute of International Law* 133–171.

4 See M.D. Fink, 'De bescherming van gezonken oorlogsschepen' (2017) 4 *Netherlands Military Law Review*, 12–16.

DOI: 10.4324/9781003307013-4

a dispute before the International Tribunal for the Law of the Sea (ITLOS).[5] In this particular case, the immunity of a warship in a foreign port was challenged in relation to the provisions of the United Nations Convention on the Law of the Sea (UNCLOS).

II. Background

The *ARA Libertad* is a tall ship, in use as a training vessel for midshipmen of the Argentine Navy. On 1 October 2012, the ship arrived at the port of Tema in Ghana as part of its goodwill West Africa tour. The visit had been notified to and was authorised by the authorities of Ghana. The vessel also had officers of several other states on board. That the ship – despite its classic, non-conventional appearance – is an Argentine warship was never in question. The day after its arrival in Ghana a court order was delivered to the vessel, which ordered that the *ARA Libertad* was to be detained and held in port. The court order was the result of a civil court action that a creditor to Argentina, NML Capital, had brought before the commercial division of the High Court of Ghana. This civil action resulted in an injunction from the High Court to detain the *ARA Libertad* in the Ghanaian port. Argentina protested through diplomatic channels[6] and appealed the court order in the Ghanaian court. Interestingly, in the appeal, both the Argentine and Ghana Foreign Affairs officials and legal advisers agreed and supported the view that a foreign warship could not be detained because of its sovereign immune status.[7] The Ghanaian executive branch, however, also viewed that it could not overturn or deny a court order of its independent judiciary branch. When in appeal Argentina was not able to persuade the judge of a breach of the warships' immunity, Argentina resorted to the dispute resolution mechanisms in UNCLOS. By the end of October, Argentina notified Ghana that it had submitted the case to the UNCLOS arbitral procedure. While the Arbitral Tribunal was being constituted, in November, Argentina also submitted a request for a provisional measures to ITLOS in order to get the vessel released.

In the meantime, the *ARA Libertad* was detained in the port of Tema. After the ship started to get short on fuel to maintain the vessel, Argentina repatriated most of the crew and foreign officers. The commander and a skeleton crew stayed onboard. The situation on the quay got more tense when, on 7 November, the Ports Authority forcibly tried to enforce another measure granted by the same court to move the ship from its present position to another berth, trying to mitigate

5 *ITLOS*, case no. 20, The "*ARA Libertad*" Case (Argentina v. Ghana), 15 December 2012.

6 An Argentine delegation that included the Minister of Defence and Interior met mid-October with officials of Ghana. See J. Kraska, 'The "ARA Libertad" (Argentina v. Ghana). ITLOS Case No. 20. Provisional Measures', in *American Journal International Law* (2013), vol. 107:1–7, at 2.

7 S. Ruiz-Cerutti, 'The UNCLOS and the Settlement of Disputes: The *ARA Libertad* Case' in L. del Castillo (ed), *Law of the Sea, from Grotius to the International Tribunal for the Law of the Sea: Liber Amicorum Judge Hugo Caminos* (Brill, 2015), 713–722, at 716.

economic losses. According to the Ports Authority, the *ARA Libertad* at its present position was financially detrimental to the Ports Authority and caused an alarming state of congestion and traffic at the port.[8] Argentina also appealed this court order.

III. Provisional measures

As a provisional measure, Argentina requested the Tribunal order that Ghana 'unconditionally enabled the Argentine warship Frigate *ARA Libertad* to leave the Ghanaian port of Tema and the jurisdictional waters of Ghana and to be resupplied to that end'.[9] Argentina held that its rights under UNCLOS were breached and lined up four UNCLOS Articles to support its view: Articles 18(1)(b), 32, 87(1)(a) and 90.[10] Ultimately, the key article was Article 32 UNCLOS, on the immunities of warships and other governmental ships operated for non-commercial purposes. Article 32 UNCLOS reads as follows: 'With such exceptions as are contained in subsection A and in Articles 30 and 31, nothing in this Convention affects the immunities of warships and other government ships operated for non-commercial purposes'.

In particular, Argentina held that immunity was breached on two points: the detainment of the vessel and the subsequent attempt of port officials to enter the vessel in order to move it to another berth. Ghana's main counter-argument was that Article 32 UNCLOS did not apply to the internal waters of a state (and in fact, nor did any of the Articles that Argentina argued had been breached),[11] and as immunity for warships in internal waters is an issue of customary international law, consequently, the issue is outside the interpretation or application of UNCLOS.[12] Ghana opined, therefore, that 'Article 32 cannot be a legal basis of Argentina's claim' and jurisdiction could not be established by an Annex VII Tribunal nor by ITLOS. Also, Ghana submitted that Argentina had waivered its immunity through the bonds agreed between Argentina and NML Capital.[13]

Two and half months after the *ARA Libertad* was first detained at the port of Tema, on 15 December 2012, the Tribunal issued its order. The Tribunal stated that, 'in light of the positions of the Parties, a difference exists between them as to the applicability of Article 32 and thus the Tribunal is of the view that a dispute

8 Written statement of the Republic of Ghana, 28 November 2015, para 5.

9 Request for the prescription of provisional measures under art 290, para 5, of the United Nations Convention on the Law of the Sea, submitted by Argentina, 14 November 2012, para 28.

10 Arts 18 (innocent passage), 87 (high seas freedoms), 90 (right of navigation) and 32 (immunities for warships). See Request for Provisional Measures (14 November 2012), para 23.

11 ITLOS order, 15 December 2012 (The'*ARA Libertad'* case), above n 5, para 52. In this context, Ghana also questioned the applicability of UNCLOS to internal waters in general. See on the issue M.G. Kohen, 'Is the Internal Waters Regime excluded from the United Nations Convention on the Law of the Sea?' in L. del Castillo (ed), *Law of the Sea, from Grotius to the International Tribunal for the Law of the Sea: Liber Amicorum Judge Hugo Caminos* (Brill, 2015), 110–124.

12 Written statement of Ghana, above n 8, para 12.

13 Ibid, para 15.

appears to exist between the Parties concerning the interpretation of the Convention', it had *prima facie* jurisdiction.[14] The Tribunal also briefly went into the merits of the case. With regard to the underlying issue of immunity for warships in foreign internal waters, it viewed that a warship is an expression of the sovereignty of the state whose flag it flies and that a warship enjoys immunity, including in internal waters.[15] ITLOS therefore ordered that the *ARA Libertad* was to be released unconditionally, that its commander and crew were able to leave the port and the maritime areas under the jurisdiction of Ghana, and that Ghana was to ensure that the vessel was resupplied to that end.[16] After new sailors from Buenos Aires arrived at the ship, the *ARA Libertad* left port on 19 December 2012.[17]

A. The immunity of warships in foreign ports

Throughout the legal proceedings, it was never a debate that a warship enjoys sovereign immunity. A warship, as the Tribunal stated, is an expression of the sovereignty of the state whose flag it flies.[18] This longstanding and generally accepted notion of customary international law is codified in Articles 32 and 95 of UNCLOS. Apart from UNCLOS, the codification of the rule goes a long way back. Immunity for warships was codified earlier in Article 8 of the Convention on the High Seas (1958), Article 22 of the Convention on the Territorial Sea and Contiguous Zone (1958) and Article 3 in the International Convention for the Unification of Certain Rules Concerning the Immunity of State Owned Ships (1926). This latter Article states that such ships [warships] shall not be subject to seizure, arrest or detention by any legal process, nor to any proceedings *in rem*. In terms of jurisprudence, immunity of warships was confirmed by the U.S. Supreme Court as early as 1812, in the *Schooner Exchange* case. After UNCLOS, immunity for warships was again recognised in Article 16 of the *Draft Articles on Jurisdictional Immunities of States* and in the *Underwater Cultural Heritage Convention* (2001).[19] Sovereign immunity for warships results in the notion that no enforcement measures can be taken against the ship, even though it is within the territory of another state.[20]

14 ITLOS order, above n 5, paras 65, 67.
15 Ibid, paras 94, 95.
16 Ibid, para 108.
17 'Detained Argentine naval ship leaves Ghana', *Reuters*, 20 December 2012 <www.reuters.com/article/us-ghana-argentina-ship-idUSBRE8BI1AF20121219>.
18 ITLOS order, above n 5, para 94.
19 2562 UNTS 3. See Article 13 of this Convention.
20 One particular example of an exception to immunity against enforcement jurisdiction in foreign waters is derived from the rules of maritime neutrality and applies only during an international armed conflict. Belligerent forces may not use neutral waters as a sanctuary or for hostile actions. Neutral states can take measures against belligerents that are in violation of the neutral waters regime during international armed conflict (see, e.g., Section 22 of the *San Remo Manual*). Article 24 of The Hague Convention XIII, concerning the rights and duties of neutral powers in naval war, also state the possibility of detaining the warship and its crew, if violations of neutral waters occur.

Immunity, therefore, manifests itself when a warship is within the sovereign waters of another state, such as internal waters or territorial sea.

Because Articles 95 and 32 UNCLOS are situated in the sections of the Convention that relate to the high seas and the territorial sea, respectively, the question that emerged before the Tribunal in this particular case was the question of whether immunity for warships exists in the internal waters of a state and what legal ground this would be based upon. The Ghanaian authorities questioned whether Article 32 UNCLOS applies to the internal waters of a state as there is nothing in UNCLOS that specifically states or implies such a view. UNCLOS is silent on the issue of warships in internal waters of another state. Interestingly, in answering this question – albeit in the context of the question whether the Tribunal had *prima facie* jurisdiction – the Tribunal's view and the opinions of individual judges on the interpretation of Article 32 UNCLOS show two different approaches to arrive at the conclusion that warships enjoy immunity in internal waters.

The first approach is the argumentation followed by the Tribunal. With regard to Article 32 UNCLOS, it viewed that 'although most of the provisions in Part II of UNCLOS relate to the territorial sea, some provisions, such as the definition of warships in Article 29 may be applicable also to the internal waters'. Here, the Tribunal applies some interesting reasoning. It views that certain provisions do not apply only to the maritime zones in which the provision is placed, but can also extend beyond that part. Article 32 UNCLOS, in the Tribunal's view, first recognises and enshrines customary international law on the immunity of warships in UNCLOS,[21] and second, the scope of this provision is not limited to the territorial sea only.[22] The Tribunal, therefore, opined that Article 32 also applies in the internal waters, providing the legal basis for the immunity of warships also in internal waters.

A second and different approach to the existence of immunity for warships in the internal waters of a state was expressed by the separate opinions of Judges Wolfrum and Cot. Although arriving at the same conclusion that immunity for warships in foreign ports exists, their approach is not to embody everything into Article 32. They disagree with both the view that Article 32 provides the immunity of warships and that the rule applies in internal waters.[23] Instead, they first argue that Article 32 does not establish immunity of warships, but 'constitutes a reference rather than a regulation in itself'.[24] As this provision does not establish immunity but its exceptions, it cannot be the source of immunity of warships. Second, they argue that Article 32 must *prima facie* be seen as limited to application in the territorial waters of a state only.[25] Third, this does not mean that immunity of warships does not exist in internal waters, but rather that immunity is based on

21 ITLOS order, above n 5, para 44.
22 Ibid, paras 45–46.
23 Joint separate opinion Wolfrum and Cot, above n 5, para 39.
24 Ibid, para 41.
25 Ibid, para 45.

customary international law, a rule which is both well established and recognised in legal doctrine.[26] Instead of an extended interpretation of Article 32 UNCLOS, this view bases immunity directly on customary international law.[27]

IV. Analysis and outcomes

After ITLOS issued its provisional measure, the Arbitral Tribunal was constituted in February 2013. The dispute took, however, another turn when, in June 2013, the Ghana Supreme Court issued a judgement on the question of whether the seizure of the *ARA Libertad* was lawful. In its judgement, it held that the local judge was in error on the issue.[28] The seizure of the vessel was a violation of international obligations to respect the immunity of warships. After this judgement, both states together requested the Arbitral Tribunal to terminate the arbitral procedure.[29]

Although the legal proceedings before the Arbitral Tribunal ended with this request, it would have been interesting to see this case dealt with on its merits as some points that were raised were not scrutinised during the ITLOS provisional measures proceedings. Primarily, it has left open the question of which interpretation with regard to Article 32 UNCLOS would be the purest interpretation to support the immunity of warships. As the ITLOS order noted that it in no way prejudges the merits of the case,[30] the Arbitral Tribunal could have endorsed one or the other view, or maybe would have come even to a wholly different approach to this matter. In this context, Judges Wolfrum and Cot and other commentators have remarked that the Tribunal may have taken the approach of centralising on the interpretation of Article 32 because the jurisdiction of the Tribunal depended heavily on Article 32.[31] Apart from the legal arguments to bolster the immunity of warships in foreign ports, also some other points brought to the fore by the Parties were not addressed in the provisional measure. One of these points is the practical extent of immunity. As mentioned, during the time when *ARA Libertad* stayed in port, the Ports Authority, based on another court order, forcibly attempted to gain

26 Ibid, para 47.

27 See on the jurisdictional discussion of the court related to this view Y. Tanaka, 'Release of a Detained Warship and Its Crew through Provisional Measures: A Comparative Analysis of the ARA Libertad and Ukraine v Russia Cases' (2020) 96 *International Law Studies* 223–256.

28 See Aide Memoire on *ARA Libertad* case (Argentina v Ghana), attached to the letter from Argentina and Ghana requesting to terminate arbitral procedures, para 5.

29 In the matter of an arbitration before an arbitral tribunal constituted under annex VII of the 1982 United Nations convention on the Law of the Sea between the Argentine Republic and the Republic of Ghana (no date).

30 ITLOS Order, above n 5, para 106. See also T.E. Robins, 'The Peculiar Case of the ARA Libertad: Provisional Measures and Prejudice to the Arbitral Tribunal's Final Result' (2015) 20 *Harvard Negotiating Law Review* 265, on discussion regarding how much a provisional measure influences the Arbitral Tribunal case.

31 Joint separate opinion Judge Wolfrum and Cot, above n 5, para 51. See also. Tanaka 'Current legal developments International Tribunal for the Law of the Sea' (2013) 28 *International Journal of Marine and Coastal Law* 375 at 378–380.

access to the vessel to move it to another berth. When the officials tried to come on board of the vessel, this was opposed by the commander, with the use of armed personnel. In this context, the words of C.J. Colombos are repeated here:

> The general doctrine is, therefore, that a warship remains under the exclusive jurisdiction of her Flag-State during her entry and stay in foreign ports and waters. No legal proceedings can be taken against her either for recovery of possession or for damages for collision or for a salvage reward, or for any other cause, and no official of the territorial State is permitted to [come onboard] the vessel against the wishes of her commander.[32]

It would have been interesting to see this doctrine reaffirmed by a court. Interestingly, if the warship does not comply with regulations issued by the foreign state and persists in it, the state's only recourse is to require the vessel to leave its sovereign waters.[33] Of note is that Article 30 UNCLOS,[34] codifying such measures for the coastal state explicitly for the purposes of the territorial sea, is another rule that is not repeated in the context of internal waters. As such, it may require the same sort of argumentation applying it to internal waters. Obviously, in this particular case, requesting the ship to depart after disregarding a court order was not an option for the Ghanaian authorities.

A second point that had no in-depth analysis in the provisional measure decision was Ghana's argument that Argentina waived immunity through the bonds.[35] Again, it would have been interesting to see how the Tribunal would have dealt with this issue at length and whether or not it would have been an actual challenge to uphold immunity in light of such agreements made by the state, or that Argentina is correct in stating that 'military assets are absolutely excluded from any kind of execution measures', or – even in the case in which it is considered that a state can waive its immunity of execution with regard to military assets – this waiver should be explicit and specific to the related military asset at stake.[36] The Ghana Supreme Court appears to have been of the same view when it reasoned that 'the waiver of immunity clause, contained in the bonds issued by Argentina to various creditors in New York were not effective to be enforced against military assets'.[37]

32 C.J. Colombos, *The International Law of the Sea* (5th rev. edition, Longmans, 1962), 242.

33 Ibid, at 249.

34 Art 30 UNCLOS reads:

> If any warship does not comply with the laws and regulations of the coastal State concerning passage through the territorial sea and disregards any requests for compliance therewith which is made to it, the coastal State may require it to leave the territorial sea.

35 See on this issue N. Peiris, 'Provisional measures in the ARA Libertad: On the margins of jurisdictional discourse' (2014) 28 *Ocean Yearbook* 134–144.

36 Request for provisional measures, 14 November 2012, para 41. See also on this issue, N. Peiris, 'ARA Libertad from ITLOS: How Provisional Can a Provisional Measure Be?' (2012) *Hague Yearbook of International Law* 159–172.

37 *Aide Memoire*, above n 28, para 5 under IV.

A third point that was not teased out, but noted as an issue in the separate opinions of Judges Rao, Lucky, Wolfrum, and Cot, is the view of the Ghanaian executive branch, who, although they held the same view as Argentina with regard to the immunity of warships, took the position of being unable to interfere in the work of its judiciary branch. The ITLOS judges in their opinions, however, opined that a state cannot shelter behind decisions of its organs as an excuse not to implement international legal obligations.[38] Interestingly, Judge Rao connects this issue to the diplomatic clearance that was given by Ghana to Argentina before arrival of the *ARA Libertad*, authorising the vessel to enter the Ghanaian port.[39] It is clear, therefore, that the judges took an opposite view from Ghana, but no in-depth legal analysis came with that view.

V. Conclusion

The significance of the *ARA Libertad* case first of all can be found in reaffirming the well-established rule that warships enjoy sovereign immunity. It furthermore upheld and clarified how immunity for warships relates to the internal waters of a state. Although the case showed two different approaches with regard to the interpretation of Article 32 UNCLOS to arrive at that conclusion, it is without doubt that immunity exists also in the internal waters of a foreign state. As such, the case has provided helpful present-day jurisprudence to strengthen the position of warships in foreign ports. James Kraska also noted that: 'the preservation of sovereign immunity for warships in this order . . . is an encouraging precedent for stability of expectations and the rule of law at sea and in port'.[40] In the context of stability, the clarification of rules on warships is important also in light of the issue the Tribunal has briefly noted in paragraph 97 of its order: 'any act which prevents by force a warship from discharging its mission and duties is a source of conflict that may endanger friendly relations among States'. Somewhat provokingly, Judge Rao pointed out that such actions should be discussed within the *ius ad bellum* spheres.[41] Although there may be something to say for this view, fortunately both states were clearly diplomatic enough not to escalate into that area of international law.

38 See, e.g., separate opinion Judge Lucky, above n 5, para 32. See discussion on this point at Peiris, 'Provisional measures in the ARA Libertad: On the margins of jurisdictional discourse', above n 35, 169–170.

39 Separate opinion of Judge Rao, above n 5, para 9.

40 Kraska, 'The "ARA Libertad" (Argentina v. Ghana). ITLOS Case No. 20. Provisional Measures', above n 6, 7.

41 Separate opinion Judge Rao, above n 5, paras 15–16.

PART II

Jurisdiction and interdiction

4

THE *MS ACHILLE LAURO* HIJACKING

Steven Haines

I. Introduction

During the Grotian era, when ocean governance was dominated by the principle of *mare liberum* (free seas), two notable areas of law prevailed against a backdrop of minimal ocean regulation: the laws of war at sea, and the law relating to sea piracy.[1] They became two essential normative pillars of *mare liberum*, simply because war and piratical acts both posed major threats to the essential rights and freedoms enshrined in the notion of 'free seas'. Each threatened peaceful trading activities and had the potential to disrupt maritime imperial access. Their regulation or suppression were significant imperatives for the great powers with seaborne empires, whose navies had a combination of war-fighting and constabulary purposes. We are clearly concerned with the suppression of violence at sea, but we are focusing in this chapter only on that violence emanating from non-state entities. Traditionally, this would have meant the suppression of piracy[2] but, in the contemporary maritime security environment, we need to broaden our focus to include other manifestations of non-state violence, including armed robbery and terrorism.

The *Achille Lauro* hijacking in 1985 provides us with a most pertinent case study, the influence of which remains significant. The seizure was effected by 'terrorists' and raised awareness of the potential for terrorist attacks within the maritime

1 I take the Grotian era to mean the three centuries from the early 17th century to the middle of the 20th century, since when fundamental and wide-ranging developments have occurred in relation to ocean governance driven by profound change in all dimensions of the ocean environment: political, institutional, economic, social, technological, physical, security, and normative.

2 Navies also had other important constabulary roles, in particular in relation to the protection of inshore fisheries and in the enforcement of customs, fiscal, and quarantine regulations. These were, however, essentially about the maintenance of order within territorial jurisdiction or relatively close to the coast. The suppression of piracy was a high seas role usually involving more distant deployment.

DOI: 10.4324/9781003307013-6

environment, something that had previously not generated substantial international concern. Importantly, however, the hijacking also fell outside the legal parameters of piracy. For that reason, it prompted serious reflection on piracy's widely accepted international legal definition. The law of sea piracy had been codified in the 1958 Geneva Convention on the High Seas.[3] In the mid-1980s, that codification had only very recently been repeated in the 1982 UN Convention on the Law of the Sea.[4] It was, as a result, rapidly coming to be regarded as the customary position on the subject.[5]

That is certainly not to suggest that this law was entirely adequate as a means of dealing with non-state violence at sea. The reason why the *Achille Lauro* incident is sufficiently significant to warrant a chapter in this volume is that, in highlighting the obvious shortcomings in the law of sea piracy, it also led directly to new treaty law on maritime security, negotiated under the auspices of the International Maritime Organisation – namely the 1988 Convention for the Suppression of Unlawful Acts Against the Safety of Maritime Navigation.[6] This is the foundation document of what can usefully be referred to as the SUA Regime.[7]

The SUA Regime has already achieved significance in relation to maritime security operations and there is certainly evidence that the utility of this new law has the potential to well exceed that of the pre-existing law of sea piracy. Could the *Achille Lauro* hijacking come to be regarded as a watershed event in maritime security law, consigning the traditional and established law of piracy to history? In order to answer that question, we need to examine the relationship between the law of piracy and the SUA Regime. We also need to give some consideration to the degree of obligation attached to those two bodies of law. Before we do that, it will be useful to provide some background comments on both the law of sea piracy and the phenomenon of 'maritime terrorism'. We will then move on briefly to describe the events of October 1985, before reaching some conclusions as to the consequences, legal and operational.

3 See 1958 Geneva High Seas Convention arts 14–21.

4 1833 UNTS 3, hereafter '*1982 UNCLOS*', arts100–107.

5 *1982 UNCLOS* arts 100–107. Relatively recent texts noting that the conventional law of piracy reflects prior customary law are Donald Rothwell and Tim Stephens, *The International Law of the Sea* (2nd ed., Hart Publishing, 2016), 171–173; and Yoshifumi Tanaka, *The International Law of the Sea* (Cambridge University Press, 2012), 355.

6 Hereafter, the 1988 SUA Convention.

7 At the same time as the 1988 SUA Convention was agreed, a protocol (essentially a separate but related treaty) was also agreed: the 1988 Protocol for the Suppression of Unlawful Acts Against the Safety of Fixed Platforms Located on the Continental Shelf (hereafter the 1988 SUA Protocol). Following the events of 11 September 2001, two further protocols were negotiated and agreed in 2005. They were intended to develop the law in the previous two instruments and broadened the range of offences to include terrorist acts and trafficking in weapons of mass destruction. While these four instruments will be referred to collectively as 'the SUA Regime' in this chapter, it should be noted that not all states party to the 1988 instruments are also party to the 2005 protocols.

II. Background

A. The law of sea piracy

Events off Somalia, in the northwestern Indian Ocean and in the Gulf of Aden, in recent years served to raise the profile of sea piracy and led to the mounting of significant multi-national naval operations to suppress it. It was not always regarded as so obviously a contemporary problem, however. Dubner, in his classic treatment of the subject published in 1980, noted that 'most international jurists and states consider the matter of "traditional" piracy a dead issue'.[8] Even more recently, the prominent international criminal lawyer, Cherif Bassiouni, remarked that 'Piracy, almost non-existent nowadays, neither threatens peace and security nor shocks the conscience of humanity, although it may have at one time'.[9] Dubner was somewhat less sanguine than Bassiouni, arguing that there ought to be some modification of the law of piracy (the treaty law from 1958) to take account of 'incidents of alleged terrorism on the seas'. Nevertheless, he also noted the difficulties likely to be experienced in obtaining any sort of international consensus to that effect.[10]

That extant law of piracy is simply stated. It concerns

> any illegal acts of violence or detention, or any act of depredation, committed for private ends by the crew or the passengers of a private ship . . . and directed on the high seas, against another ship . . . or against persons or property on board such ship.[11]

The law is a reflection of the traditional and popular perception of piracy, involving pirate vessels crewed by ruthless criminals out for private gain and attacking and seizing ships going about their lawful purpose on the high seas. It was this behaviour that the law of piracy during the Grotian era was developed to suppress, with a fundamental element of that law being the establishment of universal jurisdiction to allow the warships of any state to take action, regardless of the state of registry of the pirate vessels encountered.

8 Barry Dubner, *The Law of International Sea Piracy* (Martinus Nijhoff, 1980), 69.

9 M. Cherif Bassiouni, 'International Crimes: *Jus Cogens* and *Obligatio Erga Omnes*' (1996) *Law and Contemporary Problems* 63–74. Bassiouni's view is surprising, as piracy had certainly not ceased being a problem – see, for example, the comments made around the same time in Robin Churchill and Alan Vaughan Lowe, *The Law of the Sea* (Manchester University Press, 3rd ed, 1999), 209.

10 Dubner, *The Law of International Sea Piracy*, above n 8, 69. When Dubner was writing, the Third UN Conference on the Law of the Sea was underway but drawing to a conclusion. It had been the obvious forum for brokering any change. None was made, and the resultant 1982 UNCLOS contained precisely the same provisions on piracy as had the 1958 High Seas Convention.

11 *1982 UNCLOS* art 101. The 'high seas' is taken to mean any sea area beyond territorial jurisdiction and includes, therefore, the waters of the exclusive economic zone beyond the 12-nautical-mile territorial limit; see *1982 UNCLOS* art 58, together with art 87.

There is some evidence that 'piracy' was not previously as narrowly defined as it is today; the term being applied to various forms of criminal violence and armed robbery at sea. Indeed, during the inter-war years, a study conducted by the Harvard Research in International Law produced a draft convention on piracy that included criteria that are today excluded from the definition.[12] That draft convention was never taken forward into treaty law, however, and by the time the law of piracy was codified in the 1950s, universal jurisdiction was exercisable only in respect of the narrower definition. It was this definition, established in both conventional and customary terms, that applied in October 1985 when the *Achille Lauro* was hijacked.

The renowned 17th-century publicist Hugo Grotius addressed the issue of piracy, and the jurisdiction necessary to prosecute it, in the final paragraphs of his treatise *Mare Liberum*. He distinguished between jurisdiction over ocean space and jurisdiction over individuals to be found within it. It was emphatically the latter that he argued provided the basis for the prosecution of piracy and not any assumed dominion over the seas.[13] In establishing his argument, he referred to the classical example of Julius Caesar's capture of pirates, his attempt to achieve their prosecution by placing them within the jurisdiction of the Roman authorities ashore, and his reaction when the officiating pro-consul declined to prosecute. Caesar (at that time a private citizen) sailed back onto the high seas with the detained pirates on board and promptly crucified them, something he would not have been legally entitled to do if the seas had fallen within the territorial jurisdiction of the Roman *imperium*.

Interestingly, Caesar's reaction, two millennia ago, has echoes in the modern opinion that regards the outlawing of piracy as a *jus cogens*.[14] As a peremptory norm of international law, states do not merely have the right to act against those who have committed acts of piracy; they are arguably under an obligation to do so. Indeed, the conventional law states that 'All states shall cooperate to the fullest possible extent in the repression of piracy'.[15] This seems very clear. As Bassiouni has suggested:

> the implications of *jus cogens* are those of a duty and not of optional rights; otherwise *jus cogens* would not constitute a peremptory norm of international law. Consequently, these obligations are non-derogable in times of war as well as peace. Thus, recognising certain international crimes as *jus cogens*

12 The Harvard Research in International Law was originally published in the American Journal of International Law between 1929 and 1939. See the discussion of the 'History and Development' of piracy in Dubner, *The Law of International Sea Piracy*, above n 8 ch III, 37.

13 Hugo Grotius, *The Free Sea* (Liberty Fund, 2004), 128–129.

14 For a recent discussion of *jus cogens*, see James Crawford, *Brownlie's Principles of Public International Law* (Oxford University Press, 8th ed., 2012), 594–603. Further useful relevant discussions are: M. Cherif Bassiouni, 'International Crimes: *Jus Cogens* and *Obligatio Erga Omnes*' (1996) 59(4) *Law and Contemporary Problems*, 63–74; see also Maurizio Ragazzi, *The Concept of International Obligations Erga Omnes* (Clarendon Press, 1997).

15 *1982 UNCLOS*, art 100.

> carries with it the duty to prosecute or extradite . . . . Above all, the characterisation of certain crimes as *jus cogens* places upon states the *obligatio erga omnes* not to grant impunity to the violators of such crimes.[16]

This obligation *erga omnes* arguably provides the legal grounds for a breach of the norm of exclusive flag state jurisdiction on the high seas (which is itself a further pillar of *mare liberum*).[17] Logical though such an argument is, it is not uncontroversial; we shall return to it later in the chapter.

B. Maritime terrorism

As Walter Laqueur noted in his classic work on the subject, 'terrorism is . . . an insurrectional strategy that can be used by people of very different political convictions'.[18] It has an assumed utility in domestic political contexts but it has also long had an international dimension, with groups identified with one society or political entity often crossing and operating over political boundaries. That said, if we look back over time at manifestations of international terrorism it becomes apparent that the global socio-political and communications conditions necessary for terrorism to be seriously internationalised were not substantially in place prior to the middle of the 20th century. Indeed, the contemporary phenomenon we refer to as 'international terrorism' only became a serious international concern in the late 1960s. By then, the conditions conducive to it were in place. There was also a political cause whose leaders recognised the opportunity it provided. That cause was the product of the deep-seated animosity between the state of Israel and its Arab neighbours, exacerbated by the fate of those Muslim communities both living in, and displaced from, Palestine.

International terrorism first became a serious issue in the late 1960s and 1970s because armed groups identified with the Palestinian cause took their campaign to the international level, most dramatically by targeting civilian airliners. The hijacking of aircraft by the Popular Front for the Liberation of Palestine (PFLP) began with that of El Al Flight 426 from Rome to Tel Aviv on 23 July 1968. It continued with a number of incidents in the 1970s, including the so-called Dawson Field Hijackings in September 1970 that ended with the explosive destruction of three civil airliners on the ground in the Jordanian desert and the negotiated release of a number of PFLP fighters. Such incidents were deliberately dramatic and high profile. They demanded an international legal response.

16 Bassiouni, 'International Crimes: *Jus Cogens* and *Obligatio Erga Omnes*', above n 9, 65–66. He lists those crimes he considers have achieved *jus cogens* status and includes piracy in that list (on p 68).

17 The third, and final, pillar of *mare liberum* has been the traditional law of war at sea that permits the use of the seas for war but serves to protect the freedom to trade, especially in relation to neutral powers.

18 Walter Laqueur, *Terrorism* (Abacus, 1980), 14.

There were, however, political and practical difficulties associated with defining 'terrorist' and distinguishing between those who mounted attacks deliberately to spread fear and others who used similar techniques for other reasons. The result was an international legal response that aimed at dealing with the fact of hijacking rather than either the motives or the purpose of those committing the offence. The 1970 Hague Convention for the Suppression of the Unlawful Seizure of Aircraft was one result.[19] It entered into force quite quickly, in 1971. The word 'terrorism' did not appear anywhere in its title, preamble, or substantive text.

At that time, there was no conventional law dealing with terrorist acts that might occur at sea, essentially because it was not considered a sufficiently serious threat. Very obviously, piracy had a long history; hence, the first treaty dealing with the regulation of the high seas included provisions on piracy as an international crime.[20] While often violent and terrifying for its victims, piracy was not politically motivated terrorism, however. As a matter of record, while aircraft were being hijacked in the air, ships were certainly being seized at sea, but generally by local small-time pirates operating close inshore rather than politically or religiously motivated terrorists – and the incidents were far less dramatic, attracting little worldwide publicity.

Instances of maritime terrorism were rare, albeit not entirely unknown. In January 1961, for example, the Portuguese flagged passenger ship *Santa Maria*, with 600 passengers embarked, was seized off the Brazilian coast by a political group opposed to the Salazar-led regime in Portugal. The Third Officer and three other crew members were killed.[21] The *Achille Lauro* would not be the first cruise ship to suffer such an assault. There were also several other, largely isolated, attempted attacks on ships and offshore oil installations, none of which was especially noteworthy. In the 1970s, the Provisional Irish Republican Army (PIRA) seemed to toy with the idea of targeting ships, but nothing of real substance occurred. The placing of a bomb onboard the passenger ferry *Ulster Queen* while it was alongside in Belfast was perhaps more to do with the campaign of terror in Belfast than about taking the struggle to sea.[22] Then, in February 1981, the PIRA did suddenly go maritime and managed to sink the British registered cargo vessel, *MV Nellie M* in the approaches to the port of Londonderry. The ship was stationary in the water when it was boarded by a PIRA

19 860 UNTS 105.

20 *1958 Geneva Convention on the High Seas*; Piracy is dealt with in arts 14–22, with the international crime of piracy defined in art 15.

21 The leader of the group that seized the ship subsequently published his account of it, in Henrique Galvão, *Santa Maria. My Crusade for Portugal* (Weidenfeld & Nicolson, 1961).

22 The information quoted here is taken from Brian Parritt (ed), *Violence at Sea: A Review of Terrorism, Acts of War and Piracy, and Countermeasures to Prevent Terrorism* (ICC Publishing, 1986); see 'Chronology of Terrorist and other Attacks' 235–256. This contains mention of one PIRA attack, on the British registered passenger ferry *Ulster Queen*, damaged while alongside in Belfast by a bomb placed in its first class lounge. Despite this happening onboard a ship, its location suggests that it is probably best regarded as a part of the terrorist violence in Belfast rather than a distinctive act of 'maritime terrorism'.

unit that had seized the Moville Point Pilot Station, which serviced the port of Londonderry in Northern Ireland but which was located in County Donegal in the Republic of Ireland. Its ship's crew was taken ashore to safety before the vessel was sunk by the detonation of charges placed in its bilges. There was some press coverage of this incident, but not a great deal. Nevertheless, it was a successful attack and PIRA repeated the operation exactly 12 months later and in exactly the same location, with an equally successful attack on the *MV St Bedan*.[23] Despite the effective way in which the attacks were carried through, neither had a major impact, either in Northern Ireland or internationally. Tactical success brought with it no discernible strategic advantage for the PIRA and the organisation never thereafter repeated its attempts to mount attacks on significant maritime targets. Indeed, this strategic failure seemed to substantiate the view that terrorist acts at sea have less potential to generate public or media impact than similar scale attacks on land, especially in heavily populated areas. Terrorists feed off publicity; if there is little prospect of significant media impact following attacks on certain types of targets, they will probably be passed by in favour of more attractive options.

Operations at sea also require the skills necessary to function effectively in the maritime environment; few groups will have these as a matter of course. Terrorist acts at sea will always be challenging, will involve a measure of sea-going expertise, and may well not result in the level of publicity and political impact that may be more easily achieved in other ways. For these reasons, while much effort was put into negotiating international arrangements for dealing with aviation-related terrorism, nothing was done to put in place any international legal framework for dealing with 'maritime terrorism'. Things changed, however, in October 1985, prompted by the high-profile incident at sea in the Mediterranean that is the subject of this chapter.

C. *The* Achille Lauro *hijacking*

The *MS Achille Lauro* was a former Rotterdamsche Lloyd ocean liner transformed, in 1965, into an Italian registered cruise ship of the Flotta Lauro Line. By 1985, however, she was on charter to the Chandris Line, the Lauro Line having gone bankrupt three years earlier. The planned 12-day cruise she was undertaking at the time of the hijacking included stops in both Arab (Egyptian and Syrian) and Israeli ports. She left the Italian port of Genoa on 3 October with 748 passengers embarked and arrived in Alexandria (Egypt) on 7 October. The majority of the passengers disembarked for a sightseeing tour, leaving 97 on the ship together with the crew. The ship planned to steam from Alexandria to Port Said that day, re-embarking the other passengers on arrival in the evening.

23 The present author was the Staff Operations Officer (head of the naval operations department) in the Naval Headquarters within the Northern Ireland Security Forces at the time of the 1981 attack on the *Nellie M*. He coordinated the naval response to it and, following that experience, was in communication with the naval operational staff in Belfast in the immediate aftermath of the second attack, on the *St Bedan*, the following year.

Unknown to the master and crew, there were four members of the Palestine Liberation Front (PLF) embarked in the vessel. They were there on the orders of PLF leader Abu al-Abbas, who had conceived the attack after watching cruise ships sail in and out of ports around the Mediterranean. It appeared to him that such cruise vessels provided an easy means of accessing Israeli territory. The four men had embarked disguised as cruising tourists, their intention being to land in Israel when the ship paid its planned visit to the port of Ashdod. Their ultimate mission was to launch an attack within Israel, possibly a suicide attack (although that is by no means certain), against the Israeli military. The four had conducted dry runs on earlier cruises but, on this final voyage, they had their weapons with them. Unfortunately for them, a crew member apparently discovered them in their cabin cleaning the weapons while the ship was leaving Alexandria. The four men immediately abandoned their original plan and decided instead to hijack the ship. Their aim shifted from that of launching an attack in Israel to one of seizing the ship and somehow arranging to disembark to safety.[24]

They ordered the ship's master to steam towards the Syrian port of Tartus, where they hoped to disembark into a sympathetic Arab state. They also took the opportunity to demand the release of around 50 Palestinian fighters held in Israeli prisons, in exchange for the safe passage of the ship, its crew, and its passengers. Following diplomatic pressure from the Italian and U.S. governments, the Syrian authorities declined to cooperate, however. Nor did the Israelis respond to the demand for them to release Palestinian prisoners. The ship having been refused entry to Tartus, the terrorists killed one of the hostages, an elderly, wheel-chair bound Jewish-American tourist (Leon Klinghoffer), whose body and wheel-chair were thrown overboard. Eventually, in order to end the hijacking and secure the safety of the crew and passengers, Egyptian authorities agreed to the ship docking in Port Said, where the four Palestinians would be allowed to disembark and then take advantage of free air passage out of Egypt. This arrangement was honoured and the terrorists boarded an Egyptian commercial aircraft which took off from Egypt bound for Tunisia. There followed an interception of the Egyptian aircraft over the Mediterranean by fighter aircraft from the U.S. Sixth Fleet carrier *USS Saratoga*. The aircraft was ordered to land at a North Atlantic Treaty Organization (NATO) airbase in Sicily, where the hijackers were arrested by Italian authorities.

24 The details of the *Achille Lauro* hijacking are well documented and the facts not generally in dispute (although the precise circumstances of the decision by the four men to hijack the ship rather than land in Ashdod are still not entirely clear). See, for example, Richard Pallardy, 'Achille Lauro Hijacking', Encyclopaedia Britannica, <www.britannica.com/event/achille-lauro-hijacking>. Many of the details seem to have been confirmed by a recent account of the background to the attack and the attack itself written by Reem al-Nimer, the widow of Mohammad Abbas (aka Abu al-Abbas), the PLF leader who masterminded the operation. (Reem al-Nimer *Curse of the Achille Lauro: A Tribute to Lost Souls* [Cune Press, 2013]). Abbas was captured by U.S. forces in Iraq in 2003 and died in detention the following year. Al-Nimer's book was widely reported when published – see, for example, Robert Fisk, 'How Achille Lauro hijackers were seduced by the high life', *The Independent*, 5 May 2013.

The U.S. action prompted complaints from Egypt about the interception of an Egyptian commercial aircraft, and from Italy about the decision to force the aircraft down in Sicily (without prior approval from Rome). Although Washington would have preferred to move the detained terrorists to the United States for prosecution (which would have required extradition from Italy), the four hijackers were eventually prosecuted in Italy and sentenced to periods in jail of up to 30 years. The jurisdiction of the Italian courts in these cases relied on the *Achille Lauro* being an Italian-flagged vessel; the hijacking and murder of Leon Klinghoffer occurred, therefore, within Italian jurisdiction. Two of the convicted hijackers were released on parole in 1991 and the other two were released in 2008 and 2009.

There were a number of interesting and challenging legal issues raised by these events and the responses they provoked, all of which provide fertile ground for legal analysis. One can, for example, examine the legality of the deal brokered to allow the hijackers to disembark in Port Said and to take free passage out of Egypt, the U.S. interception of the Egyptian commercial aircraft, and the forced landing of that aircraft in Italian territory without the prior approval of Italian authorities. These each raise important questions, but they are not the reason for the inclusion of this case study in this volume. The legal questions of greatest interest here were to do with how the hijacking itself might be regarded in law. Was the seizure of the vessel an act of piracy, or not? Depending on the answer to that question, what were the jurisdictional and operational consequences?

The answer to the first of these two questions is very clear: the hijacking of the ship was emphatically not an act of piracy as defined in international law. For it to be so, the seizure would have needed to have taken place on the high seas, it would have needed to involve another vessel launching the attack, and those carrying out the hijacking would have needed to be acting for their own private ends. It failed to satisfy the piracy criteria in all senses: it was seized in Egyptian internal or territorial waters; it was seized by passengers; and the four men were politically motivated. A natural – though misplaced – perception that it was piracy served to highlight the shortcomings of the law dealing with criminal violence against shipping. Resolving those shortcomings would require either a re-drafting of the law on piracy or a quite separate development of law to do with terrorist attacks on shipping – something, indeed, like the treaty law already developed to deal with the hijacking of aircraft.

III. Analysis and outcomes

A. The SUA Regime

In December 1985, the UN General Assembly called for 'appropriate measures' to be proposed for dealing with such incidents and there began a process to develop the law.[25] The International Maritime Bureau (IMB), which had a particular role in monitoring

25 GA Res 40/61, UN GAOR, 108th plen mtg, UN Doc A/RES/40/61 (9 December 1985).

violence at sea, convened an expert workshop in San Jose, California in March 1986 to identify a way forward. One of its conclusions was that any response to maritime terrorism should avoid becoming distracted by defining terrorism, and the motives of those involved, and concentrate instead on the physical acts that could place shipping in jeopardy. This reflected the pragmatic thinking behind the conventional law developed previously to deal with aircraft hijackings. Defining 'terrorism', and dealing with the political sensitivities that discussion of motives would inevitably generate, would only serve to delay or – more likely – prevent agreement over effective action.

The IMB also discussed practical actions that could be taken to reduce the risks to shipping.[26] The workshop in San Jose explored a number of options, ranging from simple and easily implemented physical security measures to consideration of the deployment of 'sea marshals' (an idea inspired by the previous deployment of air marshals on civilian airliners). Its recommendations were fed into the Maritime Safety Committee of the International Maritime Organisation, which went on to produce interim guidance for the shipping industry that September.[27] The following year it also began to consider a draft international convention proposed jointly by Egypt, Italy and Austria, the eventual result of which was the 1988 SUA Convention agreed in Rome in March 1988. As we have already noted, this is the foundation document of the SUA Regime. Space precludes a detailed analysis of this body of law but, fortunately, this is not necessary as a most useful and comprehensive commentary has already been produced by Kraska and Pedrozo.[28]

There are two features of the SUA Regime that we need to highlight. The first is the range of offences covered by Article 3 of the 1988 SUA Convention (further expanded by the 2005 protocols). Study of these reveals that they not only more than adequately cover the offences committed onboard the *Achille Lauro*, but also subsume piracy as currently defined. States within the SUA Regime may no longer have any need to rely on the law of piracy. They are obliged to have domestic legislation in place to allow for the prosecution of SUA offences[29] – although they are under no obligation to dispense with law dealing with sea piracy.[30]

26 The outcome of which was reported in Parritt, *Violence at Sea*, above n 22. The present author was a member of the IMB expert workshop that met in San Jose and the author of the paper that argued that a response should not focus on motive but on the criminal acts themselves; see Steven Haines 'Criminal Violence at Sea: Observations on the Threat and Appropriate Responses', in Brian Parritt (ed), *Violence at Sea: A Review of Terrorism, Acts of War and Piracy, and Countermeasures to Prevent Terrorism* (ICC Publishing, 1986), 93–108.

27 IMO Documents, MSC/Circular 443 of 26 September 1986 Measures to Prevent Unlawful Acts Against Passengers and Crews Onboard Ships.

28 James Kraska and Raul Pedrozo, *International Maritime Security Law* (Martinus Nijhoff, 2013), 801–858. For simplicity, and since the 1988 SUA Convention is both the foundation document and the most ratified of the four instruments, we will tend to refer to this in the discussion that follows.

29 1988 SUA Convention, art.5.

30 In the case of the United Kingdom, for example, offences of piracy can be prosecuted using either pt II of the Aviation and Maritime Security Act 1990 (which enabled ratification of the 1988 SUA Convention) or under s 26 of the Merchant Shipping and Maritime Security Act 1997, which acknowledges the definition of piracy in the 1982 UNCLOS as 'constituting part of the law of nations'.

Since not all states are within the SUA Regime, the law of piracy still has some relevance and application. Nevertheless, the number of states within the regime – over 166 at the time of writing, including the flags of around 95% of the world's merchant ship tonnage – does mean that it is close to being universal. That being the case, there is good reason for asking what the future relevance of the law of piracy might be – could it soon become moribund?

B. The law of piracy and the SUA Regime compared

To answer this question, we need to compare and contrast the two legal regimes and consider enforcement and prosecution. There is certainly overlap because acts of piracy are effectively covered within the list of offences covered by the SUA Regime (although, very clearly, the reverse is not the case). The most important areas of contrast, however, are to do with jurisdiction and with the rights and obligations to suppress the acts included within the two regimes.

Piracy has long been subject to universal jurisdiction. Indeed, it was the first crime to be so subject, paving the way for subsequent development of the concept.[31] It does not fall within the jurisdiction of the International Criminal Court, however, and can only be prosecuted in municipal courts. That would depend, of course, on the availability of appropriate domestic law, and individual states may experience difficulty in applying it at the national level. Significantly, there is no specific international obligation on states to ensure that piracy is adequately reflected in domestic law. The effectiveness of a general ability to prosecute piracy at the municipal level could realistically only be tested if states sought to prosecute. This would itself depend on their willingness to exercise universal jurisdiction by deploying naval forces capable of enforcing the law. There has, however, been a general failure to exercise universal enforcement jurisdiction over piracy, with the naval operations in response to Somali-based piracy being quite exceptional.[32] The bulk of the cases arising from naval operations to suppress Somali piracy have been dealt with by the rendition of captured pirates from the warships of enforcing states to the jurisdiction of courts in the region.[33] In contrast, while

31 M. Cherif Bassiouni, 'The History of Universal Jurisdiction and its place in International Law' in Stephen Macedo (ed), *Universal Jurisdiction: National Courts and the Prosecution of Serious Crimes Under International Law* (University of Pennsylvania Press, 2006), 47–49. While piracy is subject to universal jurisdiction, there is some doubt as to the extent of that, including in relation to aspects of the crime that are located ashore. There is, however, the 'intrinsic difficulty of addressing maritime criminality only by taking action at sea, as inevitably, the roots of such crimes lie ashore' (see Douglas Guilfoyle, 'Policy tensions and the legal regime governing piracy' in Douglas Guilfoyle, *Modern Piracy: Legal Challenges and Responses* (Edward Elgar, 2013), 325–336, at 329.

32 See Eugene Kontorovich and Steven Art, 'An Empirical Examination of Universal Jurisdiction for Piracy' (2010) 104 *American Journal of International Law* 436–453.

33 Following agreements with regional states such as Kenya, the Seychelles, and Mauritius. See Kontorovich and Art, 'An Empirical Examination of Universal Jurisdiction for Piracy', above n 32, and Tullio Treves, 'Piracy and the International Law of the Sea', in Guilfoyle, *Modern Piracy: Legal Challenges and Responses* (Edward Elgar, 2013), 117–146.

the offences created under the SUA Regime are not subject to universal jurisdiction, they should be capable of being dealt with in the municipal courts of all states within the regime because of the obligation placed upon them to enact appropriate domestic legislation.[34]

The fact that the SUA Regime does not establish universal jurisdiction means that without the cooperation and agreement of relevant flag states, action cannot always be taken to suppress illicit activities on the high seas. Exclusive flag state jurisdiction still applies[35] – except, of course, in the case of offences that are also contrary to the law of piracy. This means that in operational and enforcement terms, there is very good reason for not consigning the law of piracy to the archives. While the offences constituting piracy are covered in the SUA Regime, the enforcement possibilities are by no means as flexible under SUA as they are under the law of piracy. If a vessel is seized by pirates, enforcement action can, if necessary, be taken without reference to the flag state. This would, for example, allow a surprise special forces operation to be mounted to end a hijacking without a high risk of compromise. Universal jurisdiction remains a valuable option which SUA does not provide.

The second issue worthy of comparison is to do with *jus cogens* and the related notion of obligations *erga omnes*. As we noted previously, it has been argued that piracy is a breach of a peremptory norm of international law (*jus cogens*) which ought to generate an obligation *erga omnes*. Bassiouni argued that if there is no such obligation, it is difficult to see how a *jus cogens* can exist. But is there an obligation *erga omnes* to suppress piracy? Article 100 of the 1982 UNCLOS certainly codifies a duty to cooperate to the fullest extent in its repression. Unfortunately, all other articles relating to piracy contain a discretionary tone rather than a mandatory one. It is by no means certain that piracy has achieved full *jus cogens* status. According to the International Law Commission, a treaty representing an agreement between two states to facilitate acts of piracy would be contrary to the law of treaties.[36] This will not mean, however, that there is a certain obligation *erga omnes* placed on all states to take positive action to suppress piracy. This is what Bassiouni seemed to be implying in the quote included earlier in this chapter. There is too great a discretionary element in the expectations placed upon states for this to be the case. In contrast, the SUA Regime contains clear obligations on states to take action, especially in relation to prosecution. In common with other counter-terrorism instruments, there is an obligation on all states party to either prosecute or extradite (to a state willing to prosecute) any pirates present within their jurisdiction. The SUA Regime obligation is seemingly stronger than that in the law of piracy.

34 See, e.g., the obligation included in art 5 of the 1988 SUA Convention.

35 There are also 'prosecute or extradite' obligations under the SUA Regime, as noted in what follows.

36 Examples mentioned by the International Law Commission as being potential breaches of art 53 of the 1969 Vienna Convention on the Law of Treaties included 'a treaty contemplating or conniving in the commission of acts, such as trade in slaves, piracy or genocide, in the suppression of which every state is called upon to cooperate' (*Yearbook of the International Law Commission*, 1966 II, 247–248).

IV. Conclusions

The SUA Regime has certainly not to date completely subsumed or replaced the existing law of piracy. It has gone some way towards doing so, but importantly, it has not established universal jurisdiction for SUA offences. What it has done, however, is create an obligation to either prosecute or extradite those who are accused of a range of unlawful acts that threaten the safety of maritime navigation. This is stronger than the discretionary nature of the universal jurisdiction contained in the law of piracy. Any future developments to do with the security of shipping are more than likely to involve further development of the SUA Regime. It is extremely difficult to imagine any serious attempt to review the law of piracy in the future. Indeed, if for any reason that became a serious possibility, it is surely the case that it would become fully subsumed within the SUA Regime. That being the case, the hijacking of the *Achille Lauro* must be regarded as a profoundly significant event that initiated a fundamental and lasting development in maritime security law. Today, the SUA Regime provides a broad legal framework for the suppression of unlawful acts against shipping and is likely to be the legal forum for developments in the future. If it does dominate in this way, the *Achille Lauro* hijacking will surely come to be seen as the seminal event in the decline of the traditional law of sea piracy – but at the time of writing, it has most certainly not consigned the law of sea piracy to history.

5

THE *SO SAN* INCIDENT

Douglas Guilfoyle

I. Introduction

On 9 December 2002, the Spanish frigates *Navarra* and *Patino* halted and boarded the cargo vessel *So San* approximately 600 nm from the coast of Yemen.[1] The *Navarra* and *Patino*, originally deployed in support of Operation Enduring Freedom to intercept Al Qaeda operatives leaving Afghanistan, were acting on U.S. and British intelligence that the *So San* was carrying a cargo of Scud missiles from North Korea to an unknown destination in the Middle East.[2] While such a cargo was discovered aboard, the vessel was eventually released to continue to Yemen.

II. Background

The *So San* displayed neither a flag nor any 'indication of its state of registry or home port', and no vessel named *So San* appeared in any available registry.[3] This obviously gave rise to uncertainty as to its nationality and suspicion as to its intentions. The captain indicated to the *Navarra* that he was carrying a cargo of concrete to Yemen. The captain resisted boarding and inspection, and warning shots were fired before the Spanish warships manoeuvred to 'cut off' the *So San*'s further progress.[4] A boarding party was then inserted by helicopter.[5]

1 Thom Shanker, 'Threats and Responses: Arms Smuggling; Scud Missiles Found on Ship of North Korea', *New York Times*, 11 December 2002, at A1.

2 Craig H. Allen, *Maritime Counterproliferation Operations and the Rule of Law* (Praeger Security International, 2007), 150; A. Fleischer, White House Press Secretary, Press Briefing, 11 December 2002, <www.presidency.ucsb.edu/ws/index.php?pid=47463>.

3 Ibid.

4 Shanker, 'Threats and Responses', above n 1.

5 Douglas Guilfoyle, *Shipping Interdiction and the Law of the Sea* (Cambridge University Press 2009), 245.

DOI: 10.4324/9781003307013-7

While the incident is commonly discussed as having been a boarding justified by suspicion that the vessel was 'without nationality' (stateless), it appears that at the 'last minute', the captain attempted to declare the vessel to be registered to Cambodia.[6] Upon enquiry, 'Cambodia could only confirm that the ship matched the description of a vessel registered in Cambodia under a different name'.[7] Cambodia nonetheless gave 'conditional consent' to the boarding of the *So San* if indeed it transpired that it was actually a Cambodian registered vessel.[8] On some reports, boarding and inspection of the ship's papers did in fact confirm its Cambodian registration.[9] Once aboard, the Spanish boarding team discovered 15 assembled Scud missiles 'with parts to make eight more missiles and 85 drums of red fuming nitric acid (an oxidiser used in Scud fuel)' underneath tonnes of bags of cement.[10] Only the cement was listed in the ship's manifest.[11]

III. Legal inquiry

The *So San* incident never resulted in a formal inquiry. Instead, it was resolved diplomatically, when Yemen publicly claimed the missiles as its own. Yemen's position (undoubtedly correct) was that it had legally purchased the Scuds from North Korea for its own defence and there was no legal basis to interdict that shipment.[12] As a result, it appears as if plans to divert the *So San* for further inspection to Diego Garcia were abandoned and the vessel was released to continue its journey.[13]

It is universally accepted that the *So San* interception was a valid exercise of the right of visit on the high seas under which, on grounds including suspicion a vessel is stateless, a warship may 'proceed to verify the ship's right to fly its flag' by sending a 'boat under the command of an officer' to inspect the ship's documents.[14] Strictly, a further search of the vessel is only permissible if 'suspicion remains after the documents have been checked'.[15] It has occasionally been doubted whether the extensive search of the *So San* which followed the boarding was legally justified, once

6 Allen, *Maritime Counterproliferation Operations and the Rule of Law*, above n 2, 150.
7 Ibid.
8 Ibid.
9 M. Byers, 'Policing the high seas: the Proliferation Security Initiative' (2004) 98 *American Journal of International Law* 526, 526 n 5.
10 Allen, *Maritime Counterproliferation Operations and the Rule of Law*, above n 2, 151.
11 M. Becker, 'The shifting order of the oceans: freedom of navigation and the interdiction of ships at sea' (2005) 46 *Harvard International Law Journal* 131–153.
12 Thom Shanker and Terence Neilan, 'Yemen Protests Seizure of North Korean Ship; Says Scuds Were Bound for Its Army', *New York Times*, 12 December 2002, <www.nytimes.com/2002/12/11/international/12CND-MISS.html>.
13 Ibid; A. Fleischer, White House Press Secretary, *Press Briefing*, 11 December 2002, <www.presidency.ucsb.edu/ws/index.php?pid=47463>.
14 Art 22(2) Geneva Convention on the High Seas 1958, 450 UNTS 82; Art. 110(2) United Nations Convention on the Law of the Sea 1982 (UNCLOS), 1833 UNTS 3.
15 Ibid.

its Cambodian nationality was confirmed.[16] Obviously, the answer to this question turns on whether Cambodia consented to the search as well as the boarding.

Nonetheless, the incident was widely taken as highlighting the lack of any legal basis to interdict or confiscate weapons delivery systems on the high seas.[17] It has also been said that the 'release of the *So San* was reflective of the seriousness with which the high seas regime [and freedom of navigation] is taken by the US'.[18] In an apparent coincidence, the United States released its national strategy to combat the proliferation of weapons of mass destruction (and their delivery systems) the next day, on 10 December 2002.[19]

IV. Analysis and outcomes

At the very least, the *So San* helped crystallise changes in international law and cooperative mechanisms aimed at the containment of the proliferation of weapons of mass destruction, their delivery systems, and precursor technologies or 'dual use' material (hereinafter, collectively, 'WMD materiel'). The most obvious examples were in the formation of the Proliferation Security Initiative (PSI) in 2003 and the passage of UN Security Council Resolution 1540 in 2004,[20] followed in due course by U.S.-led efforts to conclude bilateral and multilateral treaties providing for the consensual interdiction of vessels suspected of involvement in the proliferation of WMD or associated materiel (2004–2010).[21] Of course, it is possible that causation runs the other way and that maritime counter-proliferation was already an issue of concern to the U.S. administration and the *So San* episode was publicised in order to draw attention to the issue. Even if this were the case, the role of the incident in galvanising the international response that followed should not be underestimated.[22]

16 Becker, 'The shifting order of the oceans: freedom of navigation and the interdiction of ships at sea', above n 11, 205.

17 Cf A. Fleischer, White House Press Secretary, *Press Briefing*, 11 December 2002, <www.presidency.ucsb.edu/ws/index.php?pid=47463>.

18 See M. Byers, 'Proliferation Security Initiative (PSI)', *Max Planck Encyclopedia of Public International Law* (July 2019) para 5.

19 White House, *National Strategy to Combat Weapons of Mass Destruction* (Washington DC, 2002) <https://irp.fas.org/offdocs/nspd/nspd-17.html>.

20 See generally: D. Joyner, 'The Proliferation Security Initiative: Nonproliferation, counterproliferation and international law' (2005) 30 *Yale Journal of International Law* 507; James Kraska and Raul A Pedrozo, *International Maritime Security Law* (Martinus Nijhoff, 2013) 785–794.

21 Bilateral treaties were concluded with: Antigua and Barbuda, Bahamas, Belize, Croatia, Cyprus, Liberia, Malta, Marshall Islands, Mongolia, Panama and St. Vincent and the Grenadines. See: <https://2009-2017.state.gov/t/isn/trty/index.htm>; Kraska and Pedrozo, *International Maritime Security Law*, above n 20, 794.

22 Although the widely discussed *BBC China* incident (in which international cooperation prevented a shipment of potential uranium enrichment centrifuge components from reaching Libya) may have been as or more important. For an outline of the facts see: Guilfoyle, *Shipping Interdiction*, above n 5, 245–246; Natalie Klein, *Maritime Security and the Law of the Sea* (Oxford University Press, 2011),

A. The Proliferation Security Initiative and the Statement of Interdiction Principles

First, as indicated, the *So San* incident was widely credited with the establishment of the Proliferation Security Initiative (PSI), announced by U.S. President George W. Bush in 2003. The PSI was conceived of as an 'activity, not an organisation'[23] and represented a non-institutional political commitment to cooperate both *within* existing international law and by strengthening or creating new legal regimes where necessary.[24] Later in 2003, PSI participant states agreed a non-binding Statement of Interdiction Principles (PSI Principles) including, crucially, a commitment in principle 4 to:

> Take specific actions in support of interdiction efforts regarding cargoes of WMD, their delivery systems, or related materials, to the extent their national legal authorities permit *and consistent with their obligations under international law and frameworks*, to include:
>
> a Not to transport or assist in the transport of any such cargoes to or from states or non-state actors of proliferation concern.
>
> b At their own initiative, or at the request and good cause shown by another state, to take action to board and search any vessel flying their flag in their internal waters or territorial seas, or areas beyond the territorial seas of any other state, that is reasonably suspected of transporting such cargoes to or from states or non-state actors of proliferation concern, and to seize such cargoes that are identified.
>
> c To seriously consider providing consent under the appropriate circumstances to the boarding and searching of its own flag vessels by other states, and to the seizure of such WMD-related cargoes in such vessels that may be identified by such states.
>
> d To take appropriate actions to (1) stop and/or search in their internal waters, territorial seas, or contiguous zones (when declared) vessels that are reasonably suspected of carrying such cargoes to or from states or non-state actors of proliferation concern and to seize such cargoes that are identified; and (2) to enforce conditions on vessels entering or leaving their ports, internal waters or territorial seas that are reasonably suspected of carrying such cargoes, such as requiring that such vessels be subject to boarding, search, and seizure of such cargoes prior to entry.[25]

202–203; Y.-H. Song, 'The US-led Proliferation Security Initiative and UNCLOS: Legality, Implementation, and an Assessment', (2007) 38 *Ocean Development and International Law* 101–128.

23 J. Bolton, 'The Bush Administration's Forward Strategy for Nonproliferation' (2004–5) 5 *Chicago Journal of International Law* 395–400, at 400.

24 'Proliferation Security Initiative: Statement of Interdiction Principles', 4 September 2003, principles 3 and 4 <www.psi-online.info/psi-info-en/botschaft/-/2077920>.

25 See <www.psi-online.info/psi-info-en/botschaft/-/2077920>

As at 2021, the PSI was listed as having 107 participants.[26] While this suggests impressive coverage, it has been observed that the requirements of being a 'participant' may be 'fairly weak'.[27]

Returning to the interdiction principles, principle 4(d) raised questions (and concerns) about the extent of the legal authority of a coastal state in its territorial sea or contiguous zone to stop and search vessels, or to exercise law enforcement jurisdiction over them, on the basis that they were suspected of being engaged in proliferation of WMD materiel. Presuming that the relevant coastal state had laws in place that would make such transfers through its territory or maritime jurisdiction a crime, several cases must be distinguished. First, in internal waters, the port state has plenary sovereignty and a visiting merchant or private ship has no immunity from local law.[28] (While port states will often not enforce their laws against a foreign vessel and its crew concerning matters of the 'internal economy' of the vessel, this is usually considered a matter of comity, not legal obligation.)[29] Thus, any offences based on transportation or possession of WMD material should be capable of being enforced without difficulty. Even if there were any such difficulties, they could be cured by imposing conditions of entry upon all vessels which, as principle 4(d) notes, may be enforced in the territorial sea prior to entry or after departure.[30]

Enforcement operations in the territorial sea are more complex. A vessel not intending to call at port which is merely passing through the territorial waters of a state on its way elsewhere ordinarily enjoys the right of innocent passage. Law enforcement jurisdiction is thus usually taken to be predicated upon non-innocent activity. The list of such activities found in the UN Convention on the Law of the Sea (UNCLOS) include:

- any threat or use of force against the sovereignty, territorial integrity or political independence of the coastal State', weapons exercises, launching or landing aircraft or deploying military devices;
- research or intelligence-gathering activities; or acts aimed at causing interference with communications;
- loading or unloading 'any commodity, currency or person contrary to the customs, fiscal, immigration or sanitary laws and regulations of the coastal State';
- fishing or acts of 'wilful and serious pollution'; and
- 'any other activity not having a direct bearing on passage'.[31]

26 See <www.state.gov/proliferation-security-initiative/>.

27 M.B. Nikitin, 'Proliferation Security Initiative (PSI)', CRS Report for Congress, RL34327, 15 June 2012, 2.

28 Yoshifumi Tanaka, *The International Law of the Sea* (3rd ed., Cambridge University Press, 2019), 96–98; Donald R Rothwell and Tim Stephens, *The International Law of the Sea* (2nd ed., Hart, 2016), 56–59.

29 Ibid (Tanaka noting the different French doctrinal position taken on this point).

30 UNCLOS, above n 14, Art 25(2).

31 UNCLOS, above n 14, Art 19(2).

The obvious point is that such activities produce effects felt beyond the vessel and which directly affect the interests of the coastal state in some sense. It is not obvious that transporting materiel capable of being used in manufacturing WMD (or even fully-assembled WMD themselves) fall within any of these categories. The only form of smuggling over which coastal state jurisdiction is contemplated requires the loading or unloading of people or goods – not their mere carriage. The proposition is reinforced by Article 27 UNCLOS, which provides that the 'criminal jurisdiction of the coastal State should not be exercised on board a foreign ship passing through the territorial sea to arrest any person or to conduct any investigation in connection with any crime committed . . . during its passage' unless inter alia the consequences of the crime extend to the coastal state or are such as to disturb 'the peace of the country or the good order of the territorial sea'.[32] Again, WMD materiel destined elsewhere is unlikely to satisfy this test. However, the use of the words 'should not' rather than 'shall not' in this context appears to reflect the Anglo-Saxon legal conception of the territorial sea as a zone of plenary sovereign jurisdiction subject largely to restraints based in comity (as opposed to the Francophone limited powers theory under which a coastal state exercises only a 'bundle of servitudes' over the territorial sea).[33] Thus, under some circumstances, a coastal state could – but generally should not – step outside the limits of Article 27; indeed, given the importance attached by the international community to freedom of navigation, we can expect such cases would be rare. Compliance with a Security Council resolution might, however, be one of them. The consequences of this in the WMD counter-proliferation context are discussed in what follows.

This leaves us with the question of the contiguous zone. Any assertions of law enforcement jurisdiction in the contiguous zone must comply with Article 33 UNCLOS,[34] which provides that in a contiguous zone adjacent the territorial sea and extending no further than 24 nm from its baselines, a coastal state may 'exercise the control necessary to':

1 prevent infringement of its customs, fiscal, immigration, or sanitary laws and regulations within its territory or territorial sea;
2 punish infringement of the above laws and regulations committed within its territory or territorial sea.

The consequences of this phrasing are obvious. Enforcement jurisdiction (the power to 'punish') is distinct from a preventative jurisdiction, and is only available where an offence has already been 'committed within its territory or territorial sea'. Prevention necessarily connotes something less than full law enforcement

32 UNCLOS, above n 14, Art 27(1).

33 Daniel P. O'Connell (Ivan Shearer ed), *The International Law of the Sea*, vol. 2 (Clarendon Press, 1988), 960–961.

34 The same provision is found in: Art 24, Convention on the Territorial Sea and the Contiguous Zone 1958, 516 UNTS 206.

jurisdiction. While it might justify boarding and inspection on suspicion of a future, potential violation of customs laws, it could not justify arrest.[35] Nonetheless, such an operation could yield valuable intelligence.[36]

Such legal limitations in the contiguous zone might be thought either to circumscribe the PSI Interdiction Principles or suggest that the Principles have an exaggerated view of permissible law enforcement jurisdiction in the contiguous zone.[37] The plain text of the Principles, however, refers only to *stopping* and *searching* (not arresting) suspect vessels in the contiguous zone. This is completely compatible with the extent of coastal state preventative jurisdiction in the zone, so long as there is some reasonable suspicion justifying the measures.

B. Security Council Resolution 1540

In UNSCR 1540, acting under Chapter VII of the Charter of the United Nations, the Security Council required all states to criminalise any transfer of WMD materiel to non-state actors. Unlike the PSI, UNSCR 1540 does not target state-to-state transfers. Nonetheless, the resolution is notable as being among the very few 'legislative' Chapter VII sanctions regimes.[38] That is, it imposes wide-ranging obligations that apply to an abstract class of persons or entities for the indefinite future, as opposed to sanctions targeting a particular state, conflict, or group for a limited period.[39] Substantively, the resolution requires that states:

- 'adopt and enforce appropriate effective laws which prohibit any non-State actor to manufacture, acquire, possess, develop, transport, transfer or use nuclear, chemical or biological weapons and their means of delivery';[40]
- develop, in accordance with national and international law, 'effective border controls and law enforcement efforts to detect, deter, prevent and combat . . . illicit trafficking and brokering in such items' including through international cooperation;[41] and
- establish 'effective national export and trans-shipment controls over such items' including 'establishing and enforcing' appropriate penalties for export control violations.[42]

35 See D Guilfoyle, *Shipping Interdiction*, above n 5, 12–13; I. Shearer, 'Problems of jurisdiction and law enforcement against delinquent vessels' (1986) 35 *International and Comparative Law Quarterly* 320–330; G Fitzmaurice, 'Some results of the Geneva Conference on the Law of the Sea' (1959) 8 *International and Comparative Law Quarterly* 73–113.

36 Guilfoyle, *Shipping Interdiction*, above n 5, 243.

37 See, e.g.: Jinyuan Su, 'The Proliferation Security Initiative (PSI) and Interdiction at Sea: A Chinese Perspective' (2012) 43 *Ocean Development and International Law* 96–111.

38 The other obvious example being UN Sec Res 1373 (2001) on terrorist financing.

39 See, e.g., S. Talmon, 'The Security Council as world legislature' (2005) 99 *American Journal of International Law* 175.

40 UNSCR 1540 (2004) para 2.

41 UNSCR 1540 (2004) para 3(c).

42 UNSCR 1540 (2004) para 3(d).

It is notable that UNSCR 1540 does not directly countenance or call for maritime interdiction. However, its mandatory injunction to take effective measures – consistent with national and international law – to prevent such transfers to non-state actors may have implications for innocent passage through the territorial sea. A number of scholars have concluded that a coastal state could lawfully intercept a vessel ostensibly engaged in innocent passage through the territorial sea if it were engaged in activities contrary to UNSCR 1540.[43] The logic adopted varies, but the present author prefers the view that states have a plenary criminal law enforcement jurisdiction over their territorial sea which is normally restrained out of comity, an ordinarily permissive jurisdiction which UNSCR 1540 *obliges* them to use.[44] This view is not, however, universal.[45]

C. Bilateral and multilateral treaties on counter-proliferation by sea

Finally, the United States spearheaded an initiative to conclude a multilateral treaty on WMD and WMD materiel interdiction, as well as its own network of such bilateral agreements. The centrepiece of this effort was undoubtedly the multilateral protocol of 2005 amending the 1988 Convention for the Suppression of Unlawful Acts Against the Safety of Maritime Navigation (SUA 2005). SUA 2005 aimed at a number of offences, including the use of ships as 'floating bombs' to attack port facilities or other targets, and their potential use in the transportation of WMD or WMD materiel.[46] While SUA 2005 does contain provisions governing the boarding and search of a vessel suspected of involvement in a relevant offence, such boardings require case-by-case flag state authorisation.[47] The only exception is if the flag state has 'opted in' to provisions under which it may waive the requirement to obtain its consent either:

- by giving 'prior and general consent to the boarding and search of merchant vessels flying its flags';[48] or
- in specified circumstances (i.e. where its consent has been requested and that request is acknowledged but goes unanswered for four hours).[49]

43 See, e.g., W. Heintschel von Heinegg, 'The Proliferation Security Initiative: security vs freedom of navigation?' (2005) 35 *Israel Yearbook on Human Rights* 181, 195; Joyner, 'The Proliferation Security Initiative', above n 20, 535–536.

44 Guilfoyle, *Shipping Interdiction*, above n 5, 240–243; Cf Allen, *Maritime Counterproliferation*, above n 2, 165.

45 On the available interpretations, see Klein, *Maritime Security*, above n 22, 207–208.

46 For political reasons the treaty uses the term 'biological, chemical or nuclear weapons' or 'BCN weapons' as it was thought more specific and more neutral than 'WMD'.

47 8bis5(b), Convention for the Suppression of Unlawful Acts Against the Safety of Maritime Navigation 1988 as amended by Protocol of 2005 to the Convention for the Suppression of Unlawful. Acts against the Safety of Maritime Navigation ('SUA Convention 2005').

48 W Heintschel von Heinegg, 'Maritime Interception/Interdiction Operations' in Terry D. Gill, Dieter Fleck (eds), *The Handbook of the International Law of Military Operations* (OUP 2010), p. 382.

49 8bis5(d), SUA Convention 2005.

In parallel with its efforts to conclude a multilateral treaty on point, the United States concluded a series of 11 other bilateral treaties aimed at the interdiction of WMD materiel. Agreements were concluded with: Liberia, Marshall Islands, and Panama in 2004; Belize, Croatia, and Cyprus in 2005; Malta and Mongolia in 2007; The Bahamas in 2008; and with Antigua and Barbuda, and St. Vincent and the Grenadines, in 2010.[50] It is perhaps worth noting that as of 1 January 2011 this list included five of the world's ten largest merchant marines: Panama, Liberia, Malta, Marshall Islands, and the Bahamas.[51] Equally notable, perhaps, are the major shipping registries with which the United States did not (or could not) conclude PSI bilateral agreements: Hong Kong SAR, Greece, Singapore, China, and Cyprus.[52] The push to conclude bilateral PSI treaties has seemingly ground to a halt since 2010, perhaps reflecting a shift in U.S. priorities.[53] Like the SUA Protocol, the U.S. bilateral PSI treaties require the flag state's consent before a suspect vessel is interdicted in waters outside any state's territorial sea. Nonetheless, at the flag state's election, such consent may be presumed in certain cases. For example, some of the bilateral treaties allow boarding and inspection if, within a specified period – usually two or four hours following an *acknowledged* request to board – a flag state has made no reply.[54] However, in a nod to the *So San* incident, each treaty contains a provision permitting the interdicting state (in practice, the United States) 'to board suspect vessels claiming nationality in the other Party' that are neither flying a flag nor displaying marks of registration or nationality, and which claim to have no documentation aboard.[55] In such cases, a state party to the bilateral PSI agreement may *automatically* board the vessel for the purposes of attempting to locate any papers. In the event nationality is confirmed, permission to search the vessel may be sought from the flag state. If no documents are found, the boarding state may assimilate the vessel to a vessel without nationality. As I have observed elsewhere, such a provision 'is either simply a restatement of the right to board vessels suspected of being stateless, or an example of jurisdiction to prevent abuse of claims of nationality [delegated by the flag state to its treaty partner]'.[56]

50 See <https://2009-2017.state.gov/t/isn/trty/index.htm>.

51 United Nations Conference on Trade and Development, *Review of Maritime Transport 2011* (UN 2011), Chapter 2, 47 < http://unctad.org/en/Docs/rmt2011ch2_en.pdf> (all listed in the top ten flags by registered deadweight tonnage), the same five are still in the 2021 Review of Maritime Transport Table 2.5.

52 Ibid.

53 E. Belcher, 'The Proliferation Security Initiative: Lessons for Using Nonbinding Agreements', Council on Foreign Relations, 2011, 11 <www.cfr.org/proliferation/proliferation-securityinitiative/p25394>.

54 See, e.g., Article 4(3)(b), Agreement between the US and the Republic of Liberia concerning Cooperation to Suppress the Proliferation of Weapons of Mass Destruction, Their Delivery Systems, and Related Materials by Sea 2004 (Liberian PSI Treaty) (providing for two hour deemed consent); Article 4(3)(b), Agreement between the US and the Republic of the Marshall Islands concerning Cooperation to Suppress the Proliferation of Weapons of Mass Destruction, Their Delivery Systems, and Related Materials by Sea 2004 (Marshall Islands PSI Treaty) (providing for four hour deemed consent).

55 See, e.g., Article 4(4), Liberian PSI Treaty; Article 4(4), Marshall Islands PSI Treaty.

56 Guilfoyle, *Shipping Interdiction*, above n 5, 251.

The *So San* incident may also have served, indirectly, to increase the likelihood of further targeted restrictions on North Korean arms exports such as UNSCR 1718 (2006) and 1874 (2009). The latter resolution contemplates high seas boarding and inspection of a vessel transporting weapons covered by the earlier, but *only* with flag state consent.[57]

V. Enduring significance

Undoubtedly, the lasting significance of the *So San* incident lies in the law-making efforts of the PSI. Concern (or hope) has been expressed in some quarters that the PSI would lead to a change in customary international law permitting the interdiction of WMD materiel at sea, regardless of flag state consent.[58] Some have seen in it the potential to undermine the innocent passage regime in the territorial sea or an unwarranted expansion of coastal state jurisdiction in the contiguous zone.[59] Others have seen in it the risk of a 'Potemkin village' of legality behind which a much wider U.S.-led campaign of interdiction would occur, with consequent destabilising effects for the law of the sea.[60] Such fears (or desires) have not proven to be the case, and are not likely to become such. First, much PSI practice appears to occur unreported and effectively in secret.[61] Customary international law formation requires that state practice is publicly known.[62] Further, as I have argued elsewhere, all relevant 'PSI' law-making, be it by way of treaties or UN Security Council resolutions, is premised on the consent of the flag state: such practice could not give rise to a right to act *without* flag state consent.[63]

There has also been some debate about whether vessels transferring WMD materiel to *non-state actors* might be able to be interdicted as a countermeasure in order to indirectly enforce UNSCR 1540. The essence of countermeasures is to suspend compliance with an obligation owed to a wrongdoing state in order to induce it to

57 SC Res. 1874 (12 June 2009), paras 12 and 13. See also D. Guilfoyle, 'Counter Proliferation Activities and Freedom of Navigation' in Myron H. Nordquist and John Norton Moore (eds), *Freedom of Navigation and Globalization* (Brill Publishers, 2009), 71–87; and R. Pedrozo, 'The Impending Nuclear Disaster: Flaws in the International Counter-Proliferation Regime at Sea' (2011–12) 9 *Loyola University Chicago International Law Review* 127.

58 Cf T.V. Thomas, 'The Proliferation Security Initiative: Towards Relegation of Navigational Freedoms in UNCLOS: An Indian Perspective' (2009) 8 *Chinese Journal of International Law* 657; and J. Doolin, 'The Proliferation Security Initiative: Cornerstone of a New International Norm', (2006) 59 *Naval War College Review* 50.

59 For a thorough account of these and other criticisms see: Su, 'The Proliferation Security Initiative', above n 37, 96–118.

60 T. Perry, 'Blurring the ocean zones: The effect of the Proliferation Security Initiative on the customary international law of the sea' (2006) 37 *Ocean Development and International Law* 33, 40 and 47.

61 See M.B. Nikitin, 'Proliferation Security Initiative (PSI)', above n 27, 3 on the very general and vague reports offered by the U.S. government of PSI operational successes.

62 Klein, *Maritime Security*, above n 22, 206; compare: Song, 'The US-led Proliferation Security Initiative', above n 22, 101–112.

63 Guilfoyle, 'Counter Proliferation Activities and Freedom of Navigation', above n 57, 81.

resume compliance with its obligations. The argument goes that a flag state which allows its flag vessel to be used for such a purpose is in violation of UNSCR 1540.[64] Thus, a coastal state could then suspend an obligation owed to the flag state (such as respect for its exclusive jurisdiction over its vessels on the high seas, or their right of innocent passage in the territorial sea) to search a suspect vessel and seize any WMD materiel discovered aboard. I have set out my views on this question at length elsewhere.[65] However, the difficulty for such arguments is essentially one of standing. Where international obligations are owed to a group of states such as the members of the UN (and let us presume this is an accurate characterisation of the legal effect of Security Council resolutions, which is open to question) then only states *specially affected* by the breach may take countermeasures. It is hard to see why this category would include states other than those who would be targeted by the WMD in question. A distant, potential threat to the security of others could surely not suffice. In any event, the law of countermeasures has never been cited as the justification for such an interdiction, so to date the point remains academic.

This leaves as the major legacy of the *So San* incident the Proliferation Security Initiative itself and the network of bilateral and multilateral treaties devised to counter proliferation in WMD materiel by sea. The successes of the PSI are hard to measure because its activities are either secretive or poorly publicised – or possibly in decline. Most of its activities now seem to be 'Operational Expert Group' meetings[66] and such '[r]ecent PSI meetings have emphasised capacity-building, best practices and cooperation across agencies and governments'.[67] While in the period to 2006, the PSI was said to have played a role in some 30 interdictions, there is no evidence of similar claims from participant governments more recently.[68] This leaves us with the 'PSI treaties' and SUA 2005. Unfortunately, this treaty-based approach has not been a 'silver bullet'[69]; its coverage remains patchy at best. First, we can note of the U.S. bilateral treaties that while they have significant coverage they do not extend to some of the largest shipping registries in the world by deadweight tonnage (Hong Kong, Greece, Singapore, China, and Cyprus). Second, while SUA 2005 has come into force, its membership remains limited. It has 52 state parties, covering 40% of world shipping by tonnage.[70] These member states,

64 Heintschel von Heinegg, 'The Proliferation Security Initiative: security vs freedom of navigation?', above n 43, 200–1; and compare: S Kaye, 'The Proliferation Security Initiative in the Maritime Domain' (2005) 35 *Israel Yearbook on Human Rights* 205, 223–224.

65 D Guilfoyle, 'Interdicting Vessels to Enforce the Common Interest: Maritime Countermeasures and the Use of Force' (2007) 56 *International and Comparative Law Quarterly* 69–82.

66 See, e.g., <www.psi-online.info/>; and Kelsey Davenport, The Proliferation Security Initiative (PSI) At a Glance, Arms Control Association, March 2020 <www.armscontrol.org/factsheets/PSI>.

67 Nikitin, 'Proliferation Security Initiative', above n 27, 3.

68 Ibid.

69 W. Heintschel von Heinegg, 'The Proliferation Security Initiative: security vs freedom of navigation?', above n 43, 202.

70 See IMO Status of Conventions as at 26 October 2021: <www.imo.org/About/Conventions/StatusOfConventions/Pages/Default.aspx>.

however, do include a few states with the naval capability to conduct high seas operations (Denmark, France, Germany, Spain, Norway, the Netherlands, New Zealand, Sweden, and the United States).[71] The key point being that operationalising the maritime interdiction provisions of SUA 2005 require a state capable of doing the interdicting. Nonetheless, there would also need to be an applicable domestic implementing law before any prosecutions under the Convention (or any other mechanism) can take place. Indeed, the continued lack of specific SUA 2005 implementing legislation continues to be an obstacle to states such as Australia and the UK ratifying the Protocol.[72]

As I have noted elsewhere, a principal legacy of all these developments 'may simply be that [they have] changed the terms of debate and made ad hoc consent' by a flag state to the interdiction of a suspect shipment of WMD materiel 'more likely'. The idea of (consensual) WMD interdiction is, it seems, no longer as controversial as it was during the negotiation of SUA 2005.[73]

71 Ibid.

72 The author understands that in both countries, decision-makers have found it difficult to secure parliamentary time or space in the legislative agenda for SUA 2005 implementing laws, which are often seen as involving a degree of legal complexity out of proportion to any immediate benefit.

73 For some flavour of the protracted debate, see: IMO Doc. LEG 90/15 (2005), paras 29 ff and especially the statement of India at Annex II.

6

UNITED STATES OF AMERICA V LEI SHI

David Letts

I. Introduction

In March 2002 an incident, or series of incidents, occurred onboard the Taiwanese-owned, Seychelles-flagged fishing vessel *Full Means No. 2* while the vessel was at sea in the Pacific Ocean, which ultimately resulted in the death of the captain of the vessel and the first mate. The location of the vessel when the incidents occurred has been reported as being 'in the middle of the Pacific, 800 miles south of Hawaii'.[1] Subsequently, the vessel, with the alleged perpetrator of the crimes onboard (Lei Shi, a Chinese citizen), arrived in Hawaiian waters whereupon Shi was arrested and charged by U.S. authorities with a range of offences under U.S. domestic law relating to the crimes that had allegedly been committed at sea. Lei Shi was convicted on three counts of offences of 'violence against maritime navigation' and sentenced to 36 years in prison; Shi's appeal against conviction was dismissed. This chapter will examine the legal issues that arose in this case.

II. Background

The events that took place on the *Full Means No. 2*, and which led to Lei Shi eventually being convicted, are described in the judgement of the United States Court of Appeals, Ninth Circuit, of 24 April 2008:

> On March 14, 2002, the *Full Means No. 2*, a Taiwanese fishing vessel registered in the Republic of the Seychelles, was sailing in international waters off the coast of Hawaii. The Captain of the vessel was Taiwanese, while its

1 'Slayings at Sea', *Honolulu Star-Bulletin Hawaii News*, 2 May 2002 (accessed 4 Feb 2015).

DOI: 10.4324/9781003307013-8

> 29 crew-members, including Lei Shi, the ship's cook, were mainland Chinese. According to Shi, the Captain and First Mate beat and harassed him repeatedly and, on this date, demoted Shi from the position of cook to deck hand, punctuating the decision with a beating that was particularly severe. A few hours later, Shi responded. He retrieved two large knives from the kitchen, ascended to the deck of the ship, and fatally stabbed both men.
>
> According to the government, Shi then ordered the Second Mate to 'drive the ship' and ordered the other crewmembers to throw the captain's body overboard. Shi stated he would kill anyone who disobeyed him and refused to let his fellow crewmates use the radio. Shi retained control of the ship for two days, setting a course for China and threatening to scuttle the vessel if his instructions were not obeyed.
>
> On March 16, 2002, the crew overpowered Shi and imprisoned him in a storage compartment on the ship. The crew then set a course for Hawaii, though they never contacted the ship's parent company, apparently because none of them knew how to operate the radio. After several days of silence, the parent company notified the U.S. Coast Guard that the *Full Means No. 2* was missing and requested the Coast Guard's assistance in recovery.[2]

After the Coast Guard located the *Full Means No. 2* there was a need to establish why the vessel had been out of radio contact, but heavy seas prevented Coast Guard officials from immediately boarding the vessel.[3] A number of hours afterwards, two crew members from the *Full Means No. 2* launched a raft[4] and made their way to the Coast Guard cutter *Kiska* and delivered a letter addressed to the Hawaiian government which outlined what had, in the opinion of the crew, occurred on the vessel. The Court of Appeals' judgement notes there was an element of caution being exercised by the Coast Guard officials at this stage due to uncertainty whether the *Full Means No. 2* crew were actually dealing with a real emergency situation or 'staging an emergency to gain entry into the United States'.[5]

Before any Coast Guard officials could board the *Full Means No. 2*, there was a requirement to deal with the issue of flag state jurisdiction, as the vessel was located by the *Kiska* 'approximately 60 miles from Hilo, Hawaii'.[6] This location meant that the *Full Means No. 2* was in the U.S. exclusive economic zone (EEZ)[7] which

2 *United States v Lei Shi*, 525 F.3d 709 (9th Cir. 2008).

3 'Slayings at Sea', above n 1.

4 Reports of how the crew members reached the Coast Guard cutter vary. The Court of Appeals judgement, above n 2, refers to the men using a raft to reach the cutter; 'Slayings at Sea', above n 1, states that the crew members 'jumped ship'; 'Tales of Mutiny and Murder Unfold After a Missing Taiwanese Ship Is Found', *New York Times*, 23 March 2002 (accessed 4 Feb 2015), another report, stated that the men 'leaped into the water and were picked up by the cutter'.

5 *United States v Lei Shi*, above n 2.

6 Ibid.

7 *United Nations Convention on the Law of the Sea* (10 December 1982) 1833 UNTS 3 (hereafter '*LOSC*') entered into force 16 November 1994, Article 55 provides that'The exclusive economic

extends 200 nm[8] from the land territory of the islands that make up the state of Hawaii. In the EEZ, the jurisdiction of the United States over foreign-flagged vessels is limited,[9] with the result being that the *Full Means No. 2* was subject to the jurisdiction of the state whose flag it was flying (in this case the Republic of Seychelles) through the application of relevant provisions of the LOSC.[10] From a practical perspective, the ability of the Republic of Seychelles to adequately exercise its criminal law jurisdiction in a location that is so remote from the Seychelles land territory could reasonably be questioned. Accordingly, when the request to waive jurisdiction was received by the flag state, it was readily agreed, and this opened the way for U.S. Coast Guard officials to board the vessel with the agreement of the crew member acting as master.

After boarding the *Full Means No. 2*, the Coast Guard officials did not immediately arrest Lei Shi, as there was still a requirement to understand precisely what the circumstances onboard the vessel actually were. At this stage, the Coast Guard 'officers still considered Shi to be a prisoner of the crew . . . [and] . . . they did not immediately instruct the crew to release Shi'.[11] Discussions took place between Coast Guard officials and Shi over the next two days, during which Shi allegedly admitted that he had killed the captain and first mate, and on 21 March 2002, Shi was arrested by U.S. Federal Bureau of Investigation (FBI) agents for violating U.S. domestic legislation (18 USC 2280).[12]

III. The legal process

Chapter 4 of this volume has provided a description of the *Achille Lauro* incident,[13] including the steps that were taken by the international maritime community following that incident to deal with a circumstance whereby violence occurred on the high seas but to which the definition of piracy did not apply. As noted in Chapter 4 and Chapter 5, the outcome of these steps was the introduction of the Convention for the Suppression of Unlawful Acts Against the Safety of Maritime Navigation[14] (the 'SUA Convention'), which was accompanied by a requirement for the

zone is an area beyond and adjacent to the territorial sea, subject to the specific legal regime established in this Part, under which the rights and jurisdiction of the coastal State and the rights and freedoms of other States are governed by the relevant provisions of this Convention'.

8 Ibid, art 57.

9 See '*LOSC*', art 56 which describes the 'Rights, jurisdiction and duties of the coastal State in the exclusive economic zone'. Relevantly for this chapter, these rights do not include criminal jurisdiction over events that occur on foreign-flagged vessels located in a coastal state's EEZ.

10 See '*LOSC*', arts 58, 90–92, 94.

11 *United States v Lei Shi*, above n 2.

12 Text of 18 USC 2280 is <www.gpo.gov/fdsys/pkg/USCODE-2011-title18/pdf/USCODE-2011-title18-partI-chap111-sec2280.pdf>.

13 See Chapter 4.

14 Convention for the Suppression of Unlawful Acts Against the Safety of Maritime Navigation (10 March 1988) 1678 UNTS 221; entered into force 1 March 1992 (the 'SUA Convention').

introduction of appropriate domestic legislation by states so that the international legal obligations that were raised under the SUA Convention could be met. In the case of the United States, this requirement was met through the enactment of 18 USC 2280, which criminalises in the United States' domestic jurisdiction a number of general offences, and one specific offence of 'Threat to navigation' that are pooled together under the title of 'Violence against maritime navigation'.

Lei Shi was originally charged with a range of offences under 18 USC 2280 that included 'engaging in an act of violence against a vessel in maritime navigation; the seizure and exercise of control over a covered ship; and injuring and killing the captain and first mate in connection with the seizure and control of the vessel, in violation of 18 USC 2280(a)(1)(A)(B)(G) & (H), and 2280(b)(1)(C)'.[15] After initially pleading guilty to these charges, Shi changed his plea and a superseding indictment was filed by the prosecution which reduced the charges to:

> Count 1: 'Violence against maritime navigation by seizing and exercising control over a ship by force, threat of force and other forms of intimidation, which resulted in death' in violation of 18 USC 2280(a)(1)(A) and
> Counts 2 and 3: 'Violence against maritime navigation by performing an act of violence against a person aboard a ship which was likely to endanger the safe navigation of the ship, which resulted in death' in violation of 18 USC 2280(a)(1)(B).

Shi was subsequently found guilty by jury trial conducted in November 2005, convicted on all three counts and sentenced to 36 years in prison. He appealed against this decision to the U.S. Court of Appeals, Ninth Circuit, and this appeal was eventually dismissed.[16] An attempt to take the case to the U.S. Supreme Court pursuant to a writ of *certiorari* was also denied.[17]

A. Preliminary jurisdiction issues

Although the focus of this chapter is on the international legal issues that arose in the arrest, charging and trial(s) of Lei Shi, including analysis of the Court of Appeals' treatment of these issues, before embarking on this analysis, it is informative to consider some of the preliminary jurisdiction issues that were dealt with in the case prior to the trial proceeding. These challenges involved some interesting legal questions raised by Lei Shi which the District Court of Hawaii answered

15 *United States of America, Plaintiff, v. Lei Shi, Defendant*: Order Regarding Jurisdiction over Defendant Lei Shi dated 1 May 2003. 396 F.Supp, 2d 1132 (2003), <www.leagle.com/decision/2003152839 6FSupp2d1132_11424>.

16 Instead of describing the appeal as being 'dismissed', the Court's decision was that 'Shi's conviction and sentence imposed are AFFIRMED'.

17 *Shi v United States*, 129 S Ct 324 (2008), 6 October 2008.

by reference to both international law (primarily the SUA Convention) and U.S. domestic law (primarily 18 USC 2280).

First, and despite press speculation at the time providing commentary on the likelihood that the arrest and prosecution of Shi would place a strain on the relationship between the United States and China[18] (as Shi was a Chinese national), there appears to be no evidence that this is what actually transpired. It is not readily apparent whether Chinese authorities sought extradition of Shi to China, but court records do indicate that 'the United States Department of State has refused to inquire of the People's Republic of China whether it would exercise its jurisdiction to criminally prosecute Lei Shi'.[19] Notwithstanding, this issue was raised by Shi as part of his submissions to the District Court regarding jurisdiction. However, this line of argument was not accepted by the District Court, as it found that the combined operation of 18 USC 2280 and Article 6(4) of the SUA Convention did not create a jurisdictional hierarchy among those states that could legitimately establish a claim to exercise jurisdiction – 'neither the Seychelles nor China has a mandatory or greater claim to prosecute than the United States'.[20] Instead, the District Court found that as Lei Shi was in the custody of the United States, any 'discretion to extradite is left to the United States under both the Convention and 18 USC 2280 . . . [and] . . . both the Convention and 18 USC 2280 permit the United States to prosecute'.[21] More specifically, the fact that Lei Shi was 'later found in the United States'[22] provided sufficient basis for the United States to validly exercise jurisdiction according to the District Court in its Order of 1 May 2003.[23]

The second issue that arose during the preliminary phase of proceedings was a request lodged in 2005 for the District Court to reconsider its Order of 1 May 2003 regarding jurisdiction 'based in large part on the opinions and writings of Professor Malvina Halberstam, a law professor who was involved in the drafting of' the SUA Convention.[24] The main focus of this request was a claim that the SUA Convention, and therefore 18 USC 2280, did not apply to acts that could not be classified as acts of terrorism. On the facts, it was apparent that the actions attributed to Lei Shi onboard the *Full Means No. 2* in 2002 were criminal in nature, but they were clearly not acts of terrorism. In a decision handed down on 16 September 2005, the District Court denied the request for reconsideration, on the basis that the material presented to it did 'not provide new arguments that were not or could not have been previously raised . . . [and that the] . . . Defendant has not presented any new facts or

18 'Tales of Mutiny and Murder Unfold', above n 4; 'Captain, first mate slain in alleged mutiny at sea', *The Honolulu Advertiser*, 22 March 2002 (accessed 4 Feb 2015).

19 United States v Shi, above n 15.

20 Ibid.

21 Ibid.

22 18 USC 2280 (b)(1)(C).

23 *United States v Shi*, above n 15.

24 *United States of America, Plaintiff, v. Lei Shi, Defendant*: Order Denying Defendant's Motion for Reconsideration of the Court's May 1, 2003 Order Regarding Jurisdiction over Lei Shi, 396 F.Supp, 2d 1137 (2003), <www.leagle.com/decision/20031528396FSupp2d1132_11424>.

argument, nor pointed to intervening change in the law, warranting reconsideration of the Court's May 1, 2003 order'.[25] Although the reasoning of the District Court in both the 2003 Order and 2005 Request for Reconsideration is brief, it is clear that the Court considered that the words of the SUA Convention and 18 USC 2280 were unambiguous in their meaning when it stated that 'the conduct Lei Shi is charged with committing places him squarely within the four corners of the statute'.[26]

Reporting of the trial that occurred in November 2005 is scant, other than court documents that note the trial occurred before a jury. Shi was convicted on all three counts with which he was charged, and sentenced to 36 years imprisonment on each count (to be served concurrently).[27]

IV. Analysis and outcomes: the case on appeal

After his conviction, Shi lodged an appeal[28] which challenged:

- the jurisdiction of the District Court;
- whether the indictment against Shi contained sufficient details;
- the admissibility of a statement made by Shi to a federal agent;
- the admissibility of letters seized from Shi's bunk; and
- the reasonableness of the sentence.

All of these grounds of appeal were dismissed by the Court of Appeals. The issues raised in the four latter grounds of appeal are not particularly relevant for the subject matter of this volume, and therefore will not be addressed further. However, the reasoning applied by the court in dealing with the merits of the arguments regarding jurisdiction are relevant, and attention will now turn to the way in which they were dealt with by the Court of Appeals.

The first jurisdictional issue the court addressed was whether 18 USC 2280 was unconstitutional insofar as it applied to Shi. In a somewhat surprising turn of events, the Court of Appeals chose to deal with this topic by introducing the concept of piracy to the proceedings. The reason for describing this action by the Court of Appeals as 'surprising' is that during the six years since the murders on the *Full Means No. 2* had occurred, neither the prosecution authorities nor Shi's defence counsel had mentioned piracy as having any relevance in the proceedings. Accordingly, consideration of piracy was entirely absent from any of the pleadings that occurred before the District Court of Hawaii. It is therefore reasonable to ask

25 Ibid.

26 Ibid.

27 See, e.g., United States District Court, District of Hawaii, Judgment in a Criminal Case (Case 1:02-cr-00116-HG-KSC Document 428) and Order Granting in Part and Denying in Part Motion to Withdraw as Counsel (Case Number 1:02-cr-00116-HG-KSC Document 422).

28 The appeal was lodged with the United States Court of Appeals, Ninth Circuit, and judgement was given on 24 April 2008. See *United States v Lei Shi*, above n 2.

why the Court of Appeals decided it was necessary to answer the jurisdictional question before it by reference to a crime that did not form any part of the charges that had been brought against Shi. The answer to this question is not obvious, but nevertheless that is the approach that the Court of Appeals decided to adopt.

The Court of Appeals reasoning in describing 18 USC 2280(a)(1)(A) and (B) as 'offenses which meet the definition of piracy'[29] may be correct in terms of U.S. domestic law, but this statement does not reflect the current state of either customary international law or the applicable provision of the LOSC,[30] which is considered to be codification of the customary crime of piracy.[31] The Court of Appeals referred to the case of *United States v Smith* as providing support for the view that 'Piracy traditionally has been defined as robbery, or forcible depredations upon the sea'[32] and then immediately associated this 200-year-old case with 18 USC 2280. With respect, this line of reasoning by the Court of Appeals is difficult to comprehend. One of the key features of the modern definition of piracy is the requirement for two ships to be involved, and this was certainly not the case with the *Full Means No. 2*. Indeed, the very reason for the introduction of the SUA Convention (and the subsequent enactment of 18 USC 2280) was to address this shortfall after the events on the *Achille Lauro* had highlighted the deficiency. From a legal positivist point of view, the inclusion by the United States of offences in its domestic law that the Court of Appeals and some commentators consider fit within the realm of piracy – but that do not align with the international legal definition of this crime – creates unnecessary confusion.[33] This attempt at a wide application of the crime of piracy also seems to contradict the requirements of 18 USC 1651, which creates a specific offence of piracy that is applicable to a person who 'commits the crime of piracy as defined by the law of nations'. Accordingly, the emphasis placed upon characterising the crime committed by Lei Shi as one of piracy in order to establish a firm jurisdictional basis for the conviction is hard to understand – especially when there was another firm basis upon which jurisdiction could have been found to exist.

There are other arguments against the course chosen by the Court of Appeals in dealing with the jurisdictional question that was placed before it. One of the strongest of these arguments relates to the emphasis the Court placed on establishing jurisdiction on the basis that piracy is a crime which attracts universal jurisdiction and that an offender may be punished by any state in which the offender is located. One of the key underlying premises of universal jurisdiction is that it

29 *United States v Lei Shi*, above n 2.

30 '*LOSC*', see arts 100–107, 110.

31 See Tullio Treves, 'Piracy and the international law of the sea', in Douglas Guilfoyle (ed), *Modern Piracy, Legal Challenges and Responses* at 119–120.

32 *United States v Smith*, 5 Wheat. 153, 18 US 153, 161, 5 L.Ed. 57 (1820).

33 See, e.g., James Kraska, *Contemporary Maritime Piracy: International Law, Strategy and Diplomacy at Sea*; Praeger, 2011 at 112 where the author contends that

> Congress codified its constitutional authority to 'extradite or prosecute' offenders of maritime piracy in 18 USC 2280 . . . [and] . . . Section 2280(a)(1)(A) defines a pirate as an individual 'who unlawfully and intentionally seizes control over a ship by force or threat thereof'.

overcomes potential problems that may arise in establishing a valid arena in which a prosecution of an alleged offender can occur. However, in the case of the *Full Means No. 2*, there was no such uncertainty as the Seychelles, the flag state, was clearly able to exercise criminal jurisdiction over Lei Shi should it choose to do so.[34] There may have been lengthy extradition issues to deal with if the Seychelles had sought to exercise its criminal jurisdiction over Shi, but such potential difficulties should not be used as an excuse to circumvent valid legal processes by invoking consideration of a crime that was simply not applicable to the facts of the case. In any case, following the decision by the United States that it would not extradite Shi to the Seychelles (or China), then the mandatory language of the SUA Convention required the United States to establish its jurisdiction over Shi.[35]

Another aspect of the case was the Court of Appeals' consideration of the consequence of being 'found' within U.S. jurisdiction.[36] Part of the argument raised by Shi was that there was an implied requirement for him to be voluntarily within the United States for there to be a valid exercise of jurisdiction in relation to being 'later found in the United States'.[37] The argument put forward by Shi was that his detention onboard the *Full Means No. 2* by the crew, and his subsequent arrival in the United States, was not voluntary and therefore this created a jurisdictional deficiency. The Court of Appeals dismissed this argument in very short compass, citing both SUA Convention Article 9 and the 'Ker-Frisbie rule'[38] as international and domestic legal authority which supported the view that voluntariness of presence within the United States was not a requirement for the exercise of jurisdiction under 18 USC 2280. The Court concluded that the meaning of 'found' only imposed a requirement that the alleged offender be physically located in the United States.

Having dealt with the question of jurisdiction, the Court of Appeals then turned to the other matters raised by Shi in the challenge to his conviction, but as noted earlier, these grounds of appeal were all dismissed, and they will not be discussed further in this chapter.

V. Significance, strengths, and weaknesses of the decision

The legal action that followed the apprehension of Lei Shi in 2002 highlighted some of the complexities involved in bringing about a successful prosecution for crimes committed at sea in what could be reasonably described as fairly uncontroversial circumstances. The situation was one in which relevant international law existed under the SUA Convention, and U.S. domestic legislation under 18 USC 2280 was also

34 See '*LOSC*', art 94.

35 '*SUA Convention*', art 6 describes the measures that are to be taken by a state party to the SUA Convention to establish jurisdiction over an alleged offender.

36 18 USC 2280 (b)(1)(C) provides that 'There is jurisdiction over the activity prohibited in subsection (a) . . . in the case of a covered ship, if . . . the offender is later found in the United States after such activity is committed'.

37 *United States v Lei Shi*, above n 2.

38 *Ker v Illinios*, 119 U.S. 436, 7 S.Ct. 225, 30 L.Ed. 421 (1886); *Frisbie v Collins*, 342 U.S. 519, 522, 72 S.Ct. 509, 96 L.Ed. 541 (1952).

in place and could be used to prosecute the alleged offender. The evidence supplied by Lei Shi's shipmates, coupled with that collected by U.S. authorities when the *Full Means No. 2* berthed in Hawaii, and Shi's admissions, should have made the trial a relatively straightforward event. Nevertheless, it took more than six years for the case to be finally disposed of which occurred after Lei Shi's request to appeal his conviction in the U.S. Supreme Court was denied in 2008. In these circumstances, it can hardly be said that the case represents a watershed for the use of the SUA Convention (or U.S. domestic law) in dealing with situations of crime at sea. However, the case does show that the United States is willing to consider its international legal obligations and apply these obligations through its municipal law, in certain circumstances. What is unclear from Lei Shi's case is precisely what circumstances will trigger a prosecution, and what criteria will result in other action (or inaction) occurring.

The case also highlights that when cases that involve interplay between international and domestic law do arise, there is potential for confusion in the application of the law to appear in the reasoning adopted by the courts. Such confusion is not helpful, as it has the potential to deter subsequent prosecutions in cases when it really would be appropriate for a prosecution to take place. In this case, the Court of Appeals' foray into the subject of piracy does not provide any solace for those who call on an increase in the activism of 'Western' states in dealing with allegations of piracy. Offences that criminalise behaviour at sea which are closely connected with piracy exist in many jurisdictions. In the case of the United States, these offences are all included within the provisions of Title 18 of the U.S. Code (18 USC). However, only one of these offences (18 USC 1651 – Piracy, as defined by the law of nations) actually deals specifically with the crime of piracy as it is known under international law. The remainder deal with a large range of offences that may or may not, depending on the factual situation in each case, fall within the parameters of an act that can be legitimately described as piracy. For the sake of consistency and precision in the future, perhaps there should be revision and re-designation of such crimes so that a prosecution for piracy simply reflects a common meaning between both international and domestic law.

VI. Postscript: subsequent prosecutions for piracy

Notwithstanding the uncertainty regarding why the Court of Appeals decided that it was necessary to consider piracy in its decision in Lei Shi's case,[39] there have been a significant number of convictions in subsequent cases where U.S. courts have dealt with piracy prosecutions, and used provisions of 18 USC to obtain convictions, in circumstances when the crimes have clearly involved piracy as understood under international law.[40]

39 See, e.g., Shaun Martin, California Appellate Report: *U.S. v. Sei* (sic) (9th Cir. – April 24, 2008) <http://calapp.blogspot.com.au/2008/04/us-v-sei-9th-cir-april-24-2008.html>.

40 See, e.g., United States Attorney's Office, Eastern District of Virginia:

> Dozens of Somali pirates have been prosecuted for their roles in attacks against American vessels on the high seas and sentenced to life in prison. In April 2011, the Eastern District of Virginia

Brief mention will be made of two of these cases, as the issue is explored further in Chapter 7 of this book. Abduwali Muse[41] was involved in the *Maersk Alabama* piracy and charged with a range of offences under 18 USC, including 'piracy as defined by the Law of Nations' contrary to 18 USC 1651. The charge of piracy against Muse, which carries a mandatory life sentence, was dropped as part of a plea bargain. In the other case, Mohamed Shibin was convicted of piracy on ten counts and, among other sentences, is serving ten concurrent life sentences as a result of the piracy convictions.[42] One of the issues raised by Shibin was that he was involuntarily brought to the United States for trial, but this was not found to be a bar to prosecution – which was exactly the same outcome as occurred before the Court of Appeals in the case of Lei Shi.

---

set a new first in piracy prosecutions by capturing and charging an alleged pirate in a leadership role – Mohammad Saaili Shibin, a hostage negotiator in Somalia.

Available at <www.justice.gov/usao/vae/priorities.html>.

41 *United States v Muse,* U.S. District Court for the Southern District of New Year (Manhattan) Case 1:09-cr-00512-LAP.

42 <www.justice.gov/usao/vae/news/2012/08/20120813shibinnr.html>; see Chapter 7.

7

THE *ALI* AND *SHIBIN* CASES IN RELATION TO ARTICLE 101(C) OF UNCLOS AND THE FACILITATION OF PIRACY

Tamsin Phillipa Paige and Rob McLaughlin

I. Introduction

The situation of Somali piracy off the Horn of Africa has generated a range of modern jurisprudence referring specifically to the international crime of piracy as codified in the United Nations Convention on the Law of the Sea (UNCLOS). Most of these cases have focussed primarily (albeit not exclusively) upon the 'on-water' aspects of piracy, including attacking and detaining vessels,[1] attempted but failed attacks,[2] and participating in the operation of a pirate ship, including being positioned and prepared to engage in a pirate attack in circumstances when no attack was ultimately commenced.[3] Within this body of case law, the cases of Ali and Shibin[4] – decided in the U.S. federal court system (for the District of Columbia and the Fourth Circuit, respectively) – are significant because they are amongst

1 *Hassan M Ahmed v Republic* [2009] eKLR (High Court of Kenya at Mombassa); on Kenyan jurisdiction in relation to piracy more generally, see inter alia: James Gathii, 'Kenya's Piracy Prosecutions' (2010) 104:3 *American Journal of International Law* 416; Paul Musili Wambua, 'The jurisdictional challenges to the prosecution of piracy cases in Kenya: mixed fortunes for a perfect model in the global war against piracy' (2012) 11 *WMU Journal of Maritime Affairs* 95 at 108–110.

2 'Dutch court convicts five Somalis of piracy', *Reuters*, 18 June 2010 www.reuters.com/article/somalia-piracy-dutch-idAFLDE65G1JA20100617.

3 *Shire v R* [2015] SCCA 25 <https://seylii.org/sc/judgment/court-appeal/2015/24-0>; on select issues in Seychelles piracy jurisprudence, see generally: Jamil Ddamulira Mujuzi, 'The Prosecution in Seychelles of Piracy Committed on the High Seas and the Right to a Fair Trial' (2020) 31 *Criminal Law Forum* 1. See also, Douglas Guilfoyle and Rob McLaughlin, 'The Crime of Piracy', in C Jalloh, K Clarke & V Nmehielle (eds), *The African Court of Justice and Human and Peoples' Rights in Context Development and Challenges* (Cambridge University Press, 2019), 388–408.

4 *United States of America v Ali Mohamed Ali*, also known as Ahmed Ali Adan, also known as Ismail Ali [2013] Unreported; *United States of America v Mohammad Saaili Shibin*, a/k/a Khalif Ahmed Shibin, a/k/a Mohammad Ali, a/k/a Ali Jama [2013] Unreported.

DOI: 10.4324/9781003307013-9

the first cases to deal specifically with Article 101(c) of UNCLOS. This article defines facilitation of piracy as 'any act of inciting or intentionally facilitating an act described in subparagraph (a) or (b)'. This must be read in conjunction with the jurisdiction reflected in Article 105 of UNCLOS,[5] which states that:

> On the high seas, or in any other place outside the jurisdiction of any State, every State may seize a pirate ship or aircraft, or a ship or aircraft taken by piracy and under the control of pirates, and arrest the persons and seize the property on board. The courts of the State which carried out the seizure may decide upon the penalties to be imposed, and may also determine the action to be taken with regard to the ships, aircraft or property, subject to the rights of third parties acting in good faith.

The Ali and Shibin cases consider whether or not the concurrent municipal jurisdiction afforded to states in relation to piracy by Article 105 of UNCLOS (or as an articulation of customary international law) extends to the actions of 'on-land' piracy facilitators, and consequently also considers the scope of charges applicable under Article 101(c) of UNCLOS.[6] While the specific incidents of 'facilitation' considered in these cases is hostage ransom negotiations after a successful 'on-water' piracy action, the jurisprudence represented by these cases could easily be expanded through analogy to other forms of piracy facilitation (such as the procurement of weapons or equipment for the specific purpose of conducting piracy).

II. Background

It is important to note at the outset that while both Ali and Shibin were charged with aiding and abetting piracy, and conspiracy to commit piracy (among other things), only the case of Ali considered whether the charge of conspiracy to commit piracy fell within the scope of Article 101 (c) of UNCLOS and 18 USC § 1651. Shibin and Ali both argued that the U.S. courts lacked jurisdiction to hear the case.[7] Before getting into the facts of each case, it is worth noting that the judgement in *Ali* were appeals by the U.S. government in relation to pre-trial motions for dismissal of charges. The U.S. Department of Justice declined to retry Ali after a deadlocked jury in the initial trial.[8] In response to this, the D.C. Federal

5 Including that suspects may be transferred to third states for prosecution: See, Tamsin Phillipa Paige, 'The Impact and Effectiveness of UNCLOS on Counter-Piracy Operations' (2017) 22:1 *Journal of Conflict and Security Law* 97.

6 For a discussion on the nature of piracy jurisdiction, see: Tamsin Paige, 'Piracy and Universal Jurisdiction' (2013) 12 *Macquarie Law Journal* 131, 148–151.

7 For more detailed background on these cases, see inter alia: Graham Youngs, 'Piracy in Somalia: A Legal Analysis concerning the Prosecution of Pirate Negotiators and Pirate Facilitators under the Current US and International Framework' (2014) 24 *Indiana International & Comparative Law Review* 809.

8 Associated Press, 'U.S. to Drop Piracy Case' *Politico Magazine*, 18 January 2014 <www.politico.com/story/2014/01/us-to-drop-case-against-man-accused-of-piracy-102356>.

Court of Appeals issued a bench memorandum confirming that the reasoning in the appeal judgement was good law and would be followed in future by the U.S. federal courts.[9]

A. US v Ali

Ali was arrested in relation to the hijacking of the Danish-owned merchant vessel *CEC Future* on 7 November 2008, while it was travelling on the high seas within the Gulf of Aden.[10] The pirates then rerouted the ship to Point Ras Binna, where the defendant boarded the vessel.[11] The ship was then sailed, almost exclusively within the Somali territorial sea, to the port of Ely on the southern coast of Puntland, where it remained until the defendant had successfully negotiated a ransom of US$1.7 million with the owners, which was paid on 14 January 2009 (the initial demand having been US$7 million).[12] In June 2010, the defendant was appointed Director General of the Ministry of Education for Republic of Somaliland. It was in this capacity he was invited to attend an education conference in Raleigh, North Carolina in March 2011.[13] The invitation itself was a ruse planned and executed by U.S. federal prosecutors, and upon his arrival within U.S. territorial jurisdiction on 20 April 2011, the defendant was arrested. He was subsequently charged with, among other things, conspiracy to commit piracy against the law of nations in violation of 18 USC § 371, and aiding and abetting under 18 USC § 2 in relation to committing piracy against the law of nations in violation of 18 USC § 1651.[14] The piracy charges were subjected to a successful motion to dismiss on the basis that the U.S. federal court lacked jurisdiction over the crimes because none of the defendant's actions took place on the high seas and thus Article 105's concurrent municipal jurisdiction did not apply. The U.S. government then appealed against the motion to dismiss. The outcomes of this appeal will be discussed in further detail in what follows.

B. US v Shibin

Shibin was initially arrested by the U.S. Federal Bureau of Investigation (FBI) in relation to his role in the hijacking of the U.S.-flagged yacht *SV Quest* on 18 February 2011.[15] After his arrest, German authorities furnished the FBI with evidence of the defendant's involvement in the hijacking of the *MV Marida Marguerite* on

9 *United States of America v Ali Mohamed Ali* – Memorandum Opinion [2013] Unreported.

10 *United States of America v Ali Mohamed Ali*, above n 4, 3–4.

11 Ibid 4.

12 Ibid.

13 Ibid 5.

14 Ibid. Hostage-taking charges under the U.S. criminal code are of only slim relevance to legal practice relating to 101(c) of UNCLOS, and will not be further considered.

15 *United States of America v Mohammad Saaili Shibin*, above n 4, 2.

or around May 2010.[16] The *Quest* was making its way from India to Oman as a part of an international yacht rally when it was attacked by Somali pirates in the Arabian Sea, approximately 900 miles from Somalia and 400 miles from Oman.[17] A U.S. Navy vessel intercepted the hijacked yacht and proceeded to shadow it as it approached the Somali territorial sea in the vicinity of the Puntland region.[18] All attempts by the U.S. Navy to secure the release of the yacht and hostages were referred to the defendant for negotiation.[19] As the *Quest* approached Somali waters on 22 February 2011, the U.S. Navy boarded and seized the vessel – on some reports, because small arms fire was heard emanating from the yacht. Two Somali pirates were killed during the boarding, and 13 others (including a Yemeni national) were detained. Two additional pirate bodies were subsequently discovered. The four U.S. nationals who were hostages on board had been shot; all four ultimately died on the scene.[20] In relation to the *Marida Marguerite*, the defendant boarded the vessel after it had been hijacked, upon its arrival in Hafun, remaining on board and acting as both a guard and negotiator – for a brief period, the defendant was demoted from the role of negotiator and served only as a general guard; however, he was the individual who ultimately negotiated the final ransom of US$5 million. During this period, the vessel was held at Garaad and then Hobyo, for around seven months.[21] On 4 April 2011, the local Defence Force, working with the FBI, arrested the defendant in Bosasso.[22] The FBI interrogated Shibin while he was in Host Nation Defence Forces custody and were able to confirm that the phone number provided to the U.S. Navy in relation to hostage negotiations for the crew of the *Quest* matched the SIM card in possession of the defendant.[23] On 6 April 2011, the defendant was transferred to the custody of the Bosasso police department and then into the custody of the FBI.[24] He was then transported back to the United States and charged and convicted with piracy in relation to the *Quest* hijacking, and later in relation to the pirate attack upon the *Marida Marguerite*.[25]

III. Outcomes and analysis

In the case of *Shibin*, all appeals against conviction were dismissed by superior courts on the basis that all of the jurisdictional arguments made by the defendant were not valid, and that the trial court had full jurisdiction to hear these UNCLOS-informed

16 Ibid 6.
17 Ibid 5.
18 Ibid.
19 Ibid 6.
20 Ibid.
21 Ibid 4–5.
22 Ibid 7.
23 Ibid 8.
24 Ibid 9.
25 Ibid.

cases under U.S. domestic law. In relation to *Ali*, the appeals in relation to the dismissal of the charge of aiding and abetting piracy were upheld; however, the appeal regarding the conspiracy to commit piracy charge was dismissed as the court found that Article 101(c) of UNCLOS did not provide enough scope for such a charge. Consequently, this section will first examine the jurisdictional questions raised in *Shibin* and *Ali* in relation to concurrent municipal jurisdiction of piracy as it relates to the U.S. court system and the high seas requirement of Article 101(c). This will include consideration as to whether the presumption against extra-territoriality has an effect upon §1651 in *Ali*, and whether the forcible removal from Somalia to the United States, without formal extradition proceedings, voided U.S. jurisdiction in relation to *Shibin*. Once these matters have been considered, the analysis will then consider the legal reasoning surrounding the scope of Article 101(c) of UNCLOS in relation to the U.S. offence of conspiracy to commit piracy.

A. Jurisdiction and UNCLOS

The defendants in both *Ali* and *Shibin* argued that UNCLOS must be read in such a manner that limited concurrent municipal jurisdiction for acts committed under Article 101(c) does apply to acts of facilitation that take place on the high seas, but does not extend to jurisdiction for acts of facilitation that occur on land. Therefore, any charge of aiding and abetting piracy requires that all aiding and abetting took place on the high seas for the elements of piracy to be satisfied. Consequently, Ali and Shibin argued that because all their alleged acts of aiding and abetting piracy occurred from within Somalia (or within the Somali territorial sea), UNCLOS (or parallel customary international law) did not grant the requisite jurisdiction for prosecution to the United States. These arguments failed in both cases, with the U.S. federal court finding that the concurrent municipal jurisdiction afforded to piracy under Article 105 of UNCLOS (or reflected therein) did apply to 'on-shore' acts of facilitation of piracy, provided that the act of piracy being facilitated took place on the high seas. Further, the court confirmed that the charge of aiding and abetting piracy was available for ex post facto conduct.[26]

Additionally, in both *Ali* and *Shibin*, it was argued that a geographical limiter of the high seas should be read into Article 101(c) by virtue of the position of Article 86 and 101(c) within Part VII ('High Seas') of UNCLOS.[27] This argument was rejected on the basis that Article 101(a) specified such a geographical limitation while 101(c) did not, which indicated that the specific overruled the general: In Ali's case, the Court asserted that

26 Roger Phillips, 'Pirate Accessory Liability: Developing a Modern Legal Regime Governing Incitement and Intentional Facilitation of Maritime Piracy' (2013) 25 *Florida Journal of International Law* 271 at 306–307.

27 *United States of America v Ali Mohamed Ali*, also known as Ahmed Ali Adan, also known as Ismail Ali [2013] Unreported 13–14; *United States of America v Mohammad Saaili Shibin*, above n 4, 12 & 17.

> there are several problems with Ali's theory that article 86 imposes a strict high seas requirement on all provisions in Part VII. For one thing, [it] would result in numerous redundancies throughout UNCLOS.[28]

Further, the court in *Shibin* argued that 'Article 101(c) does not limit the facilitation acts to conduct on the high seas . . . so long as the acts specified in Article 101(a) are carried out on the high seas'.[29] This argument in *Shibin* was buttressed by reference to UN Security Council resolutions 1976 and 2020, both of which made direct statements regarding the need to prosecute 'on land' facilitators of piracy.[30] The courts were, in essence, asserting that provided the prosecution can establish a direct evidentiary link between the aiding and abetting (facilitation) on one hand, and an act of piracy that occurred on the high seas on the other hand, then Article 101(c) of UNCLOS will be satisfied materially and the jurisdiction granted by Article 105 can the exercised.[31] Finally on this point, the Memorandum Opinion released in relation to *Ali* also held that an act of piracy constituted a continuing offence that begins with the commencement of piratical acts, and – so long as those acts began on the high seas – all other contributing acts would also be caught by the concurrent municipal jurisdiction applicable to the offence of piracy.[32] As one analysis of these cases has noted, 'Ultimately, at the US appellate level, the law has been settled with respect to pirate negotiators: the US Government does not need to prove that negotiators facilitated piracy while on the high seas, even when universal jurisdiction is the theory used to prosecute the negotiator'.[33]

B. Presumption against extraterritoriality

In the *Ali* case, the defendant argued that the presumption against extraterritoriality in U.S. law (as confirmed in the case of *Kiobel*)[34] prohibited U.S. jurisdiction in relation to acts of piracy that did not occur on the high seas.[35] This argument was grounded in the wording of 18 USC § 1651, which states: 'Whoever, on the high seas, commits a crime of piracy as defined by the law of nations, and is afterward brought into or found in the United States, shall be imprisoned for life'.[36] It was this specific inclusion of a reference to 'the high seas' within this domestic criminalisation

28 *United States of America v Ali Mohamed Ali*, above n 4, 13; *United States of America v Mohammad Saaili Shibin*, above n 4, 18.

29 *United States of America v Mohammad Saaili Shibin*, above n 4, 17.

30 Ibid 18–19.

31 *United States of America v Ali Mohamed Ali*, above n 4, 20; *United States of America v Mohammad Saaili Shibin*, above n 4, 17.

32 *United States of America v Ali Mohamed Ali* – Memorandum Opinion, above n 9, 3–4.

33 Youngs, 'Piracy in Somalia: A Legal Analysis concerning the Prosecution of Pirate Negotiators and Pirate Facilitators under the Current US and International Framework', above n 7, at 842.

34 *Kiobel v. Royal Dutch Petroleum Co.* (17 April 2013) 569 US (USSC, No. 10–1491).

35 *United States of America v Ali Mohamed Ali*, above n 4, 16–17.

36 U.S. Code Title 18 Chapter 81 (United States of America) 1651 ('*18 USC*').

of piracy in the United States upon which Ali's argument was founded, and – ultimately – upon which it also foundered. This is because – much like the arguments regarding the high seas requirement reflected in the UNCLOS approach to piracy – the court found that the requirements of aiding and abetting piracy would still support a valid charge for 'on land' facilitation conduct, so long as the prosecution could 'prove that *somebody* committed piratical acts while on the high seas'.[37]

C. Need for extradition proceedings

During his defence and appeal, Shibin contended that the charges against him should have been dismissed due to a lack of personal jurisdiction over him by the U.S. courts. This lack of jurisdiction, he asserted, resulted from the fact that he was 'forcibly seized and removed from [Somalia] by agents of the United States government and was provided no opportunity to challenge either his detention, or his removal'.[38] The court dismissed this appeal by applying the Ker-Frisbie doctrine, which holds that 'the manner in which the defendant is captured and brought to the court is generally irrelevant to the court's personal jurisdiction over him'.[39] That is, a 'constructed jurisdiction' can still be a legitimate jurisdiction.[40] The court accepted that the applicability of the Ker-Frisbie doctrine was well established within U.S. law, and was applicable in this case.[41] Ultimately, the court assessed that 'Simply by virtue of being "found in" the United States, even though he was brought against his will, for the purpose of standing trial, . . . Shibin was subject to the jurisdiction of the laws of the United States'.[42] The court did note that if there had been an extradition treaty in place between Somalia and the United States, then the United States would have been bound to follow the procedure set out in that treaty; however, in the absence of such a treaty, the court's jurisdiction was not limited in relation to the manner of the defendant's arrival within it.[43]

D. Conspiracy to commit piracy

The appeals court dismissed the government's appeal regarding the conspiracy to commit piracy charge against Ali. The basis of this dismissal was grounded in U.S. domestic law rather than Article 101(c) of UNCLOS, with the court observing

37 *United States of America v Ali Mohamed Ali*, above n 4, 20. Emphasis in original.

38 *United States of America v Mohammad Saaili Shibin*, above n 4, 22–23.

39 Ibid, 23–24; For international acceptance of this doctrine in relation to *jus cogens*, see also: 'The Attorney-General of the Government of Israel v Eichmann (1961)' (1962) 56:3 *American Journal of International Law* 805.

40 Ariel Lett, 'The Meaningless Existence of Universal Jurisdiction' (2015) 23:2 *Michigan State International Law Review* 545 at 567.

41 *United States of America v Mohammad Saaili Shibin*, above n 4, 24–26.

42 Alicia Olive, 'The Enemies of All Humankind: The Fourth Circuit's Application of Universal Jurisdiction in United States v Shibin' (2014) 10:2 *South Carolina Journal of International Law and Business* 369 at 379.

43 *United States of America v Mohammad Saaili Shibin*, above n 4, 24.

that UNCLOS 'is silent on conspiratorial liability'.[44] While the common law definition of conspiracy in the U.S. system is quite confusing,[45] it was the wording of 18 USC § 371 that defeated the government's appeal in this matter. This is because 18 USC § 371 states that '[i]f two or more persons conspire . . . to commit any offence against the United States',[46] and the court held that the presumption against extraterritoriality articulated in *Kiobel* necessarily affected this charge.[47] Ultimately, the appeals court held that a prosecution of conspiracy charges in relation to piracy would first necessarily require that the United States 'have universal jurisdiction over [the relevant] offence'. However, because the court had already determined that Article 101(c) of UNCLOS was silent on conspiratorial liability, the presumption against extraterritoriality applied to the conspiracy charges; consequently, this charge was dismissed.[48] Presumably this reasoning was neither argued nor applied in Shibin's case because the *Quest* was a U.S. vessel.

IV. Contemporary significance of the cases

The *Ali* and *Shibin* cases are relatively straightforward in their jurisprudence; however, they are of enduring significance for counter-piracy operations specifically, and more broadly for maritime security operations. The primary reason for this significance is that they provide robust judicial interpretation of Article 101(c) of UNCLOS and demonstrate that international law is capable of supporting jurisdiction over 'on land' facilitators of piracy in spite of territorial jurisdiction arguments to the contrary. While the arguments in *Ali* ran counter to the expectations of those involved in these law enforcement operations regarding their ability to bring a charge of conspiracy to commit piracy against 'on-land' facilitators,[49] these arguments most likely reflect a relatively bespoke American interpretation of the nature of a conspiracy charge, rather than representing a settled international view of Article 101(c)'s scope. Further, the decision in *Ali* – where there was no clear nexus of jurisdiction apart from the general concurrent municipal jurisdiction afforded by UNCLOS – provides (at the least, U.S.) law enforcement personnel with quite clear authorities to take action and bring prosecutions. This is not to say that a fundamental imperative of international comity – that states exercise significant discretion, and be both justified and judicious, when asserting a permissive jurisdiction

44 *United States of America v Ali Mohamed Ali*, above n 4, 21.

45 Ibid, 21:

> [As] long as a substantive offence was done in furtherance of the conspiracy, and was reasonably foreseeable as a necessary or natural consequence of the unlawful agreement, then a conspirator will be held vicariously liable for the offence committed by his or her co-conspirators.

46 *18 USC* 371.

47 *United States of America v Ali Mohamed Ali*, above n 4, 22–23.

48 Ibid, 23. The original publication of the judgement contained a typographical error stating that they lacked jurisdiction to prosecute for conspiracy to commit privacy.

49 Paige, 'The Impact and Effectiveness of UNCLOS on Counter-Piracy Operations', above n 5, 106.

over conduct taking place within another state's territorial jurisdiction such as 'on-land' piracy facilitation – will not in the future present challenges to this expansive authority[50]; clearly, this is a consideration which states must heed. Nevertheless, when read in conjunction with the recent convictions of Afweyne Snr and Tiiceey in relation to the hijacking of the *Pompeii*,[51] the *Ali* and *Shibin* cases confirm that there is a strong, defensible, and judicially confirmed legal basis for maritime law enforcement and security agents to confidently seek to arrest and prosecute 'on-land' piracy facilitators where the opportunity presents.

50 See inter alia: Youngs, 'Piracy in Somalia: A Legal Analysis concerning the Prosecution of Pirate Negotiators and Pirate Facilitators under the Current US and International Framework', above n 7, at 857; Olive, 'The Enemies of All Humankind: The Fourth Circuit's Application of Universal Jurisdiction in United States v Shibin', above n 42, at 383–384.

51 '20 Years in Prison for Somali Pirate Kingpin, Belgian Court Rules' *OCEANUSLive*, 14 March 2016 <www.oceanuslive.org/main/viewnews.aspx?uid=00001112>; Ultimately, Afweyne Snr was tried under hostage taking statutes due to a direct nexus of jurisdiction that Belgium had over the incident rather than risking a piracy charge under Article 101(c) of UNCLOS: *Mohamed Abdi Hassan* [2017] Hof van Cassatie van België P. 17.0727.N.

PART III

Freedom of navigation, maritime law enforcement, and maritime security

8

THE BLACK SEA BUMPING INCIDENT

Raul (Pete) Pedrozo[1]

I. Introduction

The 1988 Black Sea bumping incident involving the United States and the Soviet Union demonstrates how the U.S. Freedom of Navigation (FON) programme has helped preserve navigational rights and freedoms for all seafaring nations, enhance safety of navigation and overflight, and reinforce the rule of law at sea. A fundamental tenet of international law is that all ships, including warships, enjoy the right of innocent passage through the territorial sea of coastal states. Soviet domestic law[2] and regulations[3] adopted in the 1980s recognised the right of innocent passage for warships in the territorial sea, but only in designated sea lanes. The United States challenged the Soviet position, both diplomatically and operationally, arguing that there was no legal basis under international law for coastal states to limit warship transits to specified sea lanes in the territorial sea. The dispute was peacefully resolved following a series of bilateral discussions between the two superpowers that ultimately resulted in the signing of the Jackson Hole Agreement in 1989.[4] A uniform interpretation

1 Captain Pedrozo was the legal adviser to the officer appointed to conduct the official Navy investigation of the Black Sea bumping incident.

2 Law of the Union of Soviet Socialist Republics on the State frontier of the USSR (24 November 1982), reprinted in United Nations, The Law of the Sea: Current Developments in State Practice (1987), 99–100 <www.un.org/Depts/los/LEGISLATIONANDTREATIES/PDFFILES/publications/E.87.V.3.pdf> [hereinafter 1982 Law].

3 *Rules for Navigation and Sojourn of Foreign Warships in the Territorial Waters and Internal Waters and Ports of the USSR*, ratified by the Council of Ministers Decree No. 384 of 25 April 1983, reprinted in 24 ILM. 1715, 1717 (1985) [hereinafter 1983 Rules].

4 United States of America-Union of Soviet Socialist Republics: Joint Statement with attached Uniform Interpretation of Rules of International Law Governing Innocent Passage, done at Jackson Hole, Wyoming, 23 September 1989, 28 ILM 1444 (1989), 14 United Nations, Law of the Sea Bulletin, 12 (December 1989), 12–13 [hereinafter Jackson Hole Agreement].

DOI: 10.4324/9781003307013-11

of rules of international law governing innocent passage attached to the agreement provides, in part, that 'all ships, including warships, regardless of cargo, armament or means of propulsion, enjoy the right of innocent passage through the territorial sea in accordance with international law, for which neither prior notification nor authorization is required'.[5] A separate agreement, designed to avoid dangerous military activities of the parties when operating in proximity of one another, was also negotiated by the two superpowers following the incident.[6]

II. Background

A. Prelude to the incident

When the Soviet Union ratified the 1958 Geneva Convention on the Territorial Sea and the Contiguous Zone[7] in 1960, it entered a reservation to Article 23[8] indicating that coastal states had 'the right to establish procedures for the authorization of the passage of foreign warships through its territorial waters'.[9] That same year, a new domestic law and implementing regulation were adopted limiting the passage of foreign warships in the Soviet territorial sea to a prior consent regime.[10] This new requirement was a dramatic change in Soviet policy. Prior to the Second World War,

5 Ibid.

6 *Agreement between the Government of the United States of America and the Government of the Union of Soviet Socialist Republic on the Prevention of Dangerous Military Activities*, signed in Moscow 1 June 1989, entered into force 1 January 1990, 28 ILM 977 (1989) [hereinafter DMA Agreement]. The DMA builds on the 1972 US-USSR Incidents at Sea Agreement, which was signed to promote safety of navigation and flight when naval forces of the parties operate in proximity of one another beyond the territorial sea. *Agreement Between the Government of The United States of America and the Government of The Union of Soviet Socialist Republics on the Prevention of Incidents On and Over the High Seas*, signed in Moscow 25 May 1972, entered into force 25 May 1972, 23 UST 1168; *Protocol to the Agreement on the Prevention of Incidents On and Over the High Seas*, 22 May 1973, 24 UST 1063 [hereinafter INCSEA Agreement].

7 516 UNTS 205 (29 April 1958).

8 Article 23 provides that

> If any warship does not comply with the regulations of the coastal State concerning passage through the territorial sea and disregards any request for compliance which is made to it, the coastal State may require the warship to leave the territorial sea.

9 Reservation of the USSR upon ratification of the *Convention on the Territorial Sea and the Contiguous Zone*, 22 November 1960, <https://treaties.un.org/pages/ViewDetails.aspx?src=TREATY&mtdsg_no=XXI-1&chapter=21&lang=en>. The Soviet reservation is consistent with Russian Judge Krylow's dissenting opinion in the Corfu Channel case ('the right to regulate passage of warships through its territorial waters appertains to the coastal State'). *Corfu Channel case* (*UK v Albania*), Merits (Judgment of 9 April) (Judge Krylow), 1949 ICJ Rep. 4, 74.

10 Article 16 of the 1960 statute on the state boundary established 'an authorization procedure for foreign warships'. Domestic regulations implementing the 1960 law required foreign warships to request permission through diplomatic channels 30 days before transiting through the Soviet territorial sea. William E. Butler, 'Innocent Passage and the 1982 Convention: The Influence of Soviet Law and Policy' (1987) 81 *American Journal of International Law* 331 at 333.

Soviet laws and regulations had always recognised the unimpeded right of innocent passage of foreign warships through the territorial sea.[11] As a result, the U.S. Navy began to conduct maritime operations in the Black Sea and elsewhere along the Soviet coast to 'show the flag' and exercise its navigational rights and freedoms.[12]

The issue appeared to resolve itself during the negotiations of the 1982 United Nations Convention on the Law of the Sea (UNCLOS).[13] During the negotiations, an attempt by some states to include prior notification or coastal state authorisation in Article 21 failed to achieve a majority vote at the conference.[14] Most countries – including the United States, the Soviet Union, and the other major maritime powers – opposed the proposal. As a result, the proponents of prior notice or consent requirements did not press their proposed amendment of Article 21 to a vote at the conclusion of the conference, as it was clear that there was not sufficient support for the provision to be adopted.[15] Shortly before the conclusion of the negotiations, the conference president, Ambassador Tommy Koh of Singapore, confirmed the point by reiterating on the record that 'the Convention is quite clear on this point. Warships do, like other ships, have a right of innocent passage through the territorial sea, and there is no need for warships to acquire the prior consent or even notification of the coastal State'.[16]

11 *The Instruction for the Navigation of Vessels in Coastal Waters within Artillery Range of Shore Batteries in Peacetime* (5 July 1924), the 1927 statute on the state boundary, the Provisional Rules for Foreign Warships Visiting USSR Waters (28 March 1931), and the 1936 Rules for the Entrance of Vessels into Areas of Restricted Movement were 'fully consistent with the prevailing customary rules of international law governing the right of innocent passage in the territorial waters of a coastal state'. Ibid 331–332.

12 From 10–13 January 1966, for example, the *USS Yarnell* (CG 17) and *USS Forrest Royal* (DD 872) conducted operations to exercise freedom of the seas and collect intelligence in the Black Sea. The U.S. warships 'were monitored with Soviet surface ships and aircraft from the time they entered the Black Sea until they exited the Bosporus'. The *USS Corry* (DD 817) entered the Black Sea on 9 February 1966, to 'show the flag' and was overflown by Soviet Air Force surveillance aircraft. James Kraska and Raul Pedrozo, *International Maritime Security Law* (Brill/Martinus Nijhoff Publishers, 2013), 257. Similarly, on 9 December 1968, the USS *Dyess* (DD/DDR 880) and USS *Turner* (DD/DDR 834) conducted a 'show the flag' operation in the Black Sea off the coasts of Turkey and the Soviet Union. The U.S. warships were closely shadowed by Soviet vessels and the Soviet government charged that the manoeuvres were a 'provocative sortie'. William J. Aceves, 'Diplomacy at Sea: U.S. Freedom of Navigation Operations in the Black Sea' (1993) 46:2 *Naval War College Review* 59 at 64.

13 *United Nations Convention on the Law of the Sea*, Montego Bay 10 December 1982 (entered into force 10 November 1994) 1833 UNTS 3 [hereinafter UNCLOS].

14 UNCLOS art 21 provides, in part, that '1. The coastal State may adopt laws and regulations, in conformity with the provisions of this Convention and other rules of international law, relating to innocent passage through the territorial sea, in respect of all or any of the following: (a) the safety of navigation and the regulation of maritime traffic' and '4. Foreign ships exercising the right of innocent passage through the territorial sea shall comply with all such laws and regulations and all generally accepted international regulations relating to the prevention of collisions at sea'.

15 *United Nations Convention on the Law of the Sea 1982: A Commentary* Vol. II 195–199. (Satya N. Nandan and Shabati Rosenne, eds, 1993).

16 Bernard H. Oxman, 'The Regime of Warships Under the United Nations Convention on the Law of the Sea' (1984) 24 *Virginia Journal of International Law* 809 at 854 n159.

Concurrently, in November 1982, the Supreme Soviet of the USSR adopted the Law of the Union of Soviet Socialist Republics on the state frontier of the USSR, which repealed the 1960 law on the state boundary.[17] Article 5 of the new law established a 2-nm territorial sea and Article 13 recognised, inter alia, the right of innocent passage for foreign warships 'in accordance with the procedures to be established by the Council of Ministers of the USSR'.[18] Implementing regulations were adopted by the USSR Council of Ministers on 28 April 1983,[19] reversing the prior consent regime instituted under the 1960 Rules. For the most part, the 1983 Rules reflected the balance of interests expressed in UNCLOS, conditioning innocent passage of warships on 'observance of the 1983 Rules, the laws and rules of the USSR relating to the regime of territorial waters, and international treaties of the USSR'.[20] One provision of the rules, however, proved to be problematic.

Article 12 provided, in part, that

> the innocent passage of foreign warships through the territorial waters of the USSR for the purpose of traversing the territorial waters of the USSR without entering internal waters and ports of the USSR shall be permitted along routes ordinarily used for international navigation:
>
> - in the Baltic Sea: according to the traffic separation systems in the area of Kypu Peninsula (Hiiumaa Island) and in the area of the Porkkala Lighthouse;
> - in the Sea of Okhotsk: according to the traffic separation schemes in the areas of Cape Aniva (Sakhalin Island) and the Fourth Kurile Strait (Paramushir and Makanrushi Islands);
> - in the Sea of Japan: according to the traffic separation system in the area of Cape Kril'on (Sakhalin Island).[21]

This provision was interpreted by Soviet officials as limiting innocent passage in the Soviet territorial sea to these five pre-designated routes.[22] Thus, innocent passage by foreign warships was purportedly prohibited along most of the Soviet coastline, including the Black Sea, a position inimical to America's freedom of navigation interests and global mobility of its armed forces.

17 1982 Law, above n 1.

18 Ibid, art 13 provides, in part, that

> Foreign warships and underwater vehicles shall enjoy the right of innocent passage through the territorial waters (territorial sea) of the USSR in accordance with the procedure to be established by the Council of Ministers of the USSR. However, submarines and other underwater vehicles are required to navigate on the surface and show their flag.

19 1983 Rules, above n 2.

20 Butler, 'Innocent Passage and the 1982 Convention', above n 19, 338.

21 1983 Rules, above n 2.

22 Butler, 'Innocent Passage and the 1982 Convention', above n 19, 340–343; Ronald D. Neubauer, 'The Right of Innocent Passage for Warships in the Territorial Sea: A Response to the Soviet Union' (1996) 68 *International Law Studies* 189, at 191–192.

Neither UNCLOS nor customary international law recognise the right of a coastal state to limit innocent passage of foreign warships to traditional or designated routes ordinarily used for international navigation, unless required for safety of navigation.[23] Accordingly, the United States considered that the Soviet law and regulations were inconsistent with international law and began to periodically challenge the new rules under the FON programme.[24]

B. U.S. Freedom of Navigation (FON) programme

The United States has worldwide security and economic interests that are dependent on the transport of goods in international trade and the free movement of its armed forces. The U.S. Navy is tasked with securing access to the world's oceans to retain global freedom of action to maintain international peace and security, as well as facilitate and enhance global trade and commerce. In response to the growing number of excessive maritime claims asserted by coastal States following the Second World War, the United States established the FON programme to influence nations to either avoid new excessive maritime claims or renounce existing ones.

Between 1948 and 1979, the United States filed about 20 diplomatic protests against excessive coastal state maritime claims. Realising that these demarches alone were ineffective and that a tangible demonstration of U.S. resolve was needed to deter excessive maritime claims, the administration of U.S. President Jimmy Carter launched the FON programme in March 1979.[25] The programme demonstrates U.S. non-acquiescence in excessive claims of other states that are designed to restrict

23 Pursuant to Article 22(1) of UNCLOS,

> the coastal State may, where necessary having regard to the safety of navigation, require foreign ships exercising the right of innocent passage through its territorial sea to use such sea lanes and traffic separation schemes as it may designate or prescribe for the regulation of the passage of ships.

24 William Aceves, 'Diplomacy at Sea', above n 11, 65. For example, in August 1979, the *USS Caron* (DD 970) and *USS Farragut* (DDG 37) conducted a 'show the flag' operations in the Black Sea. In response, the Soviets deployed a number of warplanes to stage more than 30 mock missile attacks against the U.S. warships.

25 U.S. Department of State, Bureau of Oceans and International Environmental and Scientific Affairs, Ocean and Polar Affairs, *Maritime Security and Navigation*, available at <www.state.gov/E/OES/OCNS/OPA/maritime security/>. The programme is reflected in a series of classified White House directives prepared by the National Security Council and signed by subsequent presidents: National Security Decision Directive-20 (NSDD-20), United States Law of the Sea Policy, 29 January 1982; National Security Decision Directive 265 (NSDD-265), Freedom of Navigation Program, 16 March 1987; and National Security Directive 49 (NSD-49), Freedom of Navigation Program, 12 October 1990; and the current version, Presidential Decision Directive-32 (PDD-32), Freedom of Navigation, 23 January 1995. See also, William Aceves, 'The Freedom of Navigation Program: A Study on the Relationship Between Law and Politics' (1996) 19 *Hastings International and Comparative Law Review* 259. Lincoln P. Bloomfield, National Security Council Memorandum to Zbigniew Brzezinski, Visit to the [Law of the Sea] Conference, 26 July 1979, 31 July 1979 (Secret; declassified 22 August 2000).

navigation and overflight rights and freedoms of the international community and other lawful uses of the seas related to those rights and freedoms.[26]

Operating along a triple track, the FON programme includes diplomatic communications by the State Department, operational assertions by U.S. ships and aircraft, and 'bilateral and multilateral consultations with other governments in an effort to promote maritime stability and consistency with international law'.[27] Accordingly, the programme stresses 'the need for and obligation of all States to adhere to the customary international law rules and practices reflected in . . . [UNCLOS]'.[28]

The importance of the programme was reinforced by U.S. President Ronald Reagan's ocean policy statement in March 1983, which announced that the United States would not sign UNCLOS because of several major problems in Part XI, the Convention's deep seabed mining provisions.[29] Notwithstanding the U.S. rejection of Part XI, President Reagan recognised that the Convention 'contains provisions with respect to traditional uses of the oceans which generally confirm existing maritime law and practice and fairly balance the interests of all states'.[30] Accordingly, President Reagan indicated that the United States was

> prepared to accept and act in accordance with the balance of interests relating to traditional uses of the oceans – such as navigation and overflight. In this respect, the United States will recognize the rights of other states in the waters off their coasts, as reflected in the Convention, so long as the rights and freedoms of the United States and others under international law are recognized by such coastal states.[31]

Nevertheless, President Reagan additionally announced that the United States would, consistent with the FON programme,

> exercise and assert its navigation and overflight rights and freedoms on a worldwide basis in a manner that is consistent with the balance of interests reflected in the Convention. The United States will not, however, acquiesce in unilateral acts of other states designed to restrict the rights and freedoms of the international community in navigation and overflight and other related high seas uses.[32]

26 Presidential Decision Directive-32 (PDD-32), Freedom of Navigation, 23 January 1995, unclassified excerpt reprinted in James Kraska and Raul Pedrozo, *International Maritime Security Law*, above n 11, Annex 4,213; U.S. Department of State, Bureau of Oceans and International Environmental and Scientific Affairs, Ocean and Polar Affairs, Maritime Security and Navigation, available at <www.state.gov/E/OES/OCNS/OPA/maritime security/>.

27 Ibid.

28 Ibid.

29 United States Ocean Policy, Statement by the President, 10 March 1983, *available at* <www.state.gov/documents/organization/143224.pdf>.

30 Ibid.

31 Ibid.

32 Ibid.

The FON programme is not meant or designed to be confrontational or provocative in nature. In fact, operational assertions are conducted against friends and foes alike. In 1986, Assistant Secretary of State for Oceans and International Environmental and Scientific Affairs John Negroponte explained:

> The exercise of rights – freedom to navigate on the world's oceans – is not meant to be a provocative act. Rather, in the framework of customary international law, it is a legitimate, peaceful assertion of a legal position and nothing more . . . . [T]he more aggressive and unreasonable and provocative and threatening a claim may be, the more important it is to exercise one's rights in the face of the claim. The world community can't allow itself to be coerced – coerced into lethargy in the protection of the freedom of the seas.[33]

In short, the FON programme underscores U.S. commitment to a stable legal regime for the world's oceans that carefully balances coastal and maritime state interests reflected in UNCLOS. Since its inception, the United States has conducted hundreds of operational challenges and diplomatic protests to demonstrate U.S. non-acquiescence in excessive maritime claims. A list of challenges and protests is contained in the individual country entries of the *Department of Defense Maritime Claims Reference Manual*.[34]

C. The 1986 Black Sea Affair

On 10 March 1986, the *USS Yorktown* (CG 48) and *USS Caron* (DD 970) entered the Black Sea to conduct a 'show the flag' operation and exercise the right of innocent passage in the Soviet territorial sea.[35] They were immediately shadowed by the Soviet frigate *Ladnyi* (FF 801). Three days later, the American warships entered the Soviet territorial sea 'and sailed westward along the southern Crimean Peninsula, approaching within 6 miles of the coast'.[36] The *Ladnyi* informed the *Yorktown* and *Caron* that they have violated Soviet territorial waters and ordered the U.S. warships to immediately depart the area. In addition, Soviet border guard vessels and aircraft were dispatched to the scene and the Black Sea air and naval forces were placed on alert.[37] The American ships acknowledged the warning, but maintained

33 Aceves, 'The Freedom of Navigation Program', above n 24, 287.

34 U.S. Department of Defence, *Maritime Claims Reference Manual* (MCRM), DOD 2005.1 – M, June 2008, <www.jag.navy.mil/organization/code_10_mcrm.htm>. DoD Annual FON Reports (1991–2013) are also available at <http://policy.defense.gov/OUSDPOffices/FON.aspx>.

35 Similar operations had been conducted in 1984 and 1985. Butler, 'Innocent Passage and the 1982 Convention', above n 19, 343. See also, Aceves, above n 11, 248 (On 18 February 1984, the *USS David R. Ray* (DD 971) 'was conducting FON exercises in the Black Sea near Novorossiysk when Soviet aircraft fired cannon rounds into the ship's wake and a Soviet helicopter taking photographs of the destroyer swooped within thirty feet of its deck'.

36 Butler, 'Innocent Passage and the 1982 Convention', above n 19, 343–344.

37 Ibid, 344.

their course and speed until they departed the Soviet territorial sea 2 hours and 21 minutes later.[38]

The Soviet government diplomatically protested the transit, characterising 'the incident as provocative and warned against "serious consequences" for which the United States would bear responsibility'.[39] In this regard, Admiral V. N. Chernavin, Commander in Chief of the Soviet Navy, suggested that the American warships 'might have been attacked had they remained longer in Soviet waters'.[40]

The Soviet Ministry of Foreign Affairs also held two press conferences 'to emphasize the gravity of the situation', stressing that the violation had occurred 'in the vicinity of the Soviet coast where there are no traditional seaways'.[41] Admiral Chernavin elaborated on the latter point, indicating that

> the innocent passage of foreign warships through the territorial waters of the USSR is permitted only in specially authorized coastal areas which have been announced by the Soviet Government. In a word, there are no such areas in the Black Sea off the coast of the Soviet Union.[42]

At no time, however, did the Soviet government accuse the U.S. warships of collecting intelligence during the transit, despite the fact that both ships had intelligence-gathering capacity.[43] U.S. naval authorities admitted that the *Caron* was equipped with additional electronic sensors and listening devices during the Black Sea operations, but reaffirmed that the *Yorktown* and *Caron* were simply exercising their right of innocent passage in the Soviet territorial sea consistent with international law.[44] The White House added that the operation was 'routine and not intended to be provocative or defiant', as alleged by the Soviet government.[45] A subsequent statement by the State Department similarly emphasised that the purpose of the FON programme 'was to uphold the exercise and preservation of navigation and overflight rights and freedoms around the world'.[46]

38 Ibid.
39 Butler, 'Innocent Passage and the 1982 Convention', above n 19, 334.
40 Aceves, 'Diplomacy at Sea', above n 11, 65.
41 Butler, 'Innocent Passage and the 1982 Convention', above n 19, 344–345.
42 Ibid, 345.
43 The USS *Caron* was well-known for its intelligence collection capabilities. Between 1980 and 1988, the *Caron* conducted 43 surveillance operations off the coast of numerous nations, including three operations in the Black Sea. John W. Rolph, 'Freedom of Navigation and the Black Sea Bumping Incident: How "Innocent" Must Innocent Passage Be?' (1992) 135 *Military Law Review* 137, n 17. Ships exercising the right of innocent passage may not engage in 'any act aimed at collecting information to the prejudice of the defence or security of the coastal State'. UNCLOS, Art. 19(2)(c). See also Aceves, *The Freedom of Navigation Program*, above n 24, n 38.
44 Aceves, 'Diplomacy at Sea', above n 11, 66.
45 Ibid.
46 Ibid.

III. The 1988 Black Sea bumping incident

Despite Soviet threats that violations of its laws regarding innocent passage through the territorial sea could have 'serious consequences', the U.S. government was determined to preserve its global navigation and overflight rights and decided to conduct another Black Sea FON operation in February 1988. Ironically, the two ships that conducted the operation were the *USS Yorktown* and *USS Caron*.

From the moment they entered the Black Sea on 10 February, the U.S. warships were shadowed by three Soviet ships – a *Krivak*-class frigate *Bezzavetnyi* (FFG 811), a *Mirka*-class frigate (SKR 6), and an intelligence ship. On 12 February 1988, the *Caron* and *Yorktown* intentionally crossed into the Soviet territorial sea near Sevastopol. Within minutes, the U.S. warships were surrounded by 18 Soviet naval and border guard vessels.

Caron was then informed by *Krivak* (FFG 811) that 'Soviet ships have orders to prevent violation of territorial waters, extreme measure is to strike your ship with one of ours'.[47] *Caron* replied that she was 'engaged in innocent passage consistent with international law' and continued on her planned track.[48] As *Caron* approached within 10.5 nm of the Soviet coast, *Mirka* (FFL 824) intentionally 'bumped' the U.S. warship.[49] *Caron* continued her transit and exited Soviet territorial waters about two hours later. *Caron's* closest point of approach to the Crimean Peninsula was 7.5 nm. Damage to the *Caron's* port side was minimal, and there were no injuries.[50]

Within minutes, the *Yorktown*, which was located 10.6 nm off the Soviet coast, was contacted by *Krivak* (FFG 811) and ordered to leave Soviet territorial waters or 'our ship is going to strike on yours'.[51] *Yorktown* acknowledged the transmission but continued on her track. Shortly thereafter, *Krivak* 811 intentionally 'shouldered' the U.S. warship.[52] *Yorktown* sustained minor hull damage on her port side; two Harpoon surface-to-surface missile canisters were also damaged.[53] Approximately ten minutes later, *Krivak* 811 once again contacted *Yorktown* and indicated that 'we will strike you as before if you do not clear our waters'.[54] *Yorktown* did not acknowledge the transmission and continued on her track until she exited the Soviet territorial sea an hour and a half later without further incident.

Although damage to the U.S. and Soviet warships was minimal and neither side suffered injuries, the incident drew a series of sharp diplomatic protests from both

47 'Soviets Bump 2 U.S. Warships', *Chicago Tribune*, 13 February 1988, 1

48 'U.S. Says Act was Unprovoked, Lodges Protest with Envoy, Law of the Sea', *L.A. Times*, 14 February 1988, 1.

49 'Soviets Bump 2 Navy Ships in Black Sea; U.S. Says Act was Unprovoked, Lodges Protest with Envoy, Law of the Sea', *L.A. Times*, 14 February 1988, 1.

50 Aceves, 'Diplomacy at Sea', above n 11, 68.

51 'Soviets Bump 2 U.S. Warships', *Chicago Tribune*, 13 February 1988, 1

52 'Soviets Bump 2 Navy Ships in Black Sea; U.S. Says Act was Unprovoked, Lodges Protest with Envoy, Law of the Sea', *L.A. Times*, 14 February 1988, 1.

53 Aceves, 'Diplomacy at Sea', above n 11, 68.

54 Ibid, 251–252.

sides.[55] The Soviet protest was delivered to U.S. ambassador Jack Maddock, placing blame for the incident squarely on the actions of the *Caron* and *Yorktown* – the U.S. warships:

> did not react to signals given by a Soviet border guard ship in advance to warn them of their approaching the state border of the U.S.S.R. and did not make suggested changes in their course . . . . [A] considerable distance inside Soviet territorial waters, the American naval ships executed dangerous maneuvering which led to a collision with Soviet naval ships . . . Responsibility for the provocation which has been made, which led to the collision of the warships of the two nations, lies entirely and fully on the American side.[56]

The Soviet protest was based on several points, all of which were rejected by the United States. First, the Soviets argued that the FON operation had been conducted for political purposes – that is, to undermine the 'nascent process of improvements in Soviet-American relations and heightening international relation'.[57] Second, unlike the Black Sea affair in 1986, Soviet officials claimed that the U.S. warships were collecting intelligence during the transit.[58] Third, the Soviets argued that the American ships' transit of the territorial sea was in violation of the 1982 Law and 1983 Rules because the passage of the ships had not taken place in one of five previously-designated routes ordinarily used for international navigation.[59] Finally, Soviet officials asserted that the passage was not innocent because it was 'navigationally unnecessary' – that is, the U.S. warships could have conducted their transit on the high seas instead of through Soviet territorial waters.[60]

The U.S. protest, delivered to Soviet ambassador Yuri Dubinin by Undersecretary of State for Political Affairs Michael Armacost, denied the Soviet allegations, indicating that the incident occurred as the U.S. warships were lawfully conducting innocent passage in the Soviet territorial sea.[61] Secretary of State George Shultz added that activities under the FON programme were

> fully coordinated within the Executive Branch and have the support of the President and his Cabinet. Given our sensitive political relationship with the Soviet Union, proposed operations in Soviet waters are subjected to

55 John Cushman, '2 Soviet Warships Reportedly Bump U.S. Navy Vessels', *N.Y. Times*, 13 February 1988.

56 Aceves, 'Diplomacy at Sea', above n 11, 69. A similar statement was issued by the Soviet Ministry of Defense, blaming the U.S. warships for not reacting to 'warning signals of Soviet border guard ships', and for 'dangerously maneuvering in Soviet waters'. Soviets Bump 2 U.S. Warships', *Chicago Tribune*, 13 February 1988, 1.

57 Aceves, 'Diplomacy at Sea', above n 11, 69.

58 Ibid.

59 Rolph, 'Freedom of Navigation and the Black Sea Bumping Incident', above n 42, 145.

60 Ibid, 145–146.

61 Aceves, 'Diplomacy at Sea', above n 11, 70.

> particularly rigorous scrutiny, prior to their approval, and while they are underway. But we cannot exempt the Soviets from this program – to do so would accede to their illegal maritime claims. This we do not intend to do.[62]

The U.S. protest also highlighted 'that the incident was preceded by threats from the Soviet ships that they had been authorized to strike', a clear indication that the collisions were deliberate.[63] In addition, U.S. officials vehemently denied that the *Caron* and *Yorktown* were collecting intelligence in the Soviet territorial sea.[64]

More importantly, the United States argued that there was no basis in customary international law or UNCLOS to limit innocent passage of warships to pre-designated routes as claimed by the Soviet Union. U.S. officials recognised the right of the Soviet Union to adopt laws and regulations relating to innocent passage through the territorial sea with respect to safety of navigation and the regulation of maritime traffic, as provided in UNCLOS Article 21.1(a). Additionally, the United States acknowledged that the Soviet Union could impose sea lane restrictions that limit innocent passage if they were based on safety of navigation considerations.[65] However, State Department officials asserted that the 1982 Law and 1983 Rules violated UNCLOS Articles 21 and 22 'by completely prohibiting the exercise of innocent passage in the Black Sea'.[66] Assistant Secretary of Defense for International Security Affairs Richard Armitage added that, even though the transits by the *Caron* and *Yorktown* were not operationally necessary, as long as their passage was 'continuous, expeditious, and conducted in a manner not prejudicial to the peace, good order, or security of the littoral state', it was innocent and legal.[67]

IV. Outcomes: renewed U.S.-USSR bilateral discussions

Beginning in 1986, U.S. and Soviet military officials agreed to begin a series of military exchanges outside the scope of the annual Incidents at Sea (INCSEA) review to, inter alia, improve military-to-military relations and reduce potentially

62 Ibid, 253. A similar statement was made by Secretary of Defense Frank C. Carlucci in testimony before the Senate Armed Services Committee – the U.S. operation was not a test of Soviet territorial waters, but of the right of innocent passage (Ibid, 252).

> Under international law, they had no right to attempt to impede our ships or to use force. Force is only warranted when there is a threat, and these ships were clearly engaged in innocent passage. Our view is that unless you exercise the right of freedom of navigation, inevitably you lose it. You can always find reasons for not doing it at some particular point in time, but if we start backing off we will eventually lose some of the rights that are absolutely essential for our freedom of navigation.

63 Ibid.

64 Ibid, 253.

65 UNCLOS, art 22(1) provides that

> The coastal State may, where necessary having regard to the safety of navigation, require foreign ships exercising the right of innocent passage through its territorial sea to use such sea lanes and traffic separation schemes as it may designate or prescribe for the regulation of the passage of ships.

66 Aceves, 'Diplomacy at Sea', above n 11, 70–71.

67 Rolph, 'Freedom of Navigation and the Black Sea Bumping Incident', above n 42, 146.

dangerous activities.[68] The Black Sea bumping incident reinvigorated these discussions, as both sides sought to reach a mutual understanding on the issue of innocent passage, as well as avoid dangerous manoeuvres that might lead to unintended consequences or armed conflict.[69]

A. The Agreement on the Prevention of Dangerous Military Activities (DMA Agreement)

In July 1988, the Chairman of the Joint Chiefs of Staff, Admiral William Crowe, and his Soviet counterpart Marshal Sergei Akhromeyev, Chief of the Soviet General Staff, issued a joint statement that the United States and the USSR would pursue policies and actions to assist their respective armed forces avoid dangerous military activities when operating in proximity of one another. A joint military-to-military working group was subsequently established to discuss ways to avoid unintended confrontations that might lead to conflict. The work of this group, however, would be separate and apart from the existing INCSEA structure.[70]

Less than a year later, Admiral Crowe and the new Chief of the General Staff, Colonel General Mikhail Moiseyev, signed the Agreement on the Prevention of Dangerous Military Activities (DMA Agreement).[71] Pursuant to Article II of the agreement:

> 1 . . . each Party shall take necessary measures directed toward preventing dangerous military activities, which are the following activities of personnel and equipment of its armed forces when operating in proximity to personnel and equipment of the armed forces of the other Party during peacetime:
>
> a Entering . . . the national territory of the other Party owing to circumstance brought about by force majeure, or as a result of unintentional actions . . .;

68 INCSEA Agreement, above n 5. INCSEA is a navy-to-navy agreement that was signed in 1972 by then Secretary of the Navy John Warner and Soviet Admiral Sergei Gorshkov. Article IX of the agreement requires the parties to meet annually to review the implementation of its terms. The agreement provides, in part, that each side 'avoid dangerous maneuvers, hindrance of navigation by dropping various objects near ships, and mock attacks simulating the use of weapons against aircraft or ships' when U.S. and Soviet (and later Russian) forces operate in close proximity to one another on the high seas. A Protocol extending the prohibition on simulated attacks to nonmilitary ships was signed in 1973. John H. McNeill, 'Military-to-Military Arrangements for the Prevention of U.S.-Russian Conflict' (1996) 68 *International Law Studies* 575 at 577.

69 McNeill, 'Military-to-Military Arrangements for the Prevention of U.S.-Russian Conflict', above n 67, 577; Aceves, 'Diplomacy at Sea', above n 11, 71.

70 Aceves, 'Diplomacy at Sea', above n 11, 72.

71 *DMA Agreement*, above n 5.

b Using a laser in such a manner that its radiation could cause harm to personnel or damage to equipment of the armed forces of the other Party;

c Hampering the activities . . . of the other Party in a Special Caution Area in a manner which could cause harm to personnel or damage to equipment; and

d Interfering with command and control networks in a manner which could cause harm to personnel or damage to equipment . . . .

2 The Parties shall take measures to ensure expeditious termination and resolution of peaceful means, without resort to the threat of use of force, or any incident which may arise as a result of dangerous military activities.

3 Additional provisions concerning prevention of dangerous military activities and resolutions of any incident which may arise as a result of those activities are contained in Articles III,[72] IV,[73] V[74] and VI[75] of this Agreement and the Annexes thereto.

72 Article III.2 provides that

> If, owing to circumstances brought about by force majeure or as a result of unintentional actions, as set forth in Article II, subparagraph 1(a) of this Agreement, personnel and equipment of the armed forces of one Party enter into the national territory of the other Party, such personnel shall adhere to the procedures set forth in Annexes 1 and 2 to this Agreement.

73 Article IV.2 provides that

> If personnel of the armed forces of one Party believe that personnel of the armed forces of the other Party are using a laser in a manner which could cause harm to them or damage to their equipment, they shall immediately attempt to establish communication to seek termination of such use. If the personnel of the armed forces of the Party having received such notification are actually using a laser in proximity to the area indicated in the notification, they shall investigate the relevant circumstances. If their use of a laser could in fact cause harm to personnel or damage to equipment of the armed forces of the other Party, they shall terminate such use.

74 Article V.2 provides that

> Personnel of the armed forces of the Parties present in a designated Special Caution Area shall establish and maintain communications, in accordance with Annex 1 to this Agreement, and undertake other measures as may be later agreed upon by the Parties, in order to prevent dangerous military activities and to resolve any incident which may arise as a result of such activities.

75 Article VI.1 provides that

> When personnel of the armed forces of one Party, in proximity to personnel and equipment of the armed forces of the other Party, detect interference with their command and control networks which could cause harm to them or damage to their equipment, they may inform the relevant personnel of the armed forces of the other Party if they believe that the interference is being cause by such personnel and equipment of the armed forces of that Party.

> Article VI.2 provides that 'If the personnel of the armed forces of the Party having received such information establish that this interference with the command and control networks is being caused by their activities, they shall take expeditious measure to terminate the interference'.

Like INCSEA, Article IX of the DMA established a Joint Military Commission to ensure compliance with the agreement and consider 'possible ways to ensure a higher level of safety for the personnel and equipment of their armed forces'.

Article VIII makes clear, however, that nothing in the DMA Agreement affects 'the rights and obligations of the Parties under other international agreements and arrangements in force between the Parties [e.g., INCSEA], and the rights of individual or collective self-defense and of navigation and overflight, in accordance with international law'. The latter point is reinforced in the Second Agreed Statement to the agreement: 'As indicated in Article VIII . . . this Agreement does not affect rights of navigation under international law, including the right of warships to exercise innocent passage'. It was therefore apparent that the United States would continue to conduct operational assertions under the FON programme to exercise its navigational rights under international law. Accordingly, both sides realised that there was still a need to discuss and conclude a separate arrangement on the right of innocent passage.

B. The Jackson Hole Agreement

As consultations between the two superpowers continued to resolve their differences regarding innocent passage of warships, it became evident to both sides 'that a uniform interpretation of international law on innocent passage would provide the basis for a mutually acceptable resolution'.[76] The discussions were viewed by U.S. officials as a means to reconfirm a basic understanding of the content of innocent passage. Both nations regarded UNCLOS as generally reflective of international law and practice, so the terms of the Convention were used as the point of departure for the talks.[77] Both superpowers also recognised the need to encourage all states to harmonise their domestic laws, regulations, and practices with the provisions of UNCLOS.[78]

The discussions led to the signing of the Joint Statement with attached Uniform Interpretation of Rules of International Law Governing Innocent Passage (Jackson Hole Agreement) in September 1989 by Secretary of State James Baker and Soviet Foreign Minister Eduard Shevardnadze. In the end, the Soviet Union agreed with the U.S. position that 'all ships, including warships, regardless of cargo, armament

76 McNeill, 'Military-to-Military Arrangements for the Prevention of U.S.-Russian Conflict', above n 67, 579.

77 The second paragraph of the Joint Statement provides that the two governments are guided by the provisions of UNCLOS, 'which, with respect to traditional uses of the oceans, generally constitute international law and practice and balance fairly the interests of all States'. Paragraph 1 of the Uniform Interpretation similarly provides that 'the relevant rules of international law governing innocent passage of ships in the territorial sea are stated in . . . [UNCLOS], particularly in Part II, Section 3'. *Jackson Hole Agreement*, above n 3.

78 The Joint Statement further provides in paragraph two that both sides 'recognize the need to encourage all States to harmonize their internal laws, regulations and practices, with those provisions'. *Jackson Hole Agreement*, above n 3.

or means of propulsion, enjoy the right of innocent passage through the territorial sea in accordance with international law, for which neither prior notification nor authorization is required'.[79] The parties also agreed in paragraph 3 of the Uniform Interpretation that Article 19.2 of UNCLOS contained an 'exhaustive list of activities that would render passage not innocent' and that 'a ship passing through the territorial sea that does not engage in any of those activities is in innocent passage'.

The Uniform Interpretation (paragraph 5) recognises the authority of the coastal state to adopt laws and regulations affecting innocent passage that are consistent with UNCLOS Articles 21–23 and 25. 'These include the laws and regulations requiring ships exercising the right of innocent passage . . . to use such sea lanes and traffic separation schemes as it may prescribe where needed to protect safety of navigation'.[80] However, consistent with the U.S. position, paragraph 5 further provides that 'in areas where no such sea lanes or traffic separation schemes have been prescribed, ships nevertheless enjoy the right of innocent passage'.

To avoid a repeat of the Black Sea bumping incident, paragraph 4 of the Uniform Interpretation provides that

> a coastal State which questions whether the particular passage of a ship through its territorial sea is innocent shall inform the ship of the reason why it questions the innocence of the passage and provide the ship an opportunity to clarify its intentions or correct its conduct in a reasonably short period of time.

Paragraph 7 authorises the coastal state to require a warship that engages in conduct that violates its laws or regulations or renders the ship's passage not innocent to leave its territorial sea – 'in such case, the warship shall do so immediately'. Finally, rather than resort to force, paragraph 8 calls on the parties to resolve 'all differences which may arise regarding a particular case of passage of ships through the territorial sea' through diplomatic channels or other agreed means.

Five days after the Jackson Hole Agreement was signed, the Department of State notified all U.S. diplomatic posts that the 1983 Rules had been brought into conformity with UNCLOS. Accordingly, the U.S. government had assured the USSR that U.S. warships would no longer exercise the right of innocent passage under the FON programme in the Soviet territorial sea, with the caveat that 'warships of both countries retained the right to conduct innocent passage incidental to normal navigation in the territorial sea' and that the United States 'would continue to conduct routine operations in the Black Sea'.[81]

79 *Jackson Hole Agreement*, Uniform Interpretation, above n 3, para 2.

80 Paragraph 6 of the Uniform Interpretation, however, cautions that 'such laws and regulations of the coastal State may not have the practical effect of denying or impairing the exercise of the right of innocent passage as set forth in . . . [UNCLOS]'. *Jackson Hole Agreement*, above n 3.

81 Aceves, 'Diplomacy at Sea', above n 11, 74–75.

IV. Conclusion

In combination, the DMA Agreement and the Jackson Hole Agreement were successful in defusing tensions between the United States and the USSR associated with provocative naval incidents between the two parties, such as the Black Sea bumping incident.[82] Moreover, the Soviet's reversal of their position regarding innocent passage validates the successes of the FON programme and the Black Sea 'show the flag' operations in helping to preserve freedom of navigation and establish a 'minimum world order' for use of the oceans.[83] Building on the success of INCSEA, the DMA enhanced safety of navigation and overflight by requiring the parties to avoid dangerous military activities when operating in proximity of one another. For the next 25–40 years, it all but eliminated unsafe and unprofessional aerobatics and ship handling when U.S. and Soviet (later Russian) forces encountered one another at sea or in the air. Similarly, the Jackson Hole Agreement resulted in several immediate benefits that are still relevant today. Even though the agreement was a bilateral arrangement, it represented the shared view of the world's two preeminent naval powers, and thus significantly contributed 'to the clarification of the regime of innocent passage for the entire world community'.[84] First, it provided for the unrestricted right of innocent passage for warships. Second, it encouraged compliance with UNCLOS, even though the Convention was not yet in force, by recognising that 'the relevant rules of international law governing innocent passage of ships in the territorial sea are stated in . . . [UNCLOS], particularly in Part II, Section 3'.[85] Finally, it validates that maritime 'disputes can be resolved peacefully through negotiations',[86] a model that should be applied by the parties to the ongoing disputes in the South China Sea and East China Sea.

82 Rolph, 'Freedom of Navigation and the Black Sea Bumping Incident', above n 42, 163.

83 Ibid.

84 Ibid, 164.

85 *Jackson Hole Agreement*, Uniform Interpretation, above n 3, para 1.

86 Rolph, 'Freedom of Navigation and the Black Sea Bumping Incident', above n 42, 165. See also McNeill, 'Military-to-Military Arrangements for the Prevention of U.S.-Russian Conflict', above n 67, 580 (The agreement represented a 'quiet, common sense solution to a mutual problem' that 'could be applied to other problems'.)

9

I'M ALONE

Stuart Kaye

I. Introduction

The *I'm Alone* case[1] dates from the 1930s, and represents one of the first considerations of issues such as the use of force in the enforcement of the laws of a coastal state and the doctrine of hot pursuit. In some respects, the relevance of the case today is limited, as it predates the full range of maritime zones, and the final report of the Commission is itself unfortunately very brief. Nevertheless, the case was a significant one, and is therefore worthy of consideration.

II. Background

On 16 January 1920, the Eighteenth Amendment to the U.S. Constitution came into effect throughout the United States. The amendment provided for the prohibition of the manufacture, transportation, or sale of alcoholic beverages in the United States. The Volstead Act, which was passed to support the Eighteenth Amendment, made it an offence to ship alcohol for human consumption. During the currency of the Eighteenth Amendment and the Volstead Act, the term 'Prohibition' has been applied to what was effectively one of the largest social experiments in history undertaken by a national government.

Although these measures were enshrined in part in the U.S. Constitution, there was a large illegal trade that sprang up to meet the need for alcoholic drinks, and much of this trade involved the smuggling of commercial quantities of alcoholic beverages into the United States by sea. The case in issue deals with the most notorious case of a smuggling vessel which was intercepted and subsequently sunk by the U.S. Coast Guard.

1 *SS. I'm Alone* (Canada v United States) 3 RIAA 1609.

DOI: 10.4324/9781003307013-12

The sailing ship *I'm Alone* was based in the port of Lunenberg, Nova Scotia, Canada, and was within the Canadian division of the British registry. The ship was an auxiliary schooner, with two masts and a 100-horsepower diesel engine.[2] Through the 1920s, *I'm Alone* had been suspected by American authorities of being engaged in alcohol smuggling.[3] In September 1928, she came under the command of Captain Jack Randell, a decorated veteran of both the Boer War and the First World War, who had paid off as lieutenant commander in the Royal Navy after the cessation of hostilities.[4] Randell took the ship from Halifax in Nova Scotia to operate in Caribbean waters soon after taking command, principally operating out of Belize, in what was then British Honduras. Evidence tendered in the subsequent case indicates that *I'm Alone* regularly sailed from British Honduras to waters just outside the territorial sea of the United States in the vicinity of the Louisiana coast, where she rendezvoused with small boats based in the United States, to facilitate the transference of cargo into the country.[5]

The United States territorial sea extended in the 1920s to a distance of only 3 nm, and vessels such as *I'm Alone* had long sought to avoid the jurisdiction of the Coast Guard by transhipping illegal goods for importation in waters just outside the territorial sea. The U.S. government had sought to combat this practice in two ways. First, the United States introduced what in the years after the Second World War became known as a contiguous zone. It was authorised under the Tariff Act of 1922, and provided for a stop and search zone to a distance of four leagues (12 nm) from the coast, in waters outside the territorial sea. This zone made it easier for Coast Guard vessels to catch vessels engaged in smuggling, as it took longer for them to reach the coast in waters where the Coast Guard might intervene. The lawfulness of the Tariff Act was upheld in a number of cases including in the U.S. Supreme Court.[6]

The second measure was the conclusion of a treaty with Britain to facilitate the inspection of British ships on the high seas, where they were suspected of carrying alcohol for human consumption illegally bound for the United States. In January 1924, Britain and the United States entered into a treaty,[7] referred to at the time as the Liquor Convention, which permitted the inspection of British ships on the high seas by the U.S. Coast Guard:

2 Robert Thorne, 'The Sinking of the I'm Alone' <www.newfoundlandshipwrecks.com/Im%20 Alone/documents/rumrunner_im_alone.htm> (accessed 16 November 2021).

3 For example, see Nicholas M. Poulantzas, *The Right of Hot Pursuit in International Law* (Martinus Nijhoff, 2002), 63.

4 Thorne, 'The Sinking of the I'm Alone', above n 2.

5 *SS. I'm Alone* (Canada v United States), above n 1, 1617–1618.

6 *Cook v United States* (1933) 288 US 102 at 114.

7 Convention between the United States of America and Great Britain to Aid in the Prevention of the Smuggling of Intoxicating Liquors into the United States, done at Washington 23 January 1924, entered into force 22 May 1924: US Treaty Series No.685 (hereinafter the 'Liquor Convention').

> His Britannic Majesty agrees that he will raise no objection to the boarding of private vessels under the British flag outside the limits of territorial waters by the authorities of the United States, its territories or possessions in order that enquiries may be addressed to those on board and an examination be made of the ship's papers for the purpose of ascertaining whether the vessel or those on board are endeavoring to import or have imported alcoholic beverages into the United States, its territories or possessions in violation of the laws there in force. When such enquiries and examination show a reasonable ground for suspicion, a search of the vessel may be instituted.[8]

The application of the treaty was not to all the world's oceans, but rather to waters that were within one hour's sail of the U.S. coast.[9] This was an unfortunate provision in the circumstances, as it was clearly most imprecise, as what might be one hour's sailing for a typical ship on a calm day might be one distance, but could be very different for a different vessel, or even the same vessel in different weather conditions. The difficulties of application of this provision to *I'm Alone* are especially evident given that the vessel was a sailing vessel, but also possessed an engine. Not surprisingly, this became a matter in dispute between the governments of Canada and the United States in their submissions in the case.[10] The treaty entered into force later in 1924, and was still in force at the time *I'm Alone* became active in Caribbean waters in 1928 and 1929.

The incident which forms the basis for the case occurred between 20 and 22 March 1929. The *I'm Alone* was first observed off the coast of Louisiana by the U.S. Coast Guard cutter *Wolcott*. When first observed, *I'm Alone* was reported by *Wolcott* to be a little closer than 11 nm off the coast of Louisiana. The views of the Canadian and U.S. governments differed as to whether this distance was within the scope of the 1924 treaty. The position of the Canadian government was that this was more than an hour's sail for *I'm Alone*, while the U.S. government expressed the view that *I'm Alone* was capable of speeds greater than 11 knots.[11]

Wolcott ordered *I'm Alone* to heave to and be boarded; *I'm Alone* ignored the order and sailed away from the American coast. *Wolcott* pursued, and after two days was joined by a second Coast Guard cutter, the *Dexter*. Ultimately, *Dexter* ended the pursuit after firing into *I'm Alone*. As a result, *I'm Alone* quickly sank, resulting in the total loss of the ship, and the drowning of a member of her crew, Leon Mainguy.

After diplomatic correspondence, which indicated the two governments were in disagreement over the legality of the incident, both the United States and Canada agreed to refer the incident to a Joint Commission under Article 4 of the Liquor

8 *Liquor Convention*, above n 7, art II(1).

9 *Liquor Convention*, above n 7, art II(3).

10 Canada asserted the *I'm Alone* was 14.9 nm off the U.S. coast, while the United States asserted *I'm Alone* was 10.9 nm off the coast of the United States: Poulantzas, above n 3, 63.

11 See G.G. Fitzmaurice, 'The Case of the *I'm Alone*' (1936) 17 *British Yearbook of International Law* 82 at 84–86; Poulantzas, *The Right of Hot Pursuit in International Law*, above n 3, 63–64.

Convention. Both appointed very senior judges as Commissioners, with the Chief Justice of Canada, Sir Lyman Poore Duff, and U.S. Supreme Court Associate Justice Willis van Devanter being nominated by their respective countries.

After receiving submissions from both States, the two judges delivered an interim report on 30 June 1933, before delivering a final report on 5 January 1935. They ultimately held that the action of the United States in the sinking of the *I'm Alone* was unlawful, and compensation should be payable to the ship's master and crew, as well as the family of the deceased crew member. Further compensation was limited, as it was found that *I'm Alone* was owned by and under the direction of U.S. interests who were attempting to circumvent the Volstead Act, even though the vessel was under British registration.

III. Analysis and outcomes

There are two legal issues which are fundamental to consideration of the *I'm Alone* case. First, since *I'm Alone* was ultimately fired upon more than 100 miles off the coast of the United States, had the United States a right to exercise the doctrine of hot pursuit to potentially extend what jurisdiction it might draw from the Tariff Act of 1922 or the 1924 Treaty with Britain so far offshore? Second, did the United States have the right to fire upon *I'm Alone* and sink her?

In dealing with hot pursuit first, while the *I'm Alone* case is often referred to in the context of hot pursuit, the case in reality does not deal as extensively with the issue as might be expected. Given that enforcement action took place many miles and several days' sail from the territorial sea of the United States, the Commissioners posed a question in relation to the legality of the pursuit:

> The second question relates to the right of hot pursuit. Further, it has two aspects, and it is based upon the assumption that the averments in the Answer with regard to the location and speed of the *I'm Alone* are true. The question in its first aspect is whether the Government of the United States under the Convention has the right of hot pursuit where the offending vessel is within an hour's sailing distance of the shore at the commencement of the pursuit and beyond that distance at its termination. The question in its second aspect is whether the Government of the United States has the right of hot pursuit of a vessel when the pursuit commenced within the distance of twelve miles established by the revenue laws of the United States and was terminated on the high seas beyond that distance.[12]

In the course of pleadings, the Canadian government had expressed concern that the legality of the concept of hot pursuit employed by the United States was questionable. Canada noted that the pursuit had been started by *Wolcott* but the

12 *SS. I'm Alone* (Canada v United States), above n 1, 1614.

completion of the pursuit had been effected by *Dexter*. The ability to pass the pursuit between vessels was the source of concern. The United States rejected this formulation, and also noted that although *Dexter* did complete the pursuit, *Wolcott* was still present in the vicinity.[13]

The Commissioners failed to deal with the issue at all. In their interim report they stated:

> As respects the question in its first aspect, viz., whether the Government of the United States under the Convention has the right of hot pursuit where the offending vessel is within an hour's sailing distance of the shore at the commencement of the pursuit and beyond that distance at its termination, the Commissioners are as yet not in agreement as to the proper answer, nor have they reached a final disagreement on the matter. The Commissioners, therefore, suggest that the proceeding go forward and that the evidence be produced in an orderly way, leaving the Commissioners free to give further consideration to the matter and to announce their agreement or disagreement thereon as the case may be.
>
> The question in its second aspect need not be answered because the Government of the United States has now withdrawn so much of its answer as led to the propounding of that aspect of the question.[14]

As they could not agree, they indicated the questions would be the subject of further consideration. When they returned to give the final report, the Commissioners indicated that only the first and third questions were material, and they did not address the second question, which had been the question dealing with hot pursuit. This was essentially because that regardless of whether the hot pursuit was valid or otherwise, the sinking of the *I'm Alone* at the conclusion of the chase was found by the Commissioners to be unlawful. As such, the lawfulness of the chase was irrelevant to the result.

There has been some academic debate about the effect of the failure of the Commissioners to address the issue of hot pursuit. Fitzmaurice and Garner disagreed in the years immediately after the final report as to whether their silence on the issue in the final report amounted to recognition of the doctrine or otherwise. Garner stated the Commission 'appears to have assumed that the United States was justified in exercising the right of hot pursuit in the circumstances'[15], whereas Fitzmaurice explicitly rejected this notion, noting that 'the Commissioners did not decide the point one way or the other'.[16] With respect to the late Professor Garner, Fitzmaurice's position seems stronger, given the explicit failure of the Commission

13 Fitzmaurice, 'The Case of the *I'm Alone*', above n 11, 84–85.

14 *SS. I'm Alone* (Canada v United States), above n 1, 1614.

15 James W. Garner, 'Hot Pursuit. Illegal Sinking of Vessel on the High Seas – The *I'm Alone* Case' (1935) 16 *British Yearbook of International Law* 173 at 175.

16 Fitzmaurice, 'The Case of the *I'm Alone*', above n 11 at 88–89.

to address hot pursuit in the final report, and noting the Commissioners could not agree in the interim report.[17] In hindsight, the lack of consideration by the Commission in relation to hot pursuit is not a significant concern. The contemporary formulation of hot pursuit is expressed in Article 111 of the United Nations Convention on the Law of the Sea.[18] Article 111 of the Convention envisages the passing of responsibility for the continuation of a hot pursuit between vessels and aircraft. As such, the passing of enforcement responsibility between *Wolcott* and *Dexter* would not be a matter for concern today.

The second legal issue considered by the Commissioners in the *I'm Alone* case is the use of force to bring the pursuit of *I'm Alone* to an end, which resulted in the loss of the schooner. In this case, the Commissioners did deal with the issue to a much greater extent than they did in relation to hot pursuit. The question was simply 'whether, in the circumstances, the Government of the United States was legally justified in sinking the *I'm Alone*'.

> On the assumptions stated in the question, the United States might, consistently with the Convention, use necessary and reasonable force for the purpose of effecting the objects of boarding, searching, seizing and bringing into port the suspected vessel; and if sinking should occur incidentally, as a result of the exercise of necessary and reasonable force for such purpose, the pursuing vessel might be entirely blameless. But the Commissioners think that, in the circumstances stated in paragraph eight of the Answer, the admittedly intentional sinking of the suspected vessel was not justified by anything in the Convention.[19]

This conclusion is the one most often cited in the context of the *I'm Alone* case – that the use of force was not justified and that the deliberate sinking of the vessel was unlawful. This was a formulation that has proved very influential in international law,[20] having been adopted by the Court of Inquiry in the *Red Crusader* case[21] and by the International Tribunal for the Law of the Sea in the *MV Saiga (No. 2)* case.[22]

However, the Commissioners did make an interesting differentiation on the consequences of sinking the vessel. The Commissioners noted that the sinking of *I'm Alone* was a deliberate act, and that as an intentional act, the sinking was unlawful. This, the Commissioners stated explicitly, meant that if the sinking of the *I'm Alone* had occurred incidentally, as an unintended outcome of the use of reasonable

17 Ibid, 88.

18 *United Nations Convention on the Law of the Sea*, done at Montego Bay 10 December 1982, entered into force 16 November 1994: 1833 UNTS 3.

19 *SS. I'm Alone* (Canada v United States), above n 1, 1617.

20 Louis B. Sohn, John Noyes, Erik Franckx and Kristen Juras, *Cases and Materials on the Law of the Sea* (Brill Nijhoff, 2014), 220.

21 35 ILR 485 (1962) – see Chapter 10.

22 *M/V Saiga (No. 2)* ITLOS Case No. 2, para 155 – see Chapter 11.

and necessary force, there would be nothing unlawful in the action, and no liability for the loss of the vessel.[23] This was an important development in the use of force to enforce the laws of a coastal state at sea, and set what has become the recognised standard. This was not without controversy at the time, as indicated by Sir Gerald Fitzmaurice, who expressed concern that the phrase 'necessary and reasonable' was 'unclear and ambiguous', and he noted that the effect of the judgement was apparently that regardless of whether the pursuit began within the territorial sea or beyond it, the rules for the use of force by the coastal state would effectively be as enunciated by the Commission, even though their statement was – in his view – 'not entirely clear'.[24]

As the law has developed, Fitzmaurice's concerns have not been made out, and international law now appears to clearly accept the proposition that the use of force at sea must be measured and follow a graduated escalation from warnings and shots across the bow before moving to the point where any physical action against a ship can be undertaken. Even then, necessary and reasonable force does not encompass the type of force used to sink *I'm Alone*, as in the absence of self-defence, firing at or into a vessel with solid shot will not usually be permissible.[25]

In recognition of the unlawful loss of *I'm Alone*, the Commissioners awarded funds to the surviving crew, their heirs, and the family of the sailor who was drowned. The Commissioners did not award any funds with respect to the ship or its cargo. This was because the Commissioners recognised that *I'm Alone* was owned by U.S. interests, who were using the ship to carry on an activity which was unlawful under U.S. law at the time – that is, the importation of alcoholic beverages.[26] As such, the Commissioners believed that it was not appropriate to award compensation from the U.S. government to U.S. nationals engaged in a dubious enterprise. They were willing to award a total of US$25,000 to Canada on behalf of the ship's crew, with the bulk of the funds going to the family of the drowned sailor, Leon Mainguy, and to the master of the *I'm Alone*, John Randell. Other sailors received varying amounts of compensation, without the Commissioners articulating the bases for calculation of the smaller amounts.[27]

IV. Conclusion

In conclusion, it is apparent that the *I'm Alone* case was unsatisfactory in a number of respects. The Commission avoided dealing with the key issue of hot pursuit in any meaningful way, and dealt with the use of force and the allocation of

23 Rob McLaughlin, *United Nations Peace Naval Operations in the Territorial Sea* (Martinus Nijhoff, 2009), 122; Fitzmaurice, 'The Case of the *I'm Alone*', above n 11, 99.

24 Fitzmaurice, 'The Case of the *I'm Alone*', above n 11, 99–100.

25 See Douglas Guilfoyle, *Shipping Interdiction and the Law of the Sea* (Cambridge, 2009), 293.

26 C.J. Colombos, *The International Law of the Sea* (Longmans, 1972), 177–178.

27 Mainguy's family received US$10,185 while Randell received US$7,906: *SS. I'm Alone* (Canada v United States), above n 1, 1618.

compensation very briefly. It would have been of much greater assistance to legal scholars in the years after the case for these issues to have been explored more fully. Nevertheless, the case is an important one, not for what is said, but for the influence it has had on later cases. Both the *Red Crusader* and *Saiga (No. 2)* owe a significant debt to the *I'm Alone* case in mapping out the legitimacy of the use of force at sea. *I'm Alone* marks the origin of the principle that a use of force at sea must be measured and should avoid death and injury to individuals as far as possible. This is the legacy of the *I'm Alone* case.

10

THE *RED CRUSADER* INCIDENT

Rob McLaughlin[1]

I. Introduction

The *Red Crusader* incident involved the arrest and subsequent pursuit of a UK-registered trawler (*Red Crusader*) by a Danish warship exercising Danish and Faroese fisheries jurisdiction (*Niels Ebbesen*), over the period 29–31 May 1961.[2] The incident is now generally characterised as an evolutionary step along a consistent and linear path linking *I'm Alone* to *MV Saiga*, in that it is indicative of the trending preference for more formalised initiation requirements for hot pursuit, and more controlled and gradually escalated use of force procedures. *Red Crusader* is also representative of persisting confusion in relation to interpretations of permissible levels of use of force in the form of direct fire at or into a fleeing delinquent vessel.

II. Background to the incident

A. The Faroese fisheries zone

The legal background to this incident begins with the 1901 Convention Regulating the Fisheries Outside Territorial Waters in the Ocean Surrounding the Faroe Islands and Iceland, signed at London on 24 June 1901, between the UK and Denmark.[3] Given the historic Danish, Faroese, Icelandic, and UK fisheries in the

1 This chapter is an abridged version of Rob McLaughlin, 'Revisiting the Red Crusader Incident' (2017) 35 *Australian Yearbook of International Law* 91. The author thanks the editors of the *Australian Yearbook of International Law* for their permissions associated with this chapter.

2 DHN Johnson, 'Notes: Law of the Sea' (1961) 10:3 *International and Comparative Law Quarterly* 587.

3 Convention Regulating the Fisheries Outside Territorial Waters in the Ocean Surrounding the Faroe Islands and Iceland, signed at London on 24 June 1901 UKTS 005/1903: Cd 1530.

DOI: 10.4324/9781003307013-13

area – the Faroes are approximately 180 nm northwest of the Shetland Islands, and roughly 370 nm southeast of Iceland – it was considered useful to 'regulate the police of the fisheries in the ocean surrounding the Faroe Islands and Iceland outside the territorial waters of these islands'.[4]

Article II of the 1901 Convention established for subjects of the Danish king an 'exclusive right of fishery within the distance of 3 miles from the low water mark' of the islands and their 'dependent islets, rocks, and banks'.[5] Article III defined 'miles' as 'geographical miles, whereof 60 make a degree of latitude'[6] – thus indicating what is now referred to as a nautical mile (nm). The 1901 Convention then established rules and procedures for vessel identification, and for fisheries enforcement, including that: 'the superintendence of the fisheries shall be exercised by vessels belonging to the national navies of the High Contracting Parties'[7]; that 'cruisers [of the parties] shall be competent to authenticate all infractions of the Regulations prescribed by the present convention . . . and all offences relating to fishing operations, whichever may be the nation to which the fishermen guilty of such infraction may belong'[8]; that 'the Commander of the cruiser may, if the case appears to him sufficiently serious to justify the step, take the offending boat into a port of the nation to which the fisherman belongs'[9]; and, in an early instance of cross-vesting of jurisdiction and powers in a maritime law enforcement context, that

> Resistance to the direction of Commanders of cruisers charged with the police of the fisheries, or of those who act under their orders, shall, without taking into account the nationality of the cruiser, be considered as resistance to the authority of the nation of the fishing boat.[10]

In 1954 and 1955, in the broader context of ongoing negotiations for the four 1958 Geneva Conventions[11] relating to the law of the sea, Denmark and the UK agreed to an exchange of notes amending the 1901 Convention (the 1955 Agreement).[12] One component of this amendment, settled on 22 April 1955, involved a Danish proposal – accepted by the UK – to redefine the manner in which the 3 nm

4 *1901 Convention*, above n 3, Art I – At that time, prior to the Act of Union in 1918, Iceland was exercising home rule, but was not yet the separate sovereign state of the Kingdom of Iceland in a personal union with Denmark under the Danish Crown.

5 Ibid, at Art II.

6 Ibid, at Art III.

7 Ibid, at Art XXVI.

8 Ibid, at Art XXVIII.

9 Ibid, at Art XXX.

10 Ibid, at Art XXXII.

11 Convention on the High Seas 450 UNTS 82, Convention on the Continental Shelf 499 UNTS 312, Convention on the Territorial Sea and the Contiguous Zone 516 UNTS 206, Convention on Fishing and Conservation of the Living Resources of the High Seas 559 UNTS 286.

12 Exchange of Notes amending the Convention between the United Kingdom and Denmark for regulating the fisheries outside territorial waters in the ocean surrounding the Faroe Islands of 24 June 1901, London, 23 July 1954 and 22 April 1955 UKTS 029/1955: Cmd 9452.

exclusive Faroese fishing zone was drawn, utilising a system of interlocking arcs.[13] This component of the 1955 Agreement also provided that this fisheries limit would be applied to all foreign fishing vessels, and that 'British fishing vessels shall receive treatment no less favourable than that accorded to the fishing vessels of any other foreign country'.[14]

On 2 June 1958, the government of the now independent Republic of Iceland announced that it would henceforth claim a 12 nm exclusive fishing zone. The UK vigorously protested this claim, and a number of incidents between Icelandic Coast Guard vessels and UK fishing vessels and warships – such as the 12 November 1958 *Hackness* incident[15] – followed. Contemporaneously, by memorandum dated 18 June 1958, Denmark informed the UK that 'from a long-term point of view the present state of affairs with regard to the fishery limits around the Faroe Islands was untenable', and that 'the Faroese authorities are justified in expecting to obtain an expansion of the fishing territory'. The UK disagreed with the Danish view as to the availability of a 12 nm territorial sea and fisheries area, but nevertheless proposed that the concerned governments enter into discussions, so long as they were aimed 'at a lasting settlement of the fishery questions relating to the Faroes'.[16] The Danes agreed on 5 July 1958 that 'verbal discussions held at a suitable time would be useful'.[17]

By an exchange of notes, dated 27 April 1959 (1959 Agreement), the Danish and UK governments agreed to modifications to the 1901 Convention, as amended by the 1955 Agreement. This amendment, in essence, created a generally 6 nm Faroese-only fisheries zone (a zone enclosed by a blue line in the chart annexed to the 1959 Agreement), although, as Lauterpacht observed in his initial 1962 report on the outcome of the subsequent *Red Crusader* Commission of Inquiry, the blue line at one point moves to 12 nm off the coast.[18] There was then a further 6 nm zone beyond that (effectively a zone from 6–12 nm) in which the Danish

13 Ibid, at No. 2(a) and (b).

14 Ibid, at No. 2(a), para 2B (Note from Danish Charge d'Affaires at London to Her Majesty's Principal Secretary of State for Foreign Affairs, 22 April 1955).

15 E. Lauterpacht, 'The Contemporary Practice of the United Kingdom in the Field of International Law – Survey and Comment' (1959) 8 *International and Comparative Law Quarterly* 146 at 177–182. This incident involved the hot pursuit of the British fishing vessel *Hackness* by the Icelandic Coast Guard Vessel *Thor* on 12 November 1958. *HMS Russell*, on station to monitor Icelandic conduct and assist UK vessels as required, intervened. The Icelandic protest records that: 'After consultations between the Commanding Officers of the *Thor* and *Russell*, the latter informed the *Thor's* captain that, if the *Thor* opened fire on the trawler, the *Russell* would sink her' (at 178). The UK position was that the pursuit was unlawful ab initio as *Hackness* had not been within the 3 nm territorial sea when summoned to stop. See also, Johnson, 'Notes: Law of the Sea', above n 2, at 592–597.

16 Lauterpacht, 'The Contemporary Practice of the United Kingdom in the Field of International Law – Survey and Comment', above n 15, at 175.

17 Ibid, at 175.

18 E. Lauterpacht, *The Contemporary Practice of the United Kingdom in the Field of International Law – 1962*, (ICLQ / International Law Fund, 1963), at 50–53. A copy of the Annexed chart can be found at, 20 *Heidelberg Journal of International Law* (1959/60) 83 at 85 – <www.zaoerv.de/20_1959_60/20_1959_1_2_b_83_87.pdf>; see also Johnson, 'Notes: Law of the Sea', above n 2, at 594-596.

government would 'raise no objection' to fishing by UK fishing vessels.[19] Additionally, in a set of designated areas (hatched on the annexed chart), fishing by Danish, Faroese, and UK vessels would be limited to long line and hand line between set dates each year.[20] The 1959 Agreement was also not to 'be deemed to prejudice the views held by either government as to the delimitation and limits in International Law of Territorial Waters or of exclusive jurisdiction in fishery matters'.[21]

B. Royal Navy fisheries protection operations: guidance on use of force and hot pursuit

The international law on hot pursuit as applicable between the UK and Denmark was, at that time, Article 23 of the 1958 Geneva Convention on the High Seas to which both states were signatory. The key elements of the authorisation, then as now, centred around the limitation of the authorisation to certain state vessels, requirements in relation to commencement, the valid purposes for which hot pursuit may be employed, and the termination of hot pursuit.[22] Article 23, as the provision applicable in 1961, was markedly silent (as, indeed, Article 111 of the 1982 Law of the Sea Convention remains) in relation to use of force in the exercise of the right of hot pursuit, and of its unstated culminating point – the halting and boarding of the delinquent vessel.

The affidavits and associated material collated for the UK memorial and counter-memorial submitted to the *Red Crusader* Commission of Enquiry disclose two key elements of the more detailed operational guidance provided to RN units at the time (drawn from the relevant Royal Navy publication – BR 66, Chapter 2). The first key element of operational guidance was that 'the firing of blank rounds and as a final resort the firing of shotted rounds across the bows of the offender' was acceptable operational practice.[23] Second,

> If the offending vessel fails to stop after the firing of warning shots, the fishery protection ship concerned carries on the hot pursuit until either the fishing boat stops, or she reaches the territorial waters of another power. Gunfire aimed to hit the fishing vessel would never be used unless the fishing vessel by her action was endangering life; for instance, if the fishing vessel should attempt to ram the boat carrying the boarding party.[24]

19 Exchange of Notes modifying the Convention of June 24, 1901, as later amended, concerning the Regulation of Fishing around the Faroe Islands, Copenhagen 27 April 1959, UKTS 055/1959: Cmnd 776; clauses I-II.

20 Ibid, at clause III.

21 Ibid, at clause VII.

22 1958 Convention on the High Seas, above n 11.

23 *Statement by Captain GC Leslie, OBE, Royal Navy, Captain, Fishery Protection Squadron*, para 6, citing the reference for this point as BR 66 Chapter 2 para 46 (UK National Archives File TS 58/577).

24 Ibid, at para 7; Captain Leslie, RN, specifically noted that the actions of *Niels Ebbesen* 'depart[ed] from the above policy' because, inter alia, 'the use of small arms and of shotted rounds aimed to hit was unjustified' – para 8.

III. The incident[25]

A. The initial response

On 29 May 1961, at 17:37 (local time), the Faroese Island Naval District signalled *Niels Ebbesen* (then in Torshaven harbour) that four British fishing vessels had been reported by the Myggenaes (Mykines) Lighthouse keeper at 17:25 as possibly (estimates were between 4–7 nm) within the Faroese-only (6 nm) fishing zone. Mykines is the westernmost island of the Faroes. *Niels Ebbesen* sailed about one hour later, and by 20:55 was in the area and soon detected vessels by radar ENE of her position at a range of approximately 9 nm. This placed the vessels, on *Niels Ebbesen's* calculations, within the 'blue line' that demarcated the Faroese-only fishing area. The Commission of Enquiry ultimately concluded that at 21:14, the nearest fishing vessel – which was *Red Crusader* – was 'most probably inside the blue line, possibly just on or just outside that line', but that the Commission 'fully understands and shares the view of the commanding officer (CO) of *Niels Ebbesen* that the nearest fishing vessel had been inside'.[26] The Commission concluded, on the basis of the evidence available, that *Red Crusader* had been inside the blue line, with trawl deployed, during at least the period from 20:09–21:14.[27] *Niels Ebbesen* began signalling *Red Crusader*, by siren and light, to heave to from 21:39. Although the skipper of *Red Crusader* – Mr Wood – stated that he thought the signals were for a neighbouring vessel, *Millwood* (which had a black hull), the Commission was in no doubt that the signals were clearly directed at *Red Crusader* (which had a blue hull) and that Wood must have been aware of this – not least because *Niels Ebbesen* altered course to put *Red Crusader* fine on her own port bow and illuminated *Red Crusader* directly by searchlight. At any rate, *Red Crusader* ignored the signals until *Niels Ebbesen* fired 'a blank 40mm shot . . . across her bows'. Wood subsequently claimed he had been effecting repairs to a trawl and had drifted in a south-easterly direction into the zone.[28]

B. The arrest

At approximately 22:19, Lt. Bech and Cpl. Kropp proceeded by seaboat from *Niels Ebbesen* to *Red Crusader*, and then carried out simultaneous range and bearing checks with *Niels Ebbesen* using the trawler's radar. The Danish boarding party were

25 The full report of the Commission is available as 'Investigation of certain incidents affecting the British trawler *Red Crusader*: Report of 23 March 1962 of the Commission of Enquiry established by the Government of the United Kingdom of Great Britain and Northern Ireland and the Government of the Kingdom of Denmark on 15 November 1961', 29 RIAA at 521–539 <at www.un.org/law/riaa/> ('*Red Crusader* (RIAA)'). The most commonly used citation is the very slightly abridged and edited version of the report compiled by Eli Lauterpacht: *The Red Crusader* (1967) 35 ILR 485. For ease and coherence of reference, citations for facts and conclusions drawn from the report will generally be to the ILR report ('*Red Crusader*').

26 *Red Crusader*, above n 25, at 493–494.

27 Ibid, at 494.

28 Ibid, at 495.

unarmed – this was reported at the time to have been a consequence of a Danish decision subsequent to 'confidential representations from the British Embassy [in April 1961], who had claimed that armed Danish sailors irritated the crews of British trawlers'.[29] After a meeting lasting about 20 minutes, Bech and Kropp returned to the warship with Skipper Wood, who met with the Danish commanding officer, Captain Soelling, until about 23:22, when he was returned to his trawler.

However, Skipper Wood changed his mind. At 02:58 (now on 30 May, and at the point where the two ships were about to exit Hestofjord between Hesto and Vaago Islands, in order to turn north up Molsofjord towards Torshavn on the SE coast of Stromo Island), he asked Bech to signal *Niels Ebbesen* that he would not enter Torshaven, and shortly thereafter, Bech was locked in the skipper's cabin whilst Kropp was distracted ('under courteous but efficient guard') by some of the trawler crew in quarters aft. Bech signalled *Niels Ebbesen* at 03:05 that he was locked up. At the point of the intended turn north towards Torshaven, Wood instead maintained a southerly course towards Aberdeen, and released Bech from confinement at 04:08, once *Red Crusader* was well on its way.[30]

C. The pursuit

Niels Ebbesen immediately altered course to close with *Red Crusader*, firing an initial one round of 127 mm ordnance (her main armament) astern of the trawler at 03:22, whilst at a distance of around 2,100 metres (about 1.13 nm). The copy of Chart 117 in the relevant UK National Archives file indicates that these warning shots were fired at approximately 13 nm southeast of Kirkebo Naes on the southern tip of Stromo/8 nm east of Skaalhoved on Sando Island. Siren signals followed at 03:23, followed at 03:25 by a further round of 127 mm ahead of the bows, and a further siren signal at 03:26, all at around the same range.[31] By 03:30, the range between the vessels had closed to about 0.9 nm, and by 03:38 to about 0.45 nm (approximately 900 yards). *Niels Ebbesen* delivered a loud-hailer warning and fired two 'machine gun' warning shots astern at 03:40 (assumed to have been the 20 mm machine gun, as the 40 mm armament, which was used later, was referred to specifically by calibre). The warship then fired eight further successive single 'machine-gun' shots at *Red Crusader's* 'scanner' (03:40 – two later verified hits), followed by further hailing to stop (03:41) and 21 further single shots at *Red Crusader's* mast (03:42 – no hits). *Niels Ebbesen* then escalated and fired one round of 40 mm at the masthead light (03:44 – no hit), and a further round at the mast (03:47 – no hit). The warship then warned *Red Crusader* by voice 'Stop, or I have to shoot you in your hull' (03:47). After no response, *Niels Ebbesen* fired two rounds

29 'Fisheries Dispute off the Faroes – the "Red Crusader" Incident', *Keesing's Record of World Events*, Vol 7, June 1961, at 18162; Johnson, 'Notes: Law of the Sea', above n 2, at 594–597.

30 *Red Crusader*, above n 25, at 497.

31 Ibid, at 497–498.

of 40 mm solid shot (these are not explosive rounds) at the stem (bow), with one round hitting 'a little abaft the nameplate' (03:51), followed at 03:53 by a further round of 40 mm solid shot, again at the stem (no hit): 'The range was very close – about 50 yards'.[32] In addition to two holes in the radar scanner, the report filed by one of the RN officers who inspected the damage to *Red Crusader*, at sea on 30 May, recorded damage including a hole in the hull, denting and scoring of the hull and deck, and the shattering of a pump.[33]

It was understood by the Commission that all of the shots were fired within Danish (Faroese) territorial waters.[34] Nevertheless, *Red Crusader* did not heave to, and *Niels Ebbesen* continued pursuit as *Red Crusader* made for UK territorial waters. Two Royal Navy warships – *HMS Troubridge* (a frigate) and *HMS Wotton* (a minesweeper) – were dispatched to intercept and made radio contact with *Niels Ebbesen* and *Red Crusader* at 10:30 on 30 May. *Niels Ebbesen* signalled back her position and intended course and speed at 12:12, and *Wotton* had rendezvoused with the two vessels by 14:35. They were joined by *Troubridge* soon after, 15:45.[35] A group of RN personnel, led by CO *Troubridge*, Commander Griffiths, RN, proceeded to meet with Captain Soelling in *Niels Ebbesen*, whilst other RN personnel proceeded to *Red Crusader* to inspect and report on damage, see to the welfare of the Danish boarding team, and gain Wood's side of the story. The meeting with Captain Soelling was cordial; he presented his evidence and reiterated his intention to escort *Red Crusader* back to Danish jurisdiction for investigation and trial.

Simultaneously, Wood in *Red Crusader* made it clear that he would not return to the Faeroes and intended to proceed to Aberdeen.[36] It was reported at the time that RN personnel from *Wotton* went aboard *Red Crusader* to inspect the damage, and then to *Niels Ebbesen* to discuss the situation with the Danish CO.[37] They brokered a partial solution at the scene, and despite some confusion as to orders from *Nils Ebbesen*, the Danish officer and rating – Bech and Kropp – were returned to their warship. In fact, what appears to have occurred was that an RN officer sent to inspect the damage in *Red Crusader* had offered to transfer the Danish boarding team – Bech and Kropp – back to *Niels Ebbesen* in the RN seaboat then alongside. This was not in accordance with Captain Soelling's wishes, and there was a

32 *Meeting at Admiralty 30–6–61: Red Crusader*, (UK National Archives File TS 58/577), at 7.

33 *Statement of Lt Commander Ronald Perchard, RN*, at 2 (UK National Archives File TS 58/577); an itemised list of the damages sustained can be found at *HMS Troubridge Report of Proceedings, 31 May 1961*, 46, Appendix B.

34 *Red Crusader*, above n 25, at 497–498.

35 *HMS Wotton Report of Proceedings for the Month of May 1961*, Section II, paras 11–12 (UK National Archives File TS 58/577); *Statement of Lieutenant Commander Gyles Carne, RN*, paras 13–18 (UK National Archives File TS 58/577); The Lord Privy Seal (Mr. Edward Heath), HC Deb 31 May 1961 vol 641 cc257–60.

36 HMS Wotton Report of Proceedings for the Month of May 1961, above n 35, at Section II, paras 12–14.

37 'New Fishing Dispute with Danes', *The Glasgow Herald*, 31 May 1961, at 1 <http://news.google.com/newspapers?nid=2507&dat=19610531&id=rhI1AAAAIBAJ&sjid=wqULAAAAIBAJ&pg=1695,4589439>.

subsequent Danish claim that the RN officer had in some way implied to the Danish boarding team that the offer to return to their own ship had been an instruction from Captain Soelling.[38] The RN officer insisted that this had not been the case. The issue was only finally resolved at the oral hearings, with the agreed outcome indicated in a short and relatively anodyne finding that the RN officers had at all times acted with an 'impeccable' attitude.

Upon the unexpected return to *Niels Ebbesen* of his boarding team, Captain Soelling demanded that he be allowed to place another boarding team onboard *Red Crusader*; this was then raised with Wood, who adamantly refused. Soelling asked the RN COs to order Wood to accept a new Danish boarding team, but they explained that the RN had no authority to do so.[39] Another RN officer returned to *Niels Ebbesen* to explain the likelihood 'that the *Red Crusader* would forcibly resist a boarding party'.[40] The Danish perspective on this chain of events was that the RN had in fact invited *Red Crusader* to get underway so as to frustrate a second boarding, and that this 'was an attempt at unlawful interference with the Danish naval vessel's exercise of authority over a fishing vessel under arrest'.[41] A subsequently brokered agreement (in the face of deteriorating weather) saw *Red Crusader* speed towards Aberdeen (with the UK and Danish warships in close company). *Niels Ebbesen* maintained close station on *Red Crusader* until she entered UK territorial waters. *Red Crusader* eventually arrived in Aberdeen in the evening of 31 May as *Niels Ebbesen* waited beyond the UK 3 nm limit. The Danish Ambassador in London had entered a demarche on 30 May 'demanding that the *Red Crusader* should proceed to Thorshaven' to face investigation and trial.[42] It was reported at the time that *Niels Ebbesen's* presence off Aberdeen was 'as a symbolic upholding of the arrest of *Red Crusader*', but she was eventually withdrawn on 2 June.[43]

D. The inquiry process

In order to determine what had occurred, the UK and Danish governments established a Commission of Enquiry[44] (1961 Commission Agreement) to ascertain 'the facts leading up to the arrest of the British trawler *Red Crusader* on the night of the

38 *Danish Memorial, 15 November 1961*, at 31–32 (UK National Archives File TS 58/577); *Danish Memorial, 12 January 1962*, at 12–13 (UK National Archives File TS 58/577).

39 Danish Memorial, 15 November 1961, at 31–32; HMS Wotton Report of Proceedings for the Month of May 1961, above n 35, at Section II, para13; Memorial Submitted by the Government of the United Kingdom of Great Britain and Northern Ireland – Anglo-Danish Commission of Inquiry: Case Concerning Incidents Affecting the British Trawler 'Red Crusader' (UK National Archives File TS 58/577) [25] (the 'UK Memorial'), paras 37–41.

40 Statement of Lieutenant Commander Gyles Carne, above n 35, at para 37.

41 Danish Memorial, 12 January 1962, above n 38, at 13.

42 Keesing's *Record of World Events*, above n 29, at 18162.

43 Ibid; Johnson, 'Notes: Law of the Sea', above n 2, at 596.

44 Exchange of Notes constituting an agreement establishing a Commission of Enquiry to investigate certain incidents affecting the British trawler Red Crusader, London 15 November 1961, (1962) 420 UNTS 6041 ('1961 Commission Agreement').

29th of May, 1961; . . . the circumstances of the arrest; and the facts and incidents that occurred thereafter before the *Red Crusader* reached Aberdeen'.[45] Memorials were deposited in The Hague (and exchanged in London) on 5 December 1961, with counter-memorials due on 16 January 1962. The Commission then heard oral evidence from 5–16 March 1962, and its report to the two governments was submitted on 23 March 1962.[46]

IV. Analysis and outcomes

The Commission reported its findings in three chronological 'chapters'. The major findings in the first chapter centred upon the incident from the point of first notification to *Niels Ebbesen* at 17:37 on 29 May 1961 up until, and including, the arrest of *Red Crusader*. The second chapter dealt with 'events between the arrest of the *Red Crusader* and the meeting with the British naval vessels'.[47] Chapter three dealt with the incident from the point at which the two Royal Navy warships – *Wotton* and *Troubridge* – arrived on the scene; effectively the end of the on-water aspects of the incident. The key elements of analysis in relation to hot pursuit arose primarily in the first two chapters of the report.

In regard to the incident up until the point of arrest, the Commission ultimately concluded that *Red Crusader* did, at that time, have her trawls deployed, and that it was the common practice of trawlers in the area to warn each other of a warship's approach by code word and then, given their generally poor positional fixing and plotting practices, 'to take no risks and to steam as quickly as they can in a course nearly perpendicular to the fishery limit, away from the exclusive fishery zone'.[48] As a consequence of its assessment and analysis of the evidence under this chapter, the Commission concluded 'that the *Red Crusader* was with her gear not stowed inside the blue line from about 21.00 hours until 21.14 hours on May 29th, 1961', and that 'the first signal to stop was given by *Niels Ebbesen* at 21.39 hours and that this signal and the later stop-signals were all given outside the blue line'.[49]

In relation to the hot pursuit of *Red Crusader*, the Commission made five findings – four are straightforward (findings 1, 2, 3, and 5), but one is less so (4). Finding 1 was that *Red Crusader* had been arrested.[50] Finding 2 was that Wood had subsequently put into effect a plan 'to evade the jurisdiction of an authority which he had at first, rightly, accepted'.[51] A related finding (number 3) was that Wood did 'seclude' Bech and Kropp during this escape, and intended to take them to Aberdeen.[52]

45 Ibid, at para 1(b).
46 *Red Crusader* (RIAA), above n 25, at 525.
47 *Red Crusader*, above n 25, at 495.
48 Ibid, at 492–495.
49 Ibid.
50 Ibid, at 498 finding 1.
51 Ibid, at 499 finding 2; Lauterpacht was critical of the Commission's use of the term 'rightly'.
52 Ibid, at 499 finding 3.

The final uncontentious finding (number 5) was that the Danish government, via its agent, had accepted the British damage repair estimate in relation to *Red Crusader*.[53] The more contentious of the chapter two findings – finding 4 – is worth citing in full:

> (4) that, in opening fire at 03.22 hours up to 03.53 hours, the Commanding Officer of the *Niels Ebbesen* exceeded legitimate use of armed force on two counts:
>
> (a) firing without warning of solid gun-shot;
> (b) creating danger to human life on board the *Red Crusader* without proved necessity, by the effective firing at the *Red Crusader* after 03.40 hours.
>
> The escape of the *Red Crusader* in flagrant violation of the order received and obeyed, the seclusion on board the trawler of an officer and rating of the crew of *Niels Ebbesen*, and Skipper Wood's refusal to stop may explain some resentment on the part of Captain Soelling. Those circumstances, however, cannot justify such a violent action.
>
> The Commission is of the opinion that other means should have been attempted, which, if duly persisted in, might have finally persuaded Skipper Wood to stop and revert to the normal procedure which he himself had previously followed.[54]

The first key element in this finding, it seems, was that the rounds of 40 mm solid shot aimed at the masthead light (03:44) and the mast (03:47) preceded *Niels Ebbesen's* warnings to 'Stop, or I have to shoot you in your hull' at 03:47. This finding is fairly reflective of modern practice – any use of shots aimed at or into a vessel during hot pursuit should be preceded by a warning to that effect, as it represents a significant escalation in force. On this basis, it would be arguable that the three rounds of 40 mm solid shot fired at *Red Crusader's* stem at 03:51 and 03:53 were thus not problematic, as they followed after the specific warning at 03:47.

However, the second key element of the finding complicates this analysis. The timeframe in which the Commission concluded that unjustifiable danger to human life was created 'without proved necessity', through shots aimed at or into *Red Crusader*, includes the initial shots by machine gun at the radar and mast (from 03:40), as well as the 40 mm shots. That is, the Commission found that in spite of the fact that *Red Crusader* had 'secluded' two of *Niels Ebbesen*'s crew onboard and was by then steaming for Aberdeen, and regardless of the specific warning issued at 03:47, the circumstances did not justify the use of any direct fire whatsoever. This finding places an extremely high – indeed, arguably impractical – bar on the use of direct fire. In the first place, the use of direct fire in maritime law enforcement

53 Ibid, at 499 finding 5.
54 Ibid, at 499, finding 4.

hot pursuits, after all other available mechanisms have failed to convince the fleeing vessel to heave to, is now clearly accepted as part of the escalation of force procedure, so long as it is implemented with primary consideration being given to safety of life.[55] Direct fire into unmanned areas – such as masts and the bows – remains an escalation of force option used by states,[56] recognised in a range of national laws and procedures,[57] and also utilised in UNSC maritime sanctions enforcement.[58] Second, it is unrealistic to expect of states that they would not engage in hot pursuit of a vessel, and use the full escalation of force options available, in situations when their boarding party has been detained in the fleeing vessel. In this case, there was likely little fear that Wood or the crew of *Red Crusader* would harm the Danish boarding party, but the affront to the warship and its sovereign is nevertheless severe.

Subsequent to the conclusion of the *Red Crusader* inquiry, there were a number of associated short-term commercial consequences flowing from the subsequent

55 For e.g., *MV Saiga (No. 2) (Saint Vincent and the Grenadines v Guinea)*, Judgment (1999) ITLOS Case No. 2, 156: 'It is only after appropriate actions fail that the pursuing vessel may as a last resort, use force. Even then, the appropriate warning must be issued to the ship and all efforts should be made to ensure that life is not endangered'; *Australian Defence Force Publication (ADFP) 06.1.2 Australia's Maritime Jurisdiction* (28 June 2010), para 8.32: 'The requirements for firing at or into vessels may be considered to be as follows:

a The action must be a last resort. It must be absolutely necessary evidenced by patiently exhausting all less forceful means available, including warning shots, unless an urgent threat to life demands otherwise.
b The action must follow an explicit warning that shots are to be fired into the vessel.
c That all efforts are made to ensure that life is not endangered. Any appreciable risk to life would render the use of direct fire unlawful. A death would not necessarily render the action unlawful in itself provided that the risk of death from direct fire was extremely unlikely and mitigated against'. – available at www.defence.gov.au/adfwc/Documents/DoctrineLibrary/ADFP/ADFP%20 06.1.2.pdf; Testimony of Rear Admiral Wayne E. Justice, Assistant Commandant for Capabilities, Before the House Committee on Transportation and Infrastructure, Subcommittee on Coast Guard and Maritime Transportation, 'Overview of Coast Guard Drug and Migrant Interdiction' (18 March 2009) – available at www.dhs.gov/news/2009/03/18/testimony-us-coast-guard-drug-and-migrant-interdiction.

56 See, for example, the note of a 1981 incident concerning an Australian patrol boat using direct fire in relation to a fleeing foreign fishing vessel – R Warner, 'Jurisdictional Issues for Navies Involved in Enforcing Multilateral Regimes Beyond National Jurisdiction', 14:3 *International Journal of Marine and Coastal Law* 321 (1999) at 330.

57 For example, Australia's *Maritime Powers Act (2013) (Commonwealth)*, section 54(3): 'Chasing. If the person in charge of a vessel does not comply with a requirement to stop or facilitate boarding of the vessel, a maritime officer may do one or more of the following:

(a) chase the vessel;
(b) use any reasonable means to obstruct the passage of the vessel;
(c) use any reasonable means to halt or slow the passage of the vessel, including by fouling the propellers of the vessel;
(d) after firing a warning shot, fire at or into the vessel to disable it or compel it to be brought to for boarding'

(www.comlaw.gov.au/Details/C2015C00015/Html/Text#_Toc408565816).

58 See, for example, Jane Gilliland Dalton, 'The Influence of Law on Seapower in Desert Shield/Desert Storm' (1993) 41 *Naval Law Review* 27 at 43.

Danish declaration of a 12 nm exclusive Faroese fishing zone in 1964 (which had been signalled early in 1963), in the form of a UK fishing industry declared ban on imports from the Faroes, and a Faroese reprisal ban on repairing British trawlers in Faroese harbours.[59] Further renegotiation of the fisheries arrangements followed: In 1974[60]; by decree[61] and ordinance in 1976[62]; by Act of Parliament in 1999[63]; via an Agreement relating to the Maritime Delimitation in the area between the United Kingdom and the Faroe Islands in 1999 (which dealt, inter alia, with a designated 'Special Area' in the midst of the Faroes-Shetlands-northwest Scotland triangle)[64]; further decrees on the territorial sea[65] and fishing in 2002[66]; and amendments to the Faroese fishing zone necessary after the 2 February 2007 delimitation agreement with Iceland.[67]

V. Contemporary significance of the *Red Crusader* incident

A. The progressive development of maritime law enforcement norms around hot pursuit

The key enduring legacy for maritime law enforcement operations from the *Red Crusader* incident has been refined normative and operational structures placed around use of force. In this regard, the incident continues to be a fundamental case study in the evolution of hot pursuit and use of force within that legal context. It can fairly be stated that the *Red Crusader* Commission report narrowed the liberal

59 See DHN Johnson, 'European Fishery Limits', British Institute of International and Comparative Law, *Developments in the Law of the Sea 1958–1964* (1965), 48–74 at 57–61.

60 *Act No. 597 of 17 December 1976 on the Fishing Territory of the Kingdom of Denmark* – available at www.un.org/Depts/los/LEGISLATIONANDTREATIES/PDFFILES/DNK_1976_Act.pdf – into force on 01 January 1977. The key change in this Act was that Denmark thenceforth claimed the (by now) widely anticipated 200 nm fishing zone, limited via an equidistance formulae where coasts with Iceland, Norway, and the UK were less than 400 nm distant.

61 *Decree No.598 of 21 December 1976: the Fishing territory of the Faroe Islands* (available at www.un.org/Depts/los/LEGISLATIONANDTREATIES/PDFFILES/DNK_1976_Decree.pdf.

62 Ordinance No. 599 of 21 December 1976 on the Delimitation of the Territorial Sea around the Faroe Islands – available at www.un.org/Depts/los/LEGISLATIONANDTREATIES/PDFFILES/DNK_1976_Ordinance599.pdf.

63 *Act No. 200 of 7 April 1999 on the delimitation of the territorial sea* – available at www.un.org/Depts/los/LEGISLATIONANDTREATIES/PDFFILES/DNK_1999_Act.pdf.

64 Agreement relating to the Maritime Delimitation in the area between the United Kingdom and the Faroe Islands 21 July 1999, UKTS No. 76 (1999).

65 Decree No.240 of 30 April 2002 on the Coming into Force of the Act on the Delimitation of the Territorial Sea for the Faroe Islands, www.un.org/Depts/los/LEGISLATIONANDTREATIES/PDFFILES/dnk_2002_order_and_decrees.pdf.

66 *Decree No. 241 of 30 April 2002 to Amend the Decree on the Fishing Territory of the Faroe Islands*, www.un.org/Depts/los/LEGISLATIONANDTREATIES/PDFFILES/dnk_2002_order_and_decrees.pdf.

67 See, for example, *Decree of 17 September 2009 amending the Decree on the fishing territory off the Faroe Islands*, www.un.org/Depts/los/LEGISLATIONANDTREATIES/PDFFILES/dnk_2009__decree_faroe.pdf.

I'm Alone interpretation of use of force, and particularly as to use of direct fire; as noted previously, the finding in *I'm Alone* that an 'incidental' sinking could be excusable is completely at odds with the tenor of the *Red Crusader* Commission's findings. That said, however, there have been a number of subsequent incidents in which use of force for a maritime law enforcement purpose has resulted in – or at the least contributed to — the sinking of the delinquent vessel, one recent example being the Chinese-flagged *Lu Yan Yuan Yu 10*, which sank subsequent to use of direct fire by an Argentine Coast Guard vessel on 16 March 2016.[68] However, the full details of this particular incident remain to be disclosed, and there is some potential for the level of force used (resulting in sinking) to be related to self-defence by the Argentine Coast Guard vessel, as reports have noted 'ramming' or 'collision manoeuvres' by the Chinese fishing vessel.[69] Nevertheless, in approving some of *Niels Ebbesen's* conduct and procedures (such as utilising multiple means of position fixing and ensuring that hailings were made at a range and by means that they could definitely be seen/heard on the suspect vessel), whilst criticising others (such as the timings and specificity of warnings in regard to direct fire), the Commission essentially mapped out a clear minimum baseline for escalation of force. This aspect of operational procedure has, it is fair to say, been widely accepted as a practical addendum to – or amplification of – the hot pursuit regime.[70]

B. Direct fire for maritime law enforcement purposes

The glaring inconsistency in this otherwise practical and efficient set of findings and implications was the impractical caveat placed around direct fire. The Commission's finding number 4 in chapter two clearly implies that any direct fire 'without proved necessity' automatically creates an unjustifiable danger to human life. Lauterpacht drew from this finding two rules, but effectively he distils three: 1. do not use solid shot without warning; 2. use of solid shot with warning was available, 'when arresting a foreign vessel in territorial waters', indicating by implication either that the use of – at the very least – direct fire with solid shot was limited to hot pursuit inside the Territorial Sea, or that the delinquent vessel had to have been inside the Territorial Sea at the time of its delinquent conduct; and 3. 'that firing in the course of arrest and thereby creating danger to human life is not permissible

68 'Argentina coast guard sinks Chinese fishing vessel illegally in South Atlantic', *ABC News*, 16 March 2016 – at www.abc.net.au/news/2016-03-16/argentina-coast-guard-sinks-chinese-fishing-vessel/7250208; 'Argentina Coast Guard Sinks Chinese Fishing Boat', *The Diplomat*, 16 March 2016 – at http://thediplomat.com/2016/03/argentina-coast-guard-sinks-chinese-fishing-boat/.

69 'Argentina sinks Chinese jigger which refused to stop and even tried to ram the patrol vessel', *Merco Press / South Atlantic News Agency*, 16 March 2016, http://en.mercopress.com/2016/03/16/argentina-sinks-chinese-jigger-which-refused-to-stop-and-even-tried-to-ram-the-patrol-vessel.

70 See, for example, ER Fidell, 'Hot Pursuit from a Fisheries Zone: United States v. Fishing Vessel Taiyo Maru No. 28; United States v. Kawaguchi', 70 American Journal of International Law 95 (1976)

without proved necessity – and that such necessity had not been proved in the present case'.[71]

Of these three distilled 'rules', the first remains, in general, a valid expression of one component of maritime law enforcement hot pursuit and escalation of force procedures, except insofar as it is not common practice to specify the calibre or type of ammunition that will be used when firing upon the fleeing vessel; this decision is generally left to the discretion of the on-scene commander. The second 'rule' is simply a matter of contextualised reading in that the fishing zone and the territorial sea claims were, in this situation, directly correlated. This should not be understood as an assertion, in general, that use of direct fire by a maritime law enforcement vessel was available only within its own territorial sea. Indeed, the contemporaneous hot pursuit rule – Article 23 in the 1958 Geneva Convention on the High Seas – disclosed no such limitation, stating explicitly that the hot pursuit 'may only be continued outside the territorial sea or the contiguous zone if the pursuit has not been interrupted'.[72] It is thus almost certain that the point being made was simply a reiteration of the requirement (also in Article 23) that the hot pursuit could only be legitimate if 'commenced when the foreign ship or one of its boats is within' a relevant maritime zone of 'the pursuing state'.[73]

The third 'rule', however, is problematic. The Commission did not provide any guidance on what might constitute 'proved necessity' in a maritime law enforcement context, except to say, as Lauterpacht noted, that the fact nexus in the *Red Crusader* incident did not meet the test. Craig Allen has succinctly summarised the opacity of the Commission's finding thus:

> The Commission did not specify what 'other', non-deadly means would have been appropriate in this fisheries enforcement case. Nor did it categorically rule out the use of force that might create a danger to human life in cases of 'proved necessity.'[74]

Indeed, the Commission's finding has been interpreted by some as limiting the use of direct fire only to situations of self-defence (from ramming, for example); as Francesco Francioni averred in 1985,

> The *Red Crusader* incident is probably the most restrictive precedent on the scope of legitimate use of force in the enforcement of coastal states' fishing rights. It implies the existence of an international law standard prohibiting

71 Lauterpacht, *The Contemporary Practice of the United Kingdom in the Field of International Law – 1962*, above n 18, at 53.
72 Convention on the High Seas above n 11, art 23(1).
73 Ibid.
74 Craig Allen, 'Limits on the Use of Force in Maritime Operations in Support of WMD Counter-Proliferation Initiatives' (2006) 81 *International Law Studies* 77 at 96.

> the use of force in the pursuit of an offending fishing vessel unless required by self-defense.[75]

This interpretation persisted, he noted, in the face of clear state practice that evidenced use of direct fire in maritime law enforcement contexts – some legitimate, some less so – that did not involve the immediate self-defence of the enforcing vessel.[76]

C. The threshold for direct fire for enforcement purposes

What is readily distillable from the Commission's specific findings is that the delinquent vessel's refusal to heave to – even when coupled with detention of the pursuing warship's boarding party onboard in a situation whereby it was unlikely they would come to physical harm, but whereby they could end up being taken against their will into the territorial waters, and ultimately the port and jurisdiction, of another state – did not meet the required threshold for use of direct fire. As Dan O'Connell observed,

> The difficulty in drafting fishery protection instructions is that the question of whether the use of weapons is 'excessive' remains a matter of judgment on the part of the captain. The *Red Crusader* case suggests that every device, including, presumably, harassment by navigational means, must be employed and for a sufficient period of time before force is justified. This puts the commander in a difficult position, for harassment can lead to situations where the rule of the road becomes unclear, and a collision may result.[77]

Post-1962 commentary on this issue raised a number instances of state practice which clearly indicated that firing at or into a fleeing delinquent vessel, for a maritime law enforcement purpose, was considered legitimate – if at times excessively employed (such as use of high explosive rounds by the Argentine warship *Santa*

75 Francesco Francioni, 'Peacetime Use of Force, Military Activities, and the New Law of the Sea', 18 *Cornell International Law Journal* 203 (1985) at 218–219; see also Nicholas Poulantzas, *The Right of Hot Pursuit in International Law* (1969) at 237, analysing the *Red Crusader* Commission report:

> Under these circumstances we may discover how extremely difficult it is to obtain legal approval during peace time for the use of arms against offending vessels, and how cautious coast guards should be that they do not incur the international responsibility of the coastal State by the use of unnecessary violence. However, in this case and under its special circumstances we feel that the opinion of the Commission was strict in regard to the Danish Government's position.

76 Francioni, 'Peacetime Use of Force, Military Activities, and the New Law of the Sea', above n 75, at 219–220.

77 See D.P. O'Connell, 'International Law and Contemporary Naval Operations', 44 *British Yearbook of International Law* 19 (1970) at 71–79; updated in D.P. O'Connell, *The Influence of Law on Sea Power* (Manchester, 1975) at, for example, 67.

Cruz in direct fire into the Soviet fishing vessel *Golfstrim* in June 1968).[78] Indeed, whilst the facts as yet remain unclear, the recent Argentine Coast Guard action involving a Chinese fishing vessel, noted previously, would certainly indicate an ongoing assertion of a broader right to use direct fire, including in fisheries-related cases. Fenrick – examining fisheries enforcement and hot pursuit in Canadian law as at 1980, concluded that:

> Gunfire directed at the offending vessel to disable it or otherwise force it to stop may or may not be permissible, depending on the circumstances. It must, however, be borne in mind that the law is concerned with the causing of death or grievous bodily harm to persons, and that gunfire directed at a fishing vessel which is not intended or likely to sink the vessel may still be quite likely to cause death or grievous bodily harm to persons in the vessel.[79]

To some extent, until recently, international tribunals declined to be drawn on this issue. In the 1974 *Fisheries Jurisdiction* case,[80] for example, the ICJ 'shed very little light on the question of whether Iceland could lawfully resort to force for the enforcement of its fisheries legislation'.[81] Clearly, however, state practice by Iceland was that it could – ramming being but one form of such use of force. Recall, for example, how the UK had maintained before the *Red Crusader* Commission that direct fire was not permissible in fisheries enforcement cases. However, by 1976, when faced with renewed Icelandic ramming tactics – which UK Prime Minister James Callaghan noted in one minute had 'recently led to seven collisions in one week'[82] – the UK had apparently concluded that higher levels of use of force, including use of naval gunfire, were now permissible, but ought not be employed for strategic reasons. The Ministry of Defence concluded 'that it would not be in our wider interests to relax the constraints which the present Rules of Engagement place upon the use of gunfire against this NATO ally'.[83]

In *MV Saiga (No. 2)*, however, the impractical consequences of this contentious Commission finding were finally overcome (in terms of the authority offered by an international tribunal, at any rate), as that decision clearly reflected the fact that

78 See, for example, JE Pons, 'Fishery Law Enforcement', 2 *North Carolina Journal of International Law and Commercial Regulation* 119 (1977) at 124–129 – in relation to the *Golfstrim*, Pons is citing O'Connell, and O'Connell's source is noted in *The Influence of Law on Sea Power*, above n 77, at 67 n9, as 'private'.

79 WJ Fenrick, 'Legal Limits on the Use of Force by Canadian Warships Engaged in Law Enforcement', (1980) 18 *Canadian Yearbook of International Law* 113 at 123.

80 Merits, Fisheries Jurisdiction (*U.K. v. Iceland*) (1974) ICJ 3.

81 Francioni, 'Peacetime Use of Force, Military Activities, and the New Law of the Sea', above n 75, at 217–218.

82 *The Icelandic Fisheries Dispute (PM/76/24)* (a letter signed by the Prime Minister, James Callaghan), at 2 (UK National Archives File DEFE 13/1074).

83 Iceland – Rules of Engagement and Move of Designated Fishing Area (Annex to MO 12/3/1) (UK National Archives File DEFE 13/1074), at para 7.

it was, by then, well recognised that direct fire into a fleeing delinquent vessel was acceptable as the last step in a maritime law enforcement escalation of force, so long as risk to life was minimised to the required degree.[84] This view is also reflected in decisions such as *Guyana/Suriname*,[85] and – although direct fire was not an issue – the general scheme averred to in *MV Saiga (No. 2)* was endorsed and applied by the Arbitral tribunal in *Arctic Sunrise*.[86] There is clearly, in international law, a positive and regularly utilised permission to engage in escalation of force up to and including use of direct fire for the purpose of effective maritime law enforcement, coupled with a risk management caveat relating to danger to life.[87] The U.S. Coast Guard Use of Force Policy (CGUFP), for example, requires that (as paraphrased by Allen) 'disabling fire is to be discontinued when the vessel stops, is disabled, enters the territorial sea of another state, or the situation changes in a manner that introduces substantial risk to those aboard the noncompliant vessel'.[88] Dan O'Connell,[89] Don Rothwell and Tim Stephens,[90] James Kraska and Raul (Pete) Pedrozo,[91] Cameron Moore,[92] Natalie Klein,[93] Efthymios Papastavridis,[94] Douglas Guilfoyle,[95] and Patricia Kwast[96] are but a selection of those writing *after* the *Red Crusader* who

84 For example, *MV Saiga No 2*, above n 55, at para 155.

85 See also, *Guyana v Suriname* (2008) 47 ILM 166 at 231; R Canty, 'Developing Use of Force Doctrine: A Legal Case Study of the Coast Guard's Airborne Use of Force', 31:3 *University of Miami Inter-American Law Review* 357 (2000) at 376–377; T Treves, 'Piracy, Law of the Sea, and Use of Force: Developments off the Coast of Somalia', 20:2 *European Journal of International Law* 399 (2009) at 413–414; Warner, 'Jurisdictional Issues for Navies Involved in Enforcing Multilateral Regimes Beyond National Jurisdiction', at 330.

86 Award on the Merits, *The Arctic Sunrise Arbitration (Kingdom of the Netherlands and the Russian Federation)*, 14 August 2015 (PCA Case No. 2014–02) ('*Arctic Sunrise*') at, inter alia, paras 246–275 on hot pursuit generally, § 191 on use of force specifically, and noting that 'in *M/V Saiga No. 2*, ITLOS took account of general international law rules on the use of force in considering the use of force for the arrest of a vessel', citing with approval para 155 from that judgement (at para 221).

87 For example, Ivan Shearer, 'The Development of International Law with Respect to the Law Enforcement Roles of Navies and Coast Guards in Peacetime', 71 *International Law Studies* 429 (1998) at 440–444; David Letts, 'The use of force in patrolling Australia's fishing zones', 24 *Marine Policy* 149 (2000) at 155; Allen, 'Limits on the Use of Force in Maritime Operations in Support of WMD Counter-Proliferation Initiatives', above n 74, at 105, citing the examples of *USCGC Boutwell / Encounter Bay* (1988) and *USCGC Chincoteague / MV Hermann* (1990).

88 Allen, 'Limits on the Use of Force in Maritime Operations in Support of WMD Counter-Proliferation Initiatives', above n 74, at 87.

89 O'Connell, *The Influence of law on Sea Power*, above n 77, at 65.

90 DR Rothwell and T Stephens, *The International Law of the Sea* (Hart, 2010), at 420–422.

91 J Kraska and R Pedrozo, *International Maritime Security Law* (Brill, 2013), at inter alia 552.

92 C Moore, ADF on the Beat: A Legal Analysis of Offshore Enforcement by the Australian Defence Force (2004), at 113–119.

93 N Klein, *Maritime Security and the Law of the Sea* (Oxford, 2011), at 115–117.

94 E Papastavridis, *The Interception of Vessels on the High Seas* (Hart, 2014), at 68–78.

95 D Guilfoyle, *Shipping Interdiction and the Law of the Sea* (Cambridge, 2009), at inter alia 271–272, 277–282, 287–291.

96 PJ Kwast, 'Maritime Law Enforcement and the Use of Force: Reflections on the Categorisation of Forcible Action at Sea in the Light of the *Guyana/Suriname* Award' (2008) 13 *Journal of Conflict and Security Law* 49 at inter alia 63–66.

have specifically addressed the lawfulness of direct fire. Additionally, as Kraska and Pedrozo (amongst others) have noted, the oft-cited Principle 9 of the UN Basic Principles on the Use of Force and Firearms by Law Enforcement Officials (1990) can be readily extrapolated into the maritime law enforcement context, and thus clearly permits use of – in maritime terms – direct fire at or into a vessel.[97] This is quite different than the *Red Crusader* Commission's fundamental prohibition in the absence of an ill-defined, but very high, threshold of 'necessity' that did not include either the need to ensure effective maritime law enforcement, or the fact that the delinquent vessel was steaming for its own waters with some of the pursuing vessel's boarding party secluded onboard.

The more interesting juxtaposition (and indicator of influence), consequently, is with academic analyses published *before* the *Red Crusader*; whilst references to the cumulative conditions necessary for validity in relation to precursors to the maritime doctrine of hot pursuit stretch back into the 1800s,[98] there is a marked absence of analysis of the discrete yet fundamental issue of use of force beyond warning shots. Higgins and Colombos, in 1943, analysed hot pursuit extensively, but did not address the issue of firing at or into a fleeing delinquent vessel beyond noting the iconic finding in *I'm Alone* that intentional sinking was not permissible.[99] McDougal and Burke, in their magisterial *The Public Order of the Oceans* (1962) dedicated many pages to analysing the interpretive challenges inherent within, and trends relating to, hot pursuit, but at no stage addressed the discrete issue of firing at or into a fleeing delinquent vessel.[100] In that light, perhaps the most enduring consequence of *Red Crusader* for maritime law enforcement operational practice was to bring the issue of direct fire at or into a fleeing delinquent vessel back out of the shadows, albeit in a practically fraught and limited way. Indeed, the significant

97 *Basic Principles on the Use of Force and Firearms by Law Enforcement Officials*, Adopted by the Eighth United Nations Congress on the Prevention of Crime and the Treatment of Offenders, Havana, Cuba, 27 August to 7 September 1990, Principle 9 – 'In any event, intentional lethal use of firearms may only be made when strictly unavoidable in order to protect life'.

98 In general, these relate to piracy and suppression of the slave trade, which are now matters subject to the right of visit encapsulated in Article 110 of the Law of the Sea Convention 1982; see, for example, the discussion in WE Hall, *A Treatise on International Law* (London, 1890), at ch 6; H Wheaton (R Dana editor), *Elements of International Law (Eighth Edition)* (Washington, 1866), §125–133; see also the exposition in L Sohn, 'Peacetime Use of Force on the High Seas' (1991) 64 *International Law Studies* 38. The other – more relevant and analogous – area of analysis evident in these early authorities is in relation to fisheries within territorial waters – see, for example, J Moore, *A Digest of International Law (Volume I)* (Washington, 1906), at Ch V sections IV-VI; however, again, the discrete issue of use of direct fire is almost never addressed, and where use of force for enforcement purposes is addressed, it is often couched in the terminology of 'legitimate self-defence' or 'preservation' as opposed to the more tactical concerns of maritime law enforcement.

99 P Higgins and J Colombos, *The International Law of the Sea* (London, 1943), at 103–108 (at 106 on *I'm Alone*); interestingly, the expanded treatment of hot pursuit in the 4th Edition (1959) still did not deal with this discreet issue, even in the light of the first 'Cod War' – J Colombos, *The International Law of the Sea (Fourth Revised Edition)* (London, 1959), at 141–148.

100 M McDougal and W Burke, *The Public Order of the Oceans: A Contemporary International Law of the Sea* (Yale, 1962), at 893–923.

yet opaque influence of *Red Crusader* upon this issue is a specifically noted feature of much dedicated post-*Red Crusader* analysis: As Craig Allen (along with others such as Ivan Shearer[101] and Douglas Guilfoyle[102]) has observed:

> It is clear that customary law prohibits firing into a vessel without warning. Additionally, using gunfire to intentionally sink a fleeing vessel suspected of smuggling illegal liquor, at least without first attempting to disable it, violates the established rule that force must be necessary and reasonable. Such gunfire would almost certainly pose a threat to the lives of those aboard. But the full contours of the legal limits on the use of police force at sea remain unclear . . . international law has so far failed to recognize explicitly that the level of force that is reasonable and appropriate under the circumstances will vary according to the nature of the violation and the impact alternative enforcement approaches will have on the legal regime's effectiveness. Force levels appropriate in interdicting a vessel engaged in narcotics trafficking might well be inappropriate to one suspected of violating fisheries laws in a coastal state's EEZ.[103]

Yet it is equally clear that state practice, and a number of significant international tribunals, are nevertheless fully cognizant of a permission for direct fire, with *Red Crusader* routinely cited as a foundational authority for this operational norm. This is, ultimately and somewhat paradoxically, probably the incident's most significant and enduring achievement.

V. Conclusion

From its origins as a routine fisheries enforcement operation entailing a modest damage bill, and engaging a relatively moderate diplomatic penumbra, the *Red Crusader* incident has since evolved an iconic status in the field of maritime law enforcement. Understanding why this incident – as opposed to other equally, if not more, significant incidents in terms of damage caused and diplomatic tensions exacerbated – has come to be understood as such is a function of many interlocking

101 Ivan Shearer, 'Problems of Jurisdiction and Enforcement against Delinquent Vessels' (1986) 35 *International and Comparative Law Quarterly* 320.

102 Guilfoyle, *Shipping Interdiction and the Law of the Sea*, above n 95, at 271: After reviewing the limited case law (the *I'm Alone* case, the *Red Crusader* case and *MV Saiga [No. 2]*) commentators usually conclude that under customary international law using force is a 'measure of last resort' and that any force must be 'reasonable and necessary in the circumstances'. Such general statements offer decision-makers little guidance, a difficulty compounded by the fact that the available cases generally concern instances of clearly *disproportionate* force [emphasis in original].

103 Allen, 'Limits on the Use of Force in Maritime Operations in Support of WMD Counter-Proliferation Initiatives', above n 74, at 95; Ivan Shearer has made the same point – Shearer, 'Problems of Jurisdiction and Law Enforcement against Delinquent Vessels', above n 101, at (for example) 341–342.

factors: contemporaneous tumult in the progressive development of the law of the sea, the civility of the parties in dealing with the matter, and the specific factual nexus and legal context of this particular incident. However, there are arguably two factors that have perhaps contributed disproportionately to this outcome. The first is that this incident, unlike many other more serious contemporary incidents raising similar issues, was subject to a formalised fact-finding and arbitral process which offered an unparalleled opportunity to crystallise both the state of the law, and state practice – arguably the first apposite opportunity since the *I'm Alone* arbitration in 1933–1935. The second factor is that the Commission directly addressed the use of direct fire in relation to a fleeing delinquent vessel, ending the unexplained amnesia that had apparently descended upon this fundamental issue subsequent to the scarce but direct assessment proffered in *I'm Alone*. What is perhaps more interesting, however, is that in doing so, the *Red Crusader* Commission arguably left the matter more – rather than less – opaque, apparently endorsing an operational caveat of surpassing impracticality. Yet, despite the subsequent and enduring silence of the treaties as to the issue, and thus their relative superfluity in resolving this opacity, a clear norm that mitigates – if not ultimately rejects – the *Red Crusader* Commission's approach has nevertheless crystallised in state practice, and subsequently been given expression in forums such as ITLOS via the *MV Saiga (No. 2)* case. Thus the most enduring legacy of the *Red Crusader* incident is perhaps not that it got the law right, but rather that it expressed a view on the law at all, generating a relatively opaque formulation which then served as a point of departure for a more practical and robust norm crystallisation process.

11

THE *MV SAIGA (NO. 2)* CASE

St Vincent and the Grenadines v Guinea

Phillip Drew

I. Introduction

On 1 July 1999, the International Tribunal for the Law of the Sea (ITLOS) handed down its decision on merits in the case of the *MV Saiga (No. 2) Case (St Vincent and the Grenadines v Guinea)*.[1] The judgement, which was the second ruling rendered by the Tribunal in regards to the dispute between Guinea and Saint Vincent and the Grenadines, is notable for its determinations respecting coastal state jurisdiction and the conduct of arrests in international waters.

II. Background

The MV *Saiga* is an oil tanker that, at the time of the incident in question, was provisionally registered in, and flying the flag of, Saint Vincent and the Grenadines. During the autumn of 1997, the *Saiga* was conducting bunkering operations off the west coast of Africa, refuelling and providing fresh water primarily to fishing vessels in the area.

Between 24–27 October, the *Saiga* was refuelling vessels inside of Guinea's exclusive economic zone (EEZ). On the morning of 28 October 1997, after having sailed out of Guinea's EEZ, the *Saiga* was stopped and boarded by the Guinean Navy. The Master was arrested, the crew was detained, and the

1 *The MV Saiga (No. 2) Case (St Vincent and the Grenadines v Guinea)* 1999 ITLOS Case No 2, hereinafter *Saiga* (No. 2). The first case, brought on 4 December 1997, was an application for quick release, brought under Article 292 of the *United Nations Convention on the Law of the Sea* (UNCLOS). In that case, a deeply divided court found that Guinea had failed to promptly release the *MV Saiga* and its crew, and ordered that the vessel and crew be released on the payment of a bond of US$400,000 plus the fuel that Guinea had unloaded.

DOI: 10.4324/9781003307013-14

ship was taken to Conakry, where its cargo of oil was discharged. The main charge brought against the *Saiga* by Guinea was that by conducting bunkering operations in its customs radius, the *Saiga* violated Article 1 of Law L/94/007, which prohibited the unauthorised importation of oil into Guinea's territory. On 13 November 1997, the case was referred to ITLOS on an application for prompt release (*Saiga [No. 1]*). The merits of the case were adjudicated the following year (*Saiga [No. 2]*).

Although the case of the *Saiga* is notable for several findings related to the issue of nationality of ships and the requirement for prompt release, for the purposes of this chapter, the main issues that will be addressed are the legality of the boarding operation, the amount of force used, and whether or not claims by Guinea that its vessels were in hot pursuit were valid.

A. The relevant Guinea laws

Guinea is one of the poorest states in the world.[2] In an effort to secure revenues and reduce the smuggling of fuel into the country, the Guinean government in 1994 enacted Law L/94/007, which prohibited the unauthorised importation of fuel into the country's territory and its 'customs radius', which was set out in in the *Customs Code of Guinea*. It was Guinea's position that the conduct of bunkering operations by foreign vessels within its self-declared 'customs radius' was an offence under Guinean law. The relevant provisions of the laws at issue provided as follows:

Law L/94/007

Article 1

The import, transport, storage and distribution of fuel by any natural person or corporate body not legally authorized are prohibited in the Republic of Guinea.

Article 6

Whoever illegally imports fuel into the national territory will be subject to 6 months to 2 years imprisonment, the confiscation of the means of transport, the confiscation of the items used to conceal the illegal importation and a joint and several fine equal to double the value of the subject of the illegal importation where this offence is committed by less than three individuals.[3]

2 CIA Factbook – Guinea. online: The Central Intelligence Agency <www.cia.gov/library/publications/the-world-factbook/geos/countrytemplate_gv.html>.

3 *Saiga (No. 2)*, above n 1, para 112.

The Customs Code of Guinea

Article 34

1 The customs radius includes a marine area and a terrestrial area.
2 The marine area lies between the coastline and an outer limit located at sea 250 kilometres from the coast.

B. The arrest of the Saiga

On 24 October 1997, the *Saiga* departed Dakar, Senegal, where she had taken on oil and fresh water. From Senegal, she sailed southward, taking up station in Guinea's EEZ, approximately 22 nm from Guinea's island of Alcatraz, well within Guinea's self-declared customs radius. While in that locale, the *Saiga* refuelled three vessels, two that were registered in Senegal, and one that was registered in Greece. All three of the refuelled vessels were licensed to fish in Guinea's EEZ.

On orders from its owners, the *Saiga* sailed southward during the night of 27–28 October, departing the Guinean EEZ and entering the EEZ of the neighbouring state of Sierra Leone. At approximately 09:00 hours on 28 October, Guinean naval patrol boats opened fire on the *Saiga* with large-calibre weapons. After firing on the *Saiga*, an armed Guinean boarding party boarded her. Once on board, the members of the boarding party fired their weapons indiscriminately, causing damage to the ship and seriously wounding two members of the crew. At the completion of the boarding, the *Saiga*, her Master and the crew were taken to Conakry where the Master was placed under arrest, the vessel was detained, and the cargo of approximately 4 950 metric tonnes of oil was discharged.

On 13 November 1997, Saint Vincent and the Grenadines submitted a request to ITLOS, seeking prompt release of the vessel in accordance with the requirements of Article 292 of the United Nations Convention on the Law of the Sea (UNCLOS).[4] On 4 December. the Tribunal issued its decision on the request for prompt release, ordering Guinea to release the vessel and crew upon payment of a surety of US$400,000.[5] Because of a disagreement over the terms of payment of the surety, Guinea refused to release the vessel and the Master.

The Master was tried under Guinean law for having

> imported, without declaring it, merchandise that is taxable on entering national Guinean territory, in this case diesel oil, and [refusing] to comply

4 *United Nations Convention on the Law of the Sea*, (1982) 1833 UNTS 3, art 292 [hereinafter UNCLOS]:

> Where the authorities of a State Party have detained a vessel flying the flag of another State Party and it is alleged that the detaining State has not complied with the provisions of this Convention for the prompt release of the vessel or its crew . . . the question of release from detention may be submitted to . . . the International Tribunal for the Law of the Sea

5 *Saiga (No. 2)*, above n 1, para 35.

> with injunctions by Agents of the Guinean Navy, thus committing the crimes of contraband, fraud and tax evasion.[6]

Upon conviction on 17 December 1997, the Master was fined an amount of 15,354,040,000 Guinean francs.[7] The *Saiga* and its cargo were seized as a guarantee for payment of the fine. The Master appealed his conviction and penalty to the Guinea Court of Appeal. At the conclusion of the appeal, the Master's conviction was upheld; the Court imposed a suspended sentence of six months and increased the fine by approximately 16,000 Guinea francs.

On 4 March 1998, Saint Vincent and the Grenadines arrived at an agreement with Guinea regarding the release of the *Saiga*. The release was executed in accordance with the Tribunal's order of 4 December 1997. Following the submission of written arguments, oral arguments were subsequently heard between 8 March and 20 March 1999, and the Tribunal's final decision was handed down on 1 July 1999.

III. Outcomes and analysis

Whereas during the *Saiga (No. 1)* case, the Tribunal's attention was dedicated to the issue of the prompt release of the vessel and crew, the central focus of the *Saiga (No. 2)* case was on matters related to the arrest of the *Saiga* by the Guinean Navy. In particular, the Tribunal was asked to rule on whether Guinea had jurisdiction to enforce its customs laws within its 'customs radius', whether its naval vessels had properly engaged in a hot pursuit of the *Saiga* as she departed Guinea's EEZ, and whether the amount of force used in carrying out the arrest was excessive.[8]

A. The 'customs radius'

During pleadings on the merits of the case, neither of the parties contested the basic facts pertaining to where and when the *Saiga* had engaged in bunkering operations or the location of the arrest. It was clear from the *Saiga*'s log that she had conducted bunkering operations in Guinea's EEZ and did not, at any point, enter Guinea's territorial waters.[9] Similarly, it was clear that the arrest of the *Saiga* took place in international waters within the EEZ of Sierra Leone.

Understanding that the *Saiga* had conducted its bunkering operations within Guinea's EEZ, the Tribunal's primary task was to determine whether or not

6 Ibid, para 36.

7 Ibid, para 37.

8 Of note, although both parties requested that the Tribunal make a declaration regarding the legality of conducting bunkering operations in another State's EEZ, the Tribunal decided that it would not make a determination on that issue. See *Saiga (No. 2)*, above n 1, para 138.

9 In accordance with UNCLOS Article 3, the territorial waters of Guinea extend 12 nm from its coastline. The Island of Alcatraz has a 12 nm territorial sea surrounding it. Of note, Guinea has not declared a contiguous zone.

Guinea's 'customs radius' could be enforced in its EEZ. Central to this main point of contention was Guinea's position that for the purposes of Law L/94/007, the term 'Guinea' included the customs radius as provided in the Customs Code of Guinea. In contrast, Saint Vincent and the Grenadines argued that the 'customs radius' was merely a 'special area of surveillance'[10] that did not have the effect of extending Guinea's 'national territory', and that any

> extension of the customs laws of Guinea to the exclusive economic zone is contrary to the [UNCLOS] Convention. Additionally, St Vincent and the Grenadines claimed that article 56 of [UNCLOS] does not give the right to Guinea to extend the application of its customs laws and regulations to [the EEZ].[11]

In support of its claim of jurisdiction over its 'customs radius', Guinea contended that bunkering operations in its EEZ were causing the country significant fiscal losses that were sufficient to warrant the creation of regulations made in the public interest of the state. Guinea justified its position through reference to the provision in Article 58(2) which allows states to impose regulations in the EEZ that are consistent with 'other rules of international law'.[12]

In its decision, the Tribunal found that by attempting to extend its customs and taxation scheme into its EEZ,

> Guinea acted in a manner contrary to [UNCLOS] . . . [and that consequently], the arrest and detention of the *Saiga*, the prosecution and conviction of its Master, the confiscation of the cargo and the seizure of the ship were contrary to the Convention.[13]

10 *Saiga (No. 2)*, above n 1, para 117.

11 Ibid, para 119. Article 56 of UNCLOS which, in concert with Articles 55 and 57, creates the exclusive economic zone, provides coastal states with

> rights for the purpose of exploring and exploiting, conserving and managing the natural resources, whether living or non-living, of the waters superjacent to the seabed and of the seabed and its subsoil, and with regard to other activities for the economic exploitation and exploration of the zone.

While Article 56 permits states to regulate certain activities within the EEZ, Article 58 notes that:

> In the exclusive economic zone, all States . . . enjoy, subject to the relevant provisions of this Convention, the freedoms referred to in article 87 of navigation . . . and other internationally lawful uses of the sea related to these freedoms, such as those associated with the operation of ships . . . and compatible with the other provisions of this Convention' and that 'In exercising their rights . . . States . . . shall comply with the laws and regulations adopted by the coastal State in accordance with the provisions of this Convention and other rules of international law in so far as they are not incompatible with this Part.

12 UNCLOS art 58(2).

13 *Saiga (No. 2)* para 136.

B. Hot pursuit

The arrest of the *Saiga* occurred outside of Guinea's EEZ. While UNCLOS provides the mechanism whereby a state may conduct an arrest of a vessel outside of its declared maritime zones, it also sets out the procedures for doing this in Article 111, which provides in part:

> 111.1 The hot pursuit of a foreign ship may be undertaken when the competent authorities of the coastal State have good reason to believe that the ship has violated the laws and regulations of that State. Such pursuit must be commenced when the foreign ship or one of its boats is within the internal waters, the archipelagic waters, the territorial sea or the contiguous zone of the pursuing State, and may only be continued outside the territorial sea or the contiguous zone if the pursuit has not been interrupted; and
>
> 111.2 The right of hot pursuit shall apply mutatis mutandis to violations in the exclusive economic zone . . . of the laws and regulations of the coastal State applicable in accordance with this Convention to the exclusive economic zone.
>
> 111.4 . . . The pursuit may only be commenced after a visual or auditory signal to stop has been given at a distance which enables it to be seen or heard by the foreign ship.[14]

As the Tribunal noted in its decision, the elements of hot pursuit, as set out in Article 111, are cumulative:

> First, the coastal State must reasonably believe that the pursued vessel has violated a law or regulation of that State;
>
> Second, before a pursuit is commenced the pursuing vessel must give an auditory or visual signal to the vessel ordering it to stop;
>
> Third, the pursuit must commence while the vessel is in the waters to which the law or regulation applies;
>
> Fourth, the pursuit must not be interrupted; and,
>
> Fifth, a hot pursuit may not be continued into the territorial sea of any State.

In its pleadings, Guinea stated that the pursuit of the *Saiga* had commenced on 27 October when one of its patrol vessels was sent to investigate whether the *Saiga* was conducting bunkering operations. However, when it was discovered that the *Saiga* had departed southward from its original station and could not be found, the patrol vessel was called back to port. In this instance, it was obvious that no hot pursuit had occurred.

14 UNCLOS, above n 4, art 111.

Guinea also contended that its vessels had commenced a second pursuit on the morning of 28 October. The question as to whether or not auditory or visual signals were properly employed was hotly contested between the parties, with Guinea claiming that its vessel had flashed a blue light and sounded signals, while the Master of the *Saiga* denied seeing or hearing any such signals. Ultimately, the Tribunal found that the *Saiga* was either outside of Guinea's EEZ or about to leave when it was detected by Guinean radar. The Tribunal thus found that even if the signals were communicated sometime after the *Saiga* had been detected on radar, the pursuing vessel had not properly commenced the hot pursuit while the *Saiga* was still inside Guinea's EEZ.

Finding that the provisions of Law L/94/007 contravened UNCLOS, and that the pursuit of the *Saiga* outside of Guinea's EEZ was not conducted in accordance with Article 111, the Tribunal determined that there was no hot pursuit and that the arrest of the *Saiga* was unlawful.

C. Use of force

It is well settled in international law that a government vessel that is attempting to conduct a lawful boarding of another vessel at sea may use force in order to make the vessel comply. The authority to exercise the use of force, however, is subject to very strict conditions and restrictions. Under no circumstances is a government vessel conducting law enforcement tasks entitled to employ deadly force against another vessel (considering the people in that vessel) unless that other vessel is posing a serious threat to the lives and safety of the government vessel and its personnel, or to others in the vicinity. In other words, the use of deadly force in conducting such law enforcement tasks is governed by the laws of individual self-defence; the amount of force used must be limited to that which is necessary and reasonable to overcome the threat that is posed.

The *Saiga* was unarmed when she was fired upon; nearly fully laden with gas/oil, riding low in the water, and able to maintain a speed of only 10 knots. Whereas in its original pleadings, Guinea claimed that its patrol boat fired at the *Saiga* because the *Saiga* had tried to sink it,[15] Guinea later abandoned that position, stating instead that 'the arresting officers had no alternative but to use gunfire because the *Saiga* refused to stop after repeated radio messages to it to stop and in spite of visual and auditory signals from the patrol boat P35'.[16]

In arriving at its findings on the issue of the use of force, the Tribunal referred to the case of the *I'm Alone*,[17] noting that,

> The normal practice used to stop a ship at sea is first to give an auditory or visual signal to stop, using internationally recognized signals. Where this does

15 *Saiga (No. 2)*, above n 1, para 157.

16 Ibid, para 154.

17 *S.S. I'm Alone* Case (Canada/United States) [1935] 3 RIAA 1609 – see Chapter 9.

> not succeed, a variety of actions may be taken, including the firing of shots across the bows of the ship. It is only after the appropriate actions fail that the pursuing vessel may, as a last resort, use force. Even then, appropriate warning must be issued to the ship and all efforts should be made to ensure that life is not endangered.[18]

The Tribunal also noted that, 'The basic principle concerning the use of force in the arrest of a ship at sea has been reaffirmed' by the Agreement for the Implementation of the Provisions of the United Nations Convention on the Law of the Sea of 10 December 1982 Relating to the Conservation and Management of Straddling Fish Stocks and Highly Migratory Fish Stocks. Article 22, paragraph 1(f), of the Agreement states:

> 1 The inspecting State shall ensure that its duly authorized inspectors: . . .
>
> (f) avoid the use of force except when and to the degree necessary to ensure the safety of the inspectors and where the inspectors are obstructed in the execution of their duties. The degree of force used shall not exceed that reasonably required in the circumstances.[19]

The Tribunal was unequivocal in denouncing the actions of the Guinean naval personnel who were involved in the arrest of the *Saiga*. It found that,

> although there is no evidence of the use or threat of force from the crew, [Guinean personnel] fired indiscriminately while on the deck and used gunfire to stop the engine of the ship. In using firearms in this way, the Guinean officers appeared to have attached little or no importance to the safety of the ship and the persons on board.[20]

The Tribunal concluded that, 'Guinea used excessive force and endangered human life before and after boarding the *Saiga*, and thereby violated the rights of Saint Vincent and the Grenadines under international law'.[21]

IV. Conclusion

Although Guinea's attempt to regulate bunkering activities for vessels that are fishing in its EEZ is understandable, the manner in which it chose to deal with the *Saiga* was riddled with legal errors that could not be justified or explained away. The actions of the Guinean Navy on 28 October reflected a profound misunderstanding

18 *Saiga (No. 2)*, above n 1, para 156.
19 Ibid.
20 Ibid, para 158.
21 Ibid, para 159.

of the laws respecting hot pursuit, the responsible use of force, and the exercise of coastal state jurisdiction in the exclusive economic zone. Insofar as the *Saiga (No. 2)* case permitted the Tribunal to review and comment on the myriad of errors that were committed by the Guinean authorities, it has proven to be instructive for courts and tribunals that have since faced similar issues,[22] particularly those dealing with the use of force by state authorities against civilian vessels and those state officials who are responsible for determining matters of criminal and civil jurisdiction over foreign vessels in the various maritime zones of a coastal state.

22 See, for example *The Enrica Lexie Incident (Italy v. India)*, PCA Case No. 2015–28 (21 May 2020).

12

THE 'WHISKEY ON THE ROCKS' INCIDENT

Cameron Moore[1]

I. Introduction

The 'Whiskey on the Rocks' incident involved the grounding of a Soviet *Whiskey*-class conventional submarine on the Swedish coast in 1981. It excited significant interest at the time in the context of Cold War tensions, as well as subsequent Swedish operations throughout the 1980s against unknown submerged contacts in its waters. More recently, the issue has come to prominence again as a number of Baltic states, including Sweden, are reported to be engaging in operations against unidentified submerged contacts.[2] In relation to the 'Whiskey on the Rocks' incident, there was no legal inquiry as such nor any judicial proceedings. There was some operational reporting and some limited legal writing around the time. This case is then one of applying the law to the known facts to see the extent to which it developed or confirmed state practice on the relevant issues. For the law of maritime operations, these appear mainly to relate to the rights and obligations of submarines in foreign internal and territorial waters, the sovereign

1 The views expressed in this chapter are entirely the author's own and do not represent any official view. An abbreviated treatment of this subject may be found in Cameron Moore, *Freedom of Navigation and the Law of the Sea: Warships, States and the Use of Force* (Routledge, 2021), 75–81.

2 See <www.telegraph.co.uk/news/worldnews/europe/sweden/11174169/Sweden-submarine-hunt-as-it-happened.html> concerning incidents in October 2014 and <www.canberratimes.com.au/world/finnish-military-fires-on-suspected-submarine-in-baltic-20150428-1mvhx9.html> concerning Finnish use of light depth charges as warning shots against unidentified submerged contacts in April 2015; For similar incidents in Japan, see David Axe, 'Japan Has A Plan For Dismantling China's Submarine Fleet' *Forbes Magazine* (online) 22 June 2020 <www.forbes.com/sites/davidaxe/2020/06/22/japan-has-a-plan-for-dismantling-chinas-submarine-fleet/#4065168c6d6c>; Reiji Yoshida, 'Beijing's Senkaku goal: Sub 'safe haven' in South China Sea' *Japan Times* (online) 7 November 2012 <www.japantimes.co.jp/news/2012/11/07/national/beijings-senkaku-goal-sub-safe-haven-in-south-china-sea/#.XsXmE3tS82z>.

DOI: 10.4324/9781003307013-15

immunity of warships and their crews after apparently violating coastal state sovereignty, the use of force against submerged contacts, and the law of neutrality in naval warfare.

This chapter will argue that the 'Whiskey on the Rocks' incident, and the subsequent Swedish operations against submerged contacts in Swedish waters, has enduring significance for the sovereign immunity of warships and the use of force against unidentified submerged contacts in coastal state waters. At the same time, the incident simply confirmed existing understandings of the rights and obligations of submarines in foreign coastal waters while adding nothing really to state practice in respect to the law of neutrality in naval warfare.

II. Background

The 'Whiskey on the Rocks' incident followed concerns about occasional Soviet submarine incursions into Swedish waters dating back to the 1930s,[3] but actually came at the beginning of a period of heightened tension between Sweden and the Soviet Union which lasted from 1980 until 1990.[4] This reportedly involved numerous incursions every year during the 1980s by Soviet submarines[5] and divers, as well as operations ashore in Sweden launched from the sea, as well as by other means.[6] Swedish naval units actively pursued underwater contacts, using depth charges, torpedoes, limpet mines, and fixed minefields.[7] Patrols ashore intercepted combat swimmers entering or leaving the water.[8] Although much of the naval activity occurred after the 'Whiskey on the Rocks' incident, it is important to place the incident within this context as it casts a different light on the actual character of the incident itself in retrospect. It also underlines its importance as an indicator of what was to come.

A. The incident

Froman – referring to contemporaneous news reporting – concisely described the 'Whiskey on the Rocks' incident in 1984, as follows:

> On the night of October 27, 1981, a Soviet 'whiskey' class submarine carrying a crew of 56 ran aground inside a restricted security zone nine miles southeast of the Karlskrona Naval Base, deep within Swedish territorial waters. Following an 11-day drama, which included lodging two diplomatic

3 Gordon McCormick, *Stranger Than Fiction: Soviet Submarine Operations in Swedish Waters* (Rand, 1990), 4. NB: primary sources are in Swedish, hence reliance upon secondary, mainly U.S., sources in English.

4 Ibid, 3–6.

5 Ibid.

6 Ibid, 16–17, 23.

7 Discussed in what follows.

8 McCormick, Stranger Than Fiction: Soviet Submarine Operations in Swedish Waters, above n 3.

> protests, sighting another submarine's periscope and turning back a Soviet salvage vessel both inside Swedish territorial waters, and discovering uranium 238 emanating from the submarine's hull, the Swedish government concluded 'that the submarine had intentionally violated Swedish territory to gather intelligence.' Swedish Prime Minister Thorbjorn Falldin initially called the episode 'the most grave intrusion into Swedish territory since World War II.' He later termed the violation 'all the more remarkable since in all probability the submarine has carried nuclear weapons into Swedish territory.' Its investigation closed, the Swedish Navy on November 6th escorted the submarine to the 12-mile limit, where it joined a flotilla of 20 Soviet warships waiting just outside.[9]

McCormick, in a 1990 Rand report for the U.S. Air Force on submarine incursions into Swedish waters throughout the 1980s, identified a number of aspects of the incident which are significant from a legal perspective as follows:

1 To ground where it did, U137 needed to have navigated though rocks, shallows, islands, and underwater pinnacles which would have been treacherous even to surface navigation in daylight.[10]
2 Swedish investigators boarded U137 four days after it grounded and examined its navigational instruments and found them to be in working order. They also found that entries in the logbook for the last 20 minutes of the voyage had been altered.[11]
3 The Swedes protested formally to the Soviets that the grounding was a flagrant violation of Sweden's sovereignty.[12]
4 The Soviets did not reply to the Swedish request to confirm whether nuclear weapons were on board U137, which the Swedes took as the Soviet Union being unable to deny the presence of such weapons.[13]
5 The Soviets did reply that the incident was the result of an innocent navigational error and strongly rejected Sweden's demands that it not occur again, as it was impossible to deny the possibility of future accidents at sea. Sweden's accusations were motivated by those who wished to undermine Soviet/Swedish relations.[14]
6 The Soviet Union continued to assert the sovereign immunity of U137 and demanded that it be allowed to refloat the vessel and recover it. To this end, it dispatched a surface force comprising three destroyers, a frigate, two missile

9 David Froman, 'Uncharted Waters: Non-innocent Passage of Warships in the Territorial Sea' (1984) 21 *San Diego Law Review* 625–627.
10 McCormick, *Stranger Than Fiction: Soviet Submarine Operations in Swedish Waters*, above n 3.
11 Ibid.
12 Ibid 8.
13 Ibid.
14 Ibid 8–9.

boats, a submarine salvage vessel, two electronic warfare vessels, and an oiler, which waited outside Swedish territorial waters.[15]

7 Sweden replied that it required the Soviet Union to meet four conditions for the return of the submarine:

1 The Royal Swedish Navy refloat the submarine;
2 The Soviet Union bear the cost of the salvage;
3 The Soviet Union apologise formally; and
4 That the captain of U137 submit to Swedish questioning.

8 The Soviet Union agreed reluctantly to these demands, after which Swedish investigators boarded the vessel. Ten days after it grounded, U137 proceeded to sea on the surface and under tow.[16]

A further important factual and legal point concerns Swedish internal and territorial waters. Due to the configuration of its coast, being deeply indented and with many fringing islands, Sweden claimed relatively extensive internal waters enclosed within the fringing islands. Beyond that, it claimed a 12-nm territorial sea.[17] There did not appear to be any question over the validity of Sweden's maritime claims in relation to the U137 incident or the subsequent operations against submerged contacts.

III. Analysis and outcomes

The grounding of U137 raises at least four legal issues which warrant further consideration. The first is whether the Soviet Union was acting contrary to its obligations under the United Nations Charter and the international law of the sea. The second is the extent to which U137, and, separately, its crew, enjoyed sovereign immunity from law enforcement by Sweden. The third issue is the extent to which Sweden could use force either before or after the U137 incident against unidentified submarine contacts in Swedish waters. The final issue is whether Sweden's political neutrality in the Cold War between the Warsaw Pact and the North

15 Ibid, 9.
16 Ibid.
17 Ibid, 1. Sweden's current claim appears to be the same as it was in 1981 as the United Nations Law of the Sea claims website, <www.un.org/Depts/los/LEGISLATIONANDTREATIES/STATEFILES/SWE.htm> still has the *Act Concerning the Territorial Waters of Sweden of 3 June 1966 (with amendments No 959 enacted on 18 December 1978, and No 1140, on 20 December 1979)*. It only displays section 4, which states:

> In the case of land areas, the baseline from which the territorial sea is measured is the low-water line along the coast. The territorial sea, however, is measured from skerries which rise above sea level at low-water level but not at mean water level, only if the skerries are not more than twelve/nautical miles from the land areas belonging to Sweden which are visible above water surface at mean water level. As regards internal waters along the coast, the territorial sea is measured from the outer boundaries of these water areas (straight baselines) unless such measurement is to be done in some other way because a land area is situated outside a straight baseline.

Atlantic Treaty Organization had any legal effect with respect to U137, or generally in regard to submarine incursions into Swedish waters.

A. Law of the sea obligations at the time, and the United Nations Charter

At the time that the incident occurred in 1981, the Law of the Sea Convention[18] had not yet entered into force, which did not occur until 1994, nor had the text of the convention been settled finally; the Third United Nations Conference on the Law of the Sea (UNCLOS III) process did not conclude until 1982. It is necessary therefore to look to the Convention on the Territorial Sea and Contiguous Zone of 1958[19] (1958 Convention) and customary international law to ascertain the international obligations of Sweden and the Soviet Union in this incident.

The 1958 Convention relevantly provided as follows at Article 14:

> 1 Subject to the provisions of these articles, ships of all States, whether coastal or not, shall enjoy the right of innocent passage through the territorial sea.
>
> 2 Passage means navigation through the territorial sea for the purpose either of traversing that sea without entering internal waters, or of proceeding to internal waters, or of making for the high seas from internal waters.
>
> 3 Passage includes stopping and anchoring, but only in so far as the same are incidental to ordinary navigation or are rendered necessary *by force majeure* or by distress.
>
> 4 Passage is innocent so long as it is not prejudicial to the peace, good order or security of the coastal State. Such passage shall take place in conformity with these articles and with other rules of international law. . . .
>
> 6 Submarines are required to navigate on the surface and to show their flag.

Interestingly, the USSR and the Ukrainian SSR (relevant in that the Soviet Navy was an instrument of both SSRs)[20] had both ratified the 1958 Convention, in 1960 and 1961, respectively,[21] therefore being bound when it came into effect in 1964. Sweden, on the other hand, had not even signed the 1958 Convention but appeared to view at least the effect of Article 14 to be customary international law

18 1833 UNTS 3 (entered into force 16 November 1994) ('*Law of the Sea Convention*').

19 516 UNTS 205 (entered into force 22 November 1964).

20 This chapter will otherwise refer only to the USSR or Soviet Union.

21 *United Nations Treaty Collection*, Status of Treaties <https://treaties.un.org/Pages/ViewDetails.aspx?src=UNTSONLINE&tabid=2&mtdsg_no=XXI-1&chapter=21&lang=en#Participants>.

in 1981, by virtue of its declaration on signature of the 1982 Law of the Sea Convention which stated:

> As regards those parts of the Convention which deal with innocent passage through the territorial sea, it is the intention of the Government of Sweden to continue to apply the present regime for the passage of foreign warships and other government-owned vessels used for non-commercial purposes through the Swedish territorial sea, that regime being fully compatible with the Convention.
>
> It is also the understanding of the Government of Sweden that the Convention does not affect the rights and duties of a neutral State provided for in the *Convention Concerning the Rights and Duties of Neutral Powers in Case of Naval Warfare* (XIII Convention), adopted at The Hague on 18 October 1907.[22]

Insofar as it relates to this discussion, Articles 17–20 of the 1982 Law of the Sea Convention do not provide any substantive difference to the obligations under Article 14 of the 1958 Convention. The effect is that both states viewed themselves as bound by the same obligations in respect of passage of submarines in the territorial sea, and, by implication, internal waters. (As to the reference to the law of neutrality, this chapter will discuss this further in what follows.)

It is important to establish that there appears to be no factual dispute that U137 grounded on the Swedish coast without the permission of the Swedish government. On its face, this is a breach of Swedish sovereignty by the Soviet Union. The Soviet Union was obliged under Article 2(4) of the United Nations Charter to refrain from the threat or use of force against the territorial integrity or political independence of Sweden or any other state, and, whether by virtue of the customary or conventional international law of the sea, not to prejudice the peace, good order, or security of Sweden. It is hard to see how the uninvited presence of a foreign naval unit not exercising innocent passage was consistent with these obligations. The issues, therefore, become whether the Soviet Union did not breach its obligation to respect Sweden's sovereignty because of a situation of *force majeure* or distress, or because it was acting in its own self-defence against Sweden. There is no suggestion that Sweden was engaged in an armed attack against the Soviet Union at the time, or that there was a state of belligerency between the two states. There is no basis, therefore, upon which to consider a justification of self-defence, nor of action as a component of an armed conflict.

This leaves the question of *force majeure* or distress. In the Soviet version of events, this situation was a result of navigational error. Whilst the location of the grounding and subsequent submarine incursions into Swedish waters make this improbable, if it was the case, then its negligent character makes its less serious than an intentional breach of Sweden's sovereignty. Apparently, another unofficial Soviet version of events was that the crew were in fact drunk on their return from

22 Ibid.

the successful completion of an exercise.[23] Either way, the matter is then a reasonably straightforward matter of state responsibility of the Soviet Union in international law for the negligent actions of its submarine. The international law of state responsibility is not the primary concern of this book, and thus will not be further analysed in this chapter.

The more serious question is whether U137 was in Swedish waters intentionally and in breach of the obligations of the Soviet Union under Article 2(4) of the United Nations Charter and its conventional or customary obligations under the international law of the sea. If U137 was submerged in Swedish territorial waters then it was clearly acting contrary to paragraph 6 of Article 14 of the 1958 Convention as quoted previously, as well of at least Sweden's view of customary international law.

U137 could have sailed on the surface flying its flag through Sweden's territorial waters, although whether it may have done so without any prior notification to Sweden is not clear. However, the Swedish government stated in 2013, in response to a declaration made by Ecuador upon accession to the 1982 Law of the Sea Convention, that 'no vessels or aircraft need to notify or seek prior authorization from the Coastal State to exercise the right of innocent passage in accordance with the provisions of UNCLOS'.[24] There is nothing to suggest that this was a change in policy by the Swedish government, so it was likely of the same view in 1981. On the other hand, the Soviet Union maintained that warships must seek prior notification before entering its territorial sea. The lack of prior notification of the presence of U137 in Sweden's territorial sea appeared to be contrary to the Soviet Union's own view of international law.[25]

Even so, U137 ran aground in 'a restricted security zone nine miles southeast of the Karlskrona Naval Base'.[26] Parks stated that this was in internal waters,[27] and McCormick's description of Swedish internal waters at the time is consistent with this.[28] If this was the case, there was no justification in international law for the submarine to be there intentionally, neither on Sweden's nor the Soviet Union's view of the law. If there was no basis to claim *force majeure* or distress, the presence of U137 in Sweden's internal waters was a serious breach of Sweden's sovereignty.

23 McCormick, *Stranger Than Fiction: Soviet Submarine Operations in Swedish Waters*, above n 3.

24 *United Nations Treaty Collection*, Status of Treaties, above n 21.

25 David Larson, 'National Security Aspects of the United States Extension of the Territorial Sea to Twelve Nautical Miles' (1992) 2 *Territorial Sea Journal* 189, 205–206. See also the discussion in Chapter 8 regarding the change in the Soviet Union's views regarding warship passage in the territorial sea.

26 Froman, 'Uncharted Waters: Non-innocent Passage of Warships in the Territorial Sea', above n 9, 626.

27 W. Hays Parks, 'Air War and the Law of War' (1990) 32 *Air Force Law Review* 1, 82 n 267, citing Ries, 'Sweden's Defense at the Crossroads' (1989) 22 *International Defence Review* 1617–21 and M Leitenberg, *Soviet Submarine Operations in Swedish Waters, 1980–1986* (1987).

28 Act Concerning the Territorial Waters of Sweden of 3 June 1966, above n 17.

If this was the case, did it have any implications for the sovereign immunity of U137 and its crew?

B. Sovereign immunity of warships and crew, even if in violation of coastal state laws or security

It appears that Sweden respected the sovereign immunity of U137 at all times, in that Swedish authorities did not board it until Sweden had reached an agreement with the Soviet Union. This may have been a result of pragmatism on both sides. Sweden may not have wished to provoke its large and powerful neighbour. The Soviet Union may have wished to recover its submarine as soon as possible with minimal further incident. Similarly, Swedish authorities did not question the Soviet captain, Captain Second Rank (Lieutenant Commander) Gushchin, until after it had reached agreement to do so with the Soviet Union. Even if practical concerns determined the agreement between each state, it is still the case that, despite the apparent serious breach of Sweden's sovereignty, Sweden respected the sovereign immunity of U137 as a Soviet warship.[29] Even if Sweden soon after took the view that it could attack submerged contacts in its waters, as discussed in what follows, such breaches of its sovereignty did not waive the Soviet Union's sovereign immunity in respect of U137 or its crew. This would suggest that the 'Whiskey on the Rocks' incident actually reinforced the principle of sovereign immunity of warships in situations other than armed conflict, regardless of a whether a warship has breached the sovereignty of the coastal state. It would appear then, on this view, that a coastal state can either force a vessel out of its waters or possibly prevent it from leaving, but it cannot board the vessel or question its crew without the consent of the flag state.

C. Use of force against submerged contacts

The 'Whiskey on the Rocks' incident is significant for what it led to in terms of Sweden's use of force against submerged contacts in its waters. Whilst there was no use of force against U137, Sweden relied upon its apparent violation of Swedish sovereignty to justify subsequent actions. Notably, among others, the Harsfjarden incident lasted from 1 October to 1 November 1982 and involved the Royal Swedish Navy conducting anti-submarine warfare operations against multiple contacts in the vicinity of its largest naval base.[30] There were also frequent other similar incidents throughout the 1980s.[31] The incursions were said to involve submarines, mini-submarines, combat swimmers, and even a tracked submersible capable of

29 *1958 Convention* art 23 by implication preserves sovereign immunity of warships by not prescribing the enforcement measures available to a coastal state which it provides for other categories of vessel.
30 McCormick, *Stranger Than Fiction: Soviet Submarine Operations in Swedish Waters*, above n 3, 10–11.
31 Ibid, 3–6.

travelling along the sea bed.[32] The apparent purpose of these incursions was to test Swedish coastal defences both ashore and at sea, and included interfering with minefields.[33] The Swedes took the view that they could use force to compel a submerged contact to surface or in order to drive it out of Swedish waters. Swedish naval units were not to seek lethal destruction of submerged contacts[34] (except possibly in self-defence). To this end, Swedish naval units deployed torpedoes with reduced charge warheads designed to damage only rudders and screws.[35] They also deployed limpet mines, known as the *Malin*, which would attach to a hull and give off a locating signal, as well as a shaped charge, known as an *Elma*, which would also attach to a hull but cause an explosion large enough only to flood some compartments.[36]

The Swedes did not apparently succeed in driving any submarines to the surface, but it is not known the extent to which they damaged or drove out any others.[37] The interesting legal point is the apparent lack of protest at any of this use of force. The Soviet Union, unsurprisingly, did not accept responsibility for any of the incursions into Swedish waters and presumably did not protest the use of force for this reason.[38] The situation may have been different if Sweden had caused the loss of a submarine or significant loss of life. Even so, arguably, other states seem to have acquiesced in Sweden's practice of forcibly responding to unknown submerged contacts. This would suggest that customary international law permits the use of force in defence of a coastal state's sovereignty over its internal or territorial waters. This would either be to drive such contacts to the surface or out of a coastal state's waters, but not for the purpose of lethal destruction. Arguably, this would meet the proportionality requirements of self-defence in international law, as the threat from submerged contacts in coastal state waters is not necessarily lethal.[39] If it were,

32 Ibid, 11.
33 Ibid, 11–13.
34 Ibid, 14.
35 Ibid, 13.
36 Ibid.
37 Ibid, 1, 15–20.
38 Ibid, 14–15.
39 For a word of caution on the use of force in response to non-innocent passage by warships, see Froman, 'Uncharted Waters: Non-innocent Passage of Warships in the Territorial Sea', above n 9, 673–675; Ken Booth, *Law, Force and Diplomacy at Sea* (1985, Routledge Revivals 2014), 130–136, who also noted similar problems for Norway, sees the law as 'malleable' in this area, citing D.P. O'Connell, *The Influence of Law on Sea Power* (Naval Institute Press, 1975), 142–145. In the pages cited, O'Connell himself elaborates in some detail that the practice of a number of NATO and Warsaw Pact nations was to attack submerged contacts, or at least force them to the surface. O'Connell is ambivalent about the legality of such actions, noting that submerged passage may in fact be innocent, due to factors such as weather, but that submerged passage could also amount to an armed intrusion on the coastal state's sovereignty. He accepts that some force may be used, patiently, to force a vessel to the surface, but that attacking a submerged contact directly could still give rise to a right of self-defence on the part of the submerged contact. O'Connell states that any forceful response to the submerged contact must be proportionate to the military threat prevailing at the time. This appears to be the most persuasive view of the law still. O'Connell and Shearer restate

then the use of lethal force in defence against such contacts would arguably be less problematic. The international political character of Sweden as a neutral may have influenced the international acceptability of its actions, and therefore it is useful to turn now to this issue.

D. Law of neutrality

It is important to address the issue of neutrality in this case, even if only to discount it. Sweden adopted a position of armed neutrality in the Cold War.[40] This was a political and military posture, as well as being to some extent a legal posture in so far as Sweden was not formally allied to either major bloc. As far as the law of naval operations is concerned, it does not make much difference to the 'Whiskey on the Rocks' incident or subsequent submarine incursions into Swedish waters. There was no state of armed conflict between the Warsaw Pact and NATO states as, despite the tensions, there were no actual hostilities. Sweden therefore was not a neutral in terms of the Convention Concerning the Rights and Duties of Neutral Powers in Case of Naval Warfare (XIII Convention), adopted at The Hague on 18 October 1907,[41] as this would require the existence of a naval war and belligerent parties. Even on a view that the Cold War was an actual armed conflict, it would have made little difference to the rights and obligations of Sweden and the Soviet Union in respect to U137 or the other submerged contacts in Swedish waters. Article 10 of 1907 Hague XIII states that mere passage through territorial waters of a neutral is not a violation of neutrality, which would have permitted Soviet submarines to engage in surfaced transit of Swedish territorial waters provided they showed their flag.[42] Article 5 of the same Convention prohibits the use of neutral ports and waters as a base of operations by belligerents, which would have prevented submerged Soviet operations in Swedish territorial or internal waters. As to Sweden's forceful response to incursions, Article 25 of 1907 Hague XIII states:

> A neutral Power is bound to exercise such surveillance as the means at its disposal allow to prevent any violation of the provisions of the above Articles occurring in its ports or roadsteads or in its waters.

---

these views in essentially similar terms, with an emphasis on the point that it is a submarine's behaviour that renders its passage non-innocent, rather than the mere fact of it being submerged, in D.P. O'Connell (edited by I.A. Shearer) *The International Law of the Sea: Volume I* (Clarendon, Oxford, 1982), 294–297. Yoram Dinstein has no reservations in regard to the use of force against submarines in such cases, citing state practice, but is more equivocal with regard to surface warships in *War, Aggression and Self Defence* (6th ed, Cambridge, 2017), 214–215; the German and US Commander's Handbooks are notably silent on this question.

40 McCormick, *Stranger Than Fiction: Soviet Submarine Operations in Swedish Waters*, above n 3, vii-viii.

41 205 CTS 395 (entered into force 26 January 1910). Sweden and Russia both ratified on 27 November 1909 (<https://verdragenbank.overheid.nl/en/Verdrag/Details/003328> – Netherlands Ministry of Foreign Affairs as depositary).

42 1958 Convention art 14.

This would arguably have justified Sweden trying to force submerged contacts to the surface or out of its waters. Nothing in the Convention Concerning the Rights and Duties of Neutral Powers in Case of Naval Warfare would have required a different approach to the sovereign immunity of U137 as observed by either Sweden or the Soviet Union.[43]

A final important point to note in respect of neutrality is that the only two known parties to the 'Whiskey on the Rocks' incident or the subsequent operations against submerged contacts were Sweden and the Soviet Union. Sweden could not have been a neutral third party, as there were only two parties. If there was a situation of belligerency, it was between Sweden and the Soviet Union, which renders considerations of neutrality unnecessary.

IV. Enduring relevance and conclusion

It comes now to consider the enduring relevance, or otherwise, of the legal outcomes of the 'Whiskey on the Rocks' incident and the events that followed it. They did not actually change, refine, or develop the law in any particular way. They did, however, provide some significant state practice on some important maritime operations law issues. First, the presence of a Soviet submarine aground on the Swedish coast simply reinforced that there was no internationally lawful way that this could occur. Only negligence or malign intention could have placed it there. There appeared to be no question that the international law of the sea did not permit submerged transit in foreign territorial or internal waters. Second, the respect for the sovereign immunity of U137 and the fact that its crew were not arrested, despite the appearance of a serious violation of Swedish sovereignty, places great emphasis on the importance of this principle. The pragmatic concerns on the part of the Swedes and the Soviets which may have driven this respect might actually underscore this importance. For the Swedes not to intrude upon sovereign immunity without formal agreement, or for the Soviets to acknowledge that formally conceding it to some extent was a valuable negotiating point, only reinforces the value of sovereign immunity of warships.

However, the more interesting issue, and possibly that of the most enduring significance, is the apparent widespread acceptance of the use of force against unknown submerged contacts in a coastal state's internal waters or territorial sea. The important limitation of proportionality is also significant. Sweden did not appear to kill anyone or destroy any vessel in its anti-submarine operations, so it may be that such operations are internationally acceptable provided that the use of force is proportionate to the threat faced. Lethal force may only be acceptable where the threat is lethal, whereas submerged intruders that do not pose a lethal threat may only be ejected

43 Sweden was not required to detain U137 under art 24 as this is a discretionary provision, which in any case applies to detaining non-compliant warships in port rather than those that have run aground.

with non-lethal, even if very forceful, means. On the other hand, the consequences of the 'Whiskey on the Rocks' incident and subsequent operations against submerged contacts have little significance for the law of neutrality in naval warfare. It did not appear to apply and, even if it did, it would have made little difference to the rights and obligations of Sweden and the Soviet Union.

The question then arises of the enduring significance of these incidents for maritime operations law. They are still relevant for what appear to be two main reasons. The first is that accidents with warships and military aircraft do happen. When such accidents lead to the presence of warships or military aircraft in coastal states where they are uninvited and unwelcome, quite likely because the coastal state sees itself as damaged or at least intruded upon by them, sovereign immunity can be an issue. There are some common elements between the 'Whiskey on the Rocks' incident and the landing of a U.S. EP3 maritime patrol aircraft on China's Hainan Island in 2000.[44] Both U137 and the EP3 were considered to be spying or intruding upon the coastal state, both ended up in a situation of distress in the coastal state, both likely contained sensitive information and equipment, both had crews to be repatriated, and both could claim sovereign immunity. There are some other important differences between the cases, such as the U.S. position being that it was outside Chinese territorial waters and was damaged by a Chinese fighter aircraft, but the point remains that such situations do occur and sovereign immunity will likely be an issue each time. The 'Whiskey on the Rocks' incident goes towards state practice emphasising the importance of sovereign immunity in future like cases.

The second reason for the enduring significance of the 'Whiskey on the Rocks' incident is that it enhanced the perception of the threat to Sweden of submerged contacts in its waters, which led to the forceful countermeasures in subsequent years. In a situation of rising inter-state tensions in Northeast Asia, the South China Sea, and on the borders of the Russian Federation, the presence of unknown submerged contacts in coastal state waters may excite a significant perception of threat, as recent reports suggest. Swedish operations in the 1980s against submerged contacts could well have provided the justification for the use of force against such intrusions. It could only be hoped, however, that Swedish restraint from using deliberately lethal force may also be remembered in order to prevent such incidents escalating from mere violations of sovereignty into something altogether more serious.

44 See Johnathan Odom, 'A China in the Bull Shop? Comparing the Rhetoric of a Rising China with the Reality of the International Law of the Sea' (2012) 17 *Ocean and Coastal Law Journal* 201.

PART IV
Law of naval warfare

13

RMS LUSITANIA

Cameron Moore

I. Introduction

The sinking of the Royal Mail Ship *Lusitania* on 7 May 1915 remains an infamous incident among the horrors of the First World War.[1] The significance of the loss lies in the apparently flagrant disregard for the laws of naval warfare early in the war by Germany, as much it does in the tragic and large-scale loss of innocent life aboard a prestigious passenger liner close to its port of destination. It is worth remembering that this occurred only three years after the loss of *RMS Titanic* on the same route, an incident synonymous with accidental maritime tragedy, yet in this case the action was deliberate.[2] The notoriety of the sinking of *Lusitania* defies the point that it was perhaps one merchant vessel sinking by submarines among many in that conflict.[3] It was also not the greatest loss of life in submarine warfare,[4] nor even the immediate cause of the entry of the United States into the war. The incident did, however, have a strong influence on the decision of the United States to enter the war two years later,[5] which in turn contributed to the defeat of Germany. The

1 Report of the *Wreck Commissioner's Investigation* into the Loss of Lusitania *('Wreck Commissioner's Investigation')* 17 July 1915 (Lord Mersey, Wreck Commissioner) 7.

2 David Ramsay, *Lusitania: Saga and Myth* (Norton, 2001) 2–3, 253, 266–267. See, e.g., *Wreck Commissioner's Investigation*, Transcript of the Second Day of Hearings, Examination of George Little, Third Engineer.

3 There had been at least 20 sinkings by German submarines up to that point in the war; see, e.g., *The Lusitania* 251 F 715 (SDNY 1918) 720 (Mayer J).

4 The largest loss of life was 9,400 German evacuees, half of them children, in January 1945 in the sinking of the *MV Wilhelm Gustloff* by a Soviet submarine; Timothy Nelson, 'The *Lusitania* and the Law' (25 February 2015) 253 (36) *New York Law Journal*, citing Cathryn Prince, *Death in the Baltic: The World War II Sinking of the Wilhelm Gustloff* (2013).

5 Nelson, 'The *Lusitania* and the Law', above n 4, citing President Wilson's 1917 speech to Congress in seeking a declaration of war against Germany referring to the loss of American life due to Germany's 'reckless and lawless' submarine warfare, 55 Cong. Rec. 305, 103, 104 (1917).

DOI: 10.4324/9781003307013-17

sinking of the *Lusitania* was therefore a pivotal incident in the First World War, as well as being an infamous maritime incident.

As to the incident itself, according to the report of the Wreck Commissioner's Investigation, *Lusitania* was a large, fast luxury cruise liner sailing from New York to Liverpool on its scheduled route.[6] It was a Cunard Line vessel sailing unescorted under a British flag.[7] Without warning at 2:11 pm on a clear and calm afternoon on the high seas, but within sight of the Old Head of Kinsale, Ireland, a torpedo struck the ship on the starboard side.[8] It sank 20 minutes later with the loss of 1,198 lives, most of whom drowned in the sea.[9] The torpedo came from German submarine *U20*.[10] *KapitanLeutnant* Schwieger wrote in his war diary at the time that he had only fired one torpedo but saw a second explosion.[11] He may initially have thought that he had fired into a troop ship, but could not fire a second torpedo into the mass of people he could see trying to escape the sinking ship.[12] He notes how quickly it was sinking.[13]

As to the legal significance of the incident, it gave rise to a diplomatic exchange of notes between the United States and Germany shortly afterwards,[14] a Wreck Commissioner's Court of Inquiry in 1915,[15] an insurance case against Cunard Line in New York in 1918,[16] an international arbitration between the United States and Germany in 1923,[17] and also – less relevantly for this book – salvage cases in the English Admiralty jurisdiction in 1986[18] and in the U.S. courts in the 1990s.[19]

From the incident and these cases and inquiries, three key issues emerge of most relevance to this book. The first and most obvious is whether it was lawful for the German submarine to target and sink *Lusitania* deliberately and without warning. A second issue is the presence of a quantity of munitions aboard *Lusitania*, bound for the British government. A third – but perhaps equally important – issue was the significance of the presence of 197 neutral U.S. citizens onboard, 128 of whom died.[20] It would appear that the adverse strategic consequences for Germany

6 *Wreck Commissioner's Investigation*, above n 1, 5, 6; Ramsay provides a thorough pre-war history of the ship, above n 2, 19–32.
7 *The Lusitania*, above n 3, 717.
8 *Wreck Commissioner's Investigation*, above n 1, 7.
9 Ibid, 6, 7.
10 Robert Brammer, 'The Sinking of the *Lusitania*' Law Library of Congress Blog, 29 May 2015, <https://blogs.loc.gov/law/2015/05/the-sinking-of-the-lusitania/>.
11 Ramsay, *Lusitania: Saga and Myth*, above n 2, 81–82.
12 Ibid.
13 Ibid.
14 Cited below.
15 *Wreck Commissioner's Investigation*, above n 1.
16 *The Lusitania*, above n 3.
17 Opinion in the *Lusitania* Cases, 1 November 1923, *United Nations Reports of International Arbitral Awards*, Vol VII, 32; also, Maud Thompson de Gennes (United States) v Germany, 11 March 1925, *United Nations Reports of International Arbitral Awards*, Vol VII, 166.
18 *Pierce v Bemis*; The Lusitania [1986] QB 384.
19 *Bemis v Lusitania* (1998) 523 US 1093, 140 L Ed 2d 791.
20 Opinion in the *Lusitania* Cases, 1 November 1923, 7 RIAA 32, 33.

in taking the lives of so many civilians, particularly the neutral U.S. citizens, far outweighed any tactical or operational advantage it may have gained in sinking *Lusitania*. Although the involvement of the UK and U.S. governments in transporting munitions aboard *Lusitania* does not excuse the sinking by Germany, it also raises questions as to the extent to which doing so nonetheless unnecessarily put civilian lives at risk. Questions of targeting or endangering civilians, as well as interfering with the interests of neutrals, are no less important today, so the *Lusitania* remains of enduring significance in any consideration of significant maritime operational incidents. It is also the case that, despite periods of unrestricted submarine warfare in both world wars, the law as it would apply to the sinking of *Lusitania* has not really changed. If anything, the sinking of the *Lusitania* still underscores the value of the rule against attacking merchant ships, particularly passenger ships, without warning. However, before addressing these legal issues, it is important to place the sinking of *Lusitania* in the broader factual context of the First World War in 1915.

II. Background

The sinking of *Lusitania* occurred less than a year into the war. It appeared to be a completely unexpected turn of events, as far as the travelling public was concerned. Germany had declared a war zone around the British Isles[21] and the Imperial German Embassy had even placed advertisements in U.S. newspapers, published on the day of sailing, directly next to the advertisement for passage on the *Lusitania*. The advertisement read:

> Travellers intending to embark on the Atlantic voyage are reminded that a state of war exists between Germany and her allies and Great Britain and her allies; that the zone of war includes the waters adjacent to the British Isles; that, in accordance with formal notice given by the Imperial German Government, vessels flying the flag of Great Britain or of any of her allies are liable to destruction in these waters, and that travellers sailing in the war zone on ships of Great Britain or her allies do so at their own risk.
> Imperial German Embassy, April 22, 1915. Washington, D. C.[22]

Even so, in finding that Cunard Line was not negligent in the 1918 insurance case titled *The Lusitania*, Mayer J stated 'No trans-Atlantic passenger liner, and certainly none carrying American citizens, had been torpedoed up to that time'.[23] No one apparently thought that the German notice to the public meant that passenger ships would be attacked without warning. The expectation appeared to be that international law would still be observed in the terms stated in a diplomatic note to Germany of 9 June 1915:

21 *The Lusitania*, above n 3, 721.
22 Ibid.
23 Ibid, 731.

> Only her actual resistance to capture or refusal to stop when ordered to do so for the purpose of visit and search could have afforded the commander of the submarine any justification for so much as putting the lives of those on board the ship in jeopardy.[24]

It is important to recognise that the British government had tested the patience of the U.S. government as much as the German government had in relation to respect for the interests of neutrals, but Germany's action in sinking *Lusitania* decidedly shifted American opinion in Britain's favour.[25] O'Connell discusses British Admiralty orders of January and February 1915 that its merchant ships should show neutral colours as a *ruse de guerre* and resemble neutral vessels as much as possible, and that they should also attempt to ram enemy submarines.[26] Further, the Admiralty restricted neutral passage through the North Sea to channels where blockade supervision would be possible, while mining the other approaches.[27] There had also been an exchange of notes between the United States and Germany with respect to submarine warfare prior to the sinking of *Lusitania*. The German Note of 4 February 1915 stated:

Proclamation

1. The waters surrounding Great Britain and Ireland, including the whole English Channel, are hereby declared to be a war zone. On and after the 18th of February, 1915, every enemy merchant ship found in the said war zone will be destroyed without its being always possible to avert the dangers threatening the crews and passengers on that account.
2. Even neutral ships are exposed to danger in the war zone, as in view of the misuse of neutral flags ordered on January 31 by the British government, and of the accidents of naval war, it cannot always be avoided to strike even neutral ships in attacks that are directed at enemy ships.
3. Northward navigation around the Shetland Islands, in the eastern waters of the North Sea, and in a strip of not less than 30 miles width along the Netherlands coast is in no danger.

Von Pohl
Chief of the Admiral Staff of the Navy
Berlin, February 4, 1915[28]

24 Ibid, 733.
25 O'Connell, *The Influence of Law on Sea Power* (Manchester, 1975), 45–47.
26 Ibid.
27 Ibid.
28 *The Lusitania*, above n 3, 719.

The United States protested in its reply of 10 February 1915.[29] Importantly, Mayer J notes that on the same day, the United States also protested to Britain. This was in relation to *Lusitania* flying the U.S. flag on its voyage from New York to Liverpool on 30 January 1915. Britain responded that this was done at the request of embarking passengers who were U.S. citizens, to ensure their safety in light of the risk of the ship being torpedoed without warning.[30]

In noting these exchanges and that, since 30 January 1915 and in the vicinity of the *Lusitania's* trans-Atlantic route, German submarines had sunk 20 merchant vessels, chased two more which escaped, and damaged another, Mayer J still took the view that Germany had not indicated it would act contrary to settled international law that obliged it to safeguard the lives of passengers.[31]

III. Analysis and outcomes

A. The lawfulness of the sinking of the Lusitania*: law of naval warfare obligations at the time*

Despite the various Hague Conventions of 1907, no treaty existed in 1915 governing attacks on enemy merchant vessels. The Convention Relative to Certain Restrictions with Regard to the Exercise of the Right of Capture in Naval Warfare (XI Convention)[32] did not address attacks on merchant ships. It only provided for exemption of certain vessels from capture, inviolability of postal correspondence, and the prisoner-of-war status of captured crew depending on their enemy or neutral national status. Indeed, the issue may have been so settled in customary international law as not to justify a specific treaty rule. The preamble states that the treaty only addresses 'principles which have hitherto remained in the uncertain domain of controversy'. The London Declaration Concerning the Laws of Naval War of 1909, to which Germany, Britain and the United States were signatories,[33] only addressed capture – rather than destruction – of enemy merchant vessels. Even though it did not formally enter into force, it reflected customary international law at the time and was actually formally abandoned by the Allied Powers on 7 July 1916.[34] In 1912, Oppenheim's second edition of *International Law: Volume*

29 Ibid.

30 Ibid.

31 Ibid, 720.

32 205 CTS 367 (entered into force 26 January 1910). Germany, Britain and the United States all ratified on 27 November 1909 <www.icrc.org/applic/ihl/ihl.nsf/States.xsp?xp_viewStates=XPages_NORMStatesParties&xp_treatySelected=230>.

33 <www.icrc.org/applic/ihl/ihl.nsf/INTRO/255>.

34 The Maritime Rights Order in Council of 1916 (7 July 1916) as reproduced in H A Smith, *The Law and Customs of the Sea* (3rd ed, Stevens & Sons, 1959) 250; Adam Roberts and Richard Guelff, *Documents on the Laws of War* (3rd ed, Oxford, 2000), 127, being the Prefatory Note to the *1936 London Procès-Verbal Relating to the Rules of Submarine Warfare Set Forth in Part IV of the Treaty of London of 22 April 1930* (opened for signature 6 November 1936) UKTS 29 (1936) Cmd 5302 (entered into force 6 November 1936).

II – War and Neutrality is unequivocal in stating that 'Enemy merchantmen may be attacked only if they refuse to submit to visit after having been duly signalled to do so'.[35]

Each proceeding arising from the sinking of *Lusitania* takes a similar position, including the eventual German admission of liability. Lord Mersey, as Wreck Commissioner, stated:

> Sir Edward Carson, when opening the case, described the course adopted by the German Government in directing this attack as 'contrary to International Law and the usages of war,' and as constituting, according to the law of all civilized countries, 'a deliberate attempt to murder the passengers on board the ship.'
>
> This statement is, in my opinion, true, and it is made in language not a whit too strong for the occasion . . . . German authorities on the laws of war at sea themselves establish beyond all doubt that though in some cases the destruction of an enemy trader may be permissible, there is always an obligation first to secure the safety of the lives of those on board.[36]

Mayer J also cited abundant references to this effect.[37] His Honour also noted the consistency in the British, U.S., Russian, and Japanese prize laws before quoting section 116 of the *German Prize Code*, in force at the time of the sinking:

> Before proceeding to a destruction of the vessel, the safety of all persons on board, and, so far as possible, their effects, is to be provided for, and all ship's papers and other evidentiary material, which, according to the views of the persons at interest, is of value for the formulation of the judgment of the prize court, are to be taken over by the commander.[38]

There appears to have been little question as to the existence and content of the rule in customary international law. The 1923 arbitration between the United States and Germany proceeded on the basis that Germany had admitted liability

35 L. Oppenheim, *International Law: A Treatise: Volume II: War and Neutrality* (2nd ed, Longmans, 1912), 226.

36 *Wreck Commissioner's Investigation*, above n 1, 7–8.

37 *The Lusitania*, above n3, 734: Phillimore on International Law (3rd Ed.) vol. 3, p. 584; Sir Sherston Baker on First Steps in International Law, p. 236; G. B. Davis on Elements of International Law, pp. 358, 359; A. Pearce Higgins on War and the Private Citizen, pp. 33, 78, referring to proceedings of Institute of International Law at Turin in 1882; Creasy on International Law, p. 562, quoting Chief Justice Cockburn in his judgement in the Geneva Arbitration; L.A. Atherby-Jones on Commerce in War, p. 529; Professor Holland's article, Naval War College, 1907, p. 82; Oppenheim on International Law (2nd Ed.) vol. 2, pp. 244, 311; Taylor on International Law, p. 572; Westlake on International Law (2nd Ed.) p. 309, part II; Halleck on International Law, vol. 2, pp. 15, 16; Vattel's Law of Nations (Chitty's Ed.) 362.

38 *The Lusitania*, above n 3, 736

in its diplomatic note of 4 February 1916 and therefore primarily concerned itself with the measure of damages.[39]

Germany did not admit liability straight away, however, and in the subsequent exchange of notes with the United States, provided a defence of its actions. As this chapter will discuss, these arguments have continued to have resonance in respect to the sinking of *Lusitania*, and in respect of unrestricted submarine warfare generally, ever since. It is worth quoting the initial German diplomatic note of 28 May 1915 reasonably fully before analysing these arguments.

> The Imperial Government begs in this connection to point out that the *Lusitania* was one of the largest and fastest English commerce steamers, constructed with Government funds as auxiliary cruisers, and is expressly included in the navy list published by the British Admiralty.
>
> It is, moreover, known to the Imperial Government from reliable information furnished by its officials and neutral passengers that for some time practically all the more valuable English merchant vessels have been provided with guns, ammunition and other weapons, and reinforced with a crew specially practiced in manning guns. According to reports at hand here, the *Lusitania* when she left New York undoubtedly had guns on board which were mounted under decks and masked . . . .
>
> High rewards have been offered by the British Government as a special incentive for the destruction of the submarines by merchant vessels, and such rewards have already been paid out. In view of these facts, which are satisfactorily known to it, the Imperial Government is unable to consider English merchant vessels any longer as 'undefended territory' in the zone of maritime war designated by the Admiralty Staff of the Imperial German Navy, the German commanders are consequently no longer in a position to observe the rules of capture otherwise usual and with which they invariably complied before this.
>
> Lastly, the Imperial Government must specially point out that on her last trip the *Lusitania*, as on earlier occasions, had Canadian troops and munitions on board, including no less than 5,400 cases of ammunition destined for the destruction of brave German soldiers.
>
> The German Government believes that it acts in just self-defence when it seeks to protect the lives of its soldiers by destroying ammunition destined for the enemy with the means of war at its command. The English steamship company must have been aware of the dangers to which passengers on board the *Lusitania* were exposed under the circumstances.[40]

39 Opinion in the *Lusitania* Cases, above n 20, 32 and 33, which became an oft-cited authority in U.S. case law on awards of damages; Nelson, 'The *Lusitania* and the Law', above n 4.

40 United States, *Foreign Relations of the United States*, Washington DC, 1915 Supplement, 419–421. The *Wreck Commissioner's Investigation* addresses the substance, without reproducing the text, of the note, 6.

B. The significance of Lusitania's contribution to the war effort

Should the points made by the German government have made any difference to the lawfulness of the sinking of *Lusitania*? The British government did not deny the points with respect to the carriage of some munitions (being 4,200 rifle cartridges),[41] the ship's design – although not its use – for Admiralty purposes,[42] and the instructions to British merchant ships in respect of countering German submarines.[43] The key differences in the German argument are that *Lusitania* was actually armed and that she was carrying troops and explosives. Even if all the German factual assertions are accepted, would they have authorised the attack without warning?

The carriage of explosives would have created no exception to the rule about attacks on merchant ships. As discussed, the only exception was when a merchant ship resisted visit and search by an enemy warship. There is no suggestion of resistance to a request for visit and search on the part of *Lusitania*, so the remaining question then is whether she could have been classified as a naval auxiliary rather than a merchant ship. If she had been classified as a naval auxiliary, then the rules would have been different.

There is no evidence to support the view that *Lusitania* was armed, which raises the question of what level of certainty Germany would have to have had to argue successfully that it was attacking a naval auxiliary, even if mistakenly. The Convention Relating to the Conversion of Merchant Ships into Warships (VII Convention)[44] required that *Lusitania* be under the direct authority of the British government, bear the external distinguishing marks of a warship of the Royal Navy, be under the command of a commissioned naval officer, the crew subject to military discipline, observe the laws and customs of war, and be announced as a conversion in the list of warships. *Lusitania* only really met the first criteria in that her sailing was under Admiralty direction.[45] It would have been difficult for Germany to argue that it was mistaken about the other criteria. *Lusitania's* listing as

41 *Wreck Commissioner's Investigation*, above n 1, 6. In *The Lusitania*, above n 3, Mayer J stated, at 717: 'She did carry some 18 fuse cases and 125 shrapnel cases, consisting merely of empty shells, without any powder charge, 4,200 cases of safety cartridges, and 189 cases of infantry equipment, such as leather fittings, pouches, and the like'.

42 *Wreck Commissioner's Investigation*, above n1, 1; Ramsay, Lusitania: Saga and Myth, above n 2, 33–36.

43 *Wreck Commissioner's Investigation*, above n 1, 9.

44 205 CTS 319 (entered into force 26 January 1910). Germany and Britain ratified on 27 November 1909. The United States neither signed nor ratified. <www.icrc.org/applic/ihl/ihl.nsf/States.xsp?xp_viewStates=XPages_NORMStatesParties&xp_treatySelected=210>.

45 *Wreck Commissioner's Investigation*, above n1, 9. During the war, Cunard was not permitted to communicate directly with her whilst she was at sea; only the Admiralty could, *Wreck Commissioner's Investigation*, Transcript of the Second Day of Hearings, Examination of Alfred Booth, Chairman of Cunard Line.

an auxiliary indicated that she could be converted into a warship rather than that she was.[46]

Could the German government have argued that *Lusitania* was a lawful target by virtue of her employment rather than her formal status? This is more a question of evidence. The German government could point to *Lusitania's* use in carrying munitions,[47] and the arming of other auxiliary cruisers and merchantmen and their belligerent actions such as ramming.[48] (There was no evidence to suggest that *Lusitania* was carrying Canadian troops at this or any other time.[49]) Was this enough to excuse the attack on *Lusitania*? There was at the time no proportionality test for attacks on military objectives as now found in Additional Protocol I to the Geneva Conventions,[50] but even so, the risk to the lives of so many innocent passengers had to weigh against the military advantage to be gained from an attack without warning. The law at the time provided for stop, visit, and search to address the use of *Lusitania* to support the war effort and to take forceful action only if she resisted. Even so, there was a serious risk to the German submarine from gunfire and ramming if it surfaced to carry out the visit and search.[51] Was this simply an acceptable risk to the submarines if they were to be employed in intercepting passenger ships? Alternatively, noting that the first U.S. protest of 13 May 1915 commented upon 'the practical impossibility of employing submarines in the destruction of commerce without disregarding those rules of fairness, reason, justice, and humanity, which all modern opinion regards as imperative', should submarines be employed in intercepting passenger ships at all?[52] The answer to both questions at the time appears to have been in the negative. In June 1915, the Kaiser ordered that no more passenger ships were to be sunk.[53] The note from the German Ambassador in Washington admitting liability to the United States Secretary of State of 4 February 1916 advised that:

> The Imperial German Government having subsequent to the event issued to its naval officers the new instructions which are now prevailing, expresses

46 Ramsay, *Lusitania: Saga and Myth*, above n 2, 33–36.

47 Article 6 of the Convention Concerning the Rights and Duties of Neutral Powers in Case of Naval Warfare (XIII Convention) did prevent the supply of munitions, adopted at The Hague on 18 October 1907 (opened for signature 18 October 1907) 205 CTS 395 (entered into force 26 January 1910). Germany ratified on 27 November 1909. The United States ratified on 3 December 1909. Britain signed on 18 October 1907 but did not ratify. (<https://verdragenbank.overheid.nl/en/Verdrag/Details/003328> – Netherlands Ministry of Foreign Affairs as depositary).

48 O'Connell, The Influence of Law on Sea Power, above n 25, 46.

49 Ramsay, *Lusitania: Saga and Myth*, above n 2, 194–195.

50 Protocol Additional to the Geneva Conventions of 12 August 1949 and Relating to the Protection of Victims of International Armed Conflicts, (opened for signature 8 June 1977) 1125 UNTS 3 (entered into force 7 December 1978) ('Additional Protocol I') art 52(2).

51 O'Connell, The Influence of Law on Sea Power, above n 25, 46.

52 United States, *Foreign Relations of the United States*, Washington DC, 1915 Supplement, 393, 395.

53 O'Connell, *The Influence of Law on Sea Power*, above n 25, 46; Ramsay, *Lusitania: Saga and Myth*, above n 2, 219. The German Note to the United States of 8 July 1915 addressing safe passage for

> profound regret that citizens of the United States suffered by the sinking of the *Lusitania* and assuming liability therefor offers to make reparation for the life of the citizens of the United States who were lost by the payment of a suitable indemnity.[54]

On 4 May 1916, the German Foreign Office advised U.S. Ambassador Gerard:

> The German submarine forces have had, in fact, orders to conduct submarine warfare in accordance with the general principles of visit and search and destruction of merchant vessels as recognised by international law; the sole exception being the conduct of warfare against the enemy trade carried on enemy freight ships that are encountered in the war zone surrounding Great Britain . . . . The German government, guided by this idea, notifies the government of the United States that the German naval forces have received the following orders: In accordance with the general principles of visit and search and destruction of merchant vessels recognized by international law, such vessels, both within and without the area declared as naval war zone, shall not be sunk without warning and without saving human lives, unless these ships attempt to escape or offer resistance.[55]

This admission of liability and change of practice was to the U.S. government rather than the British government but was still an admission by Germany that firing torpedoes into *Lusitania* without warning was unacceptable. This raises the question of whether the presence of United States citizens onboard *Lusitania*, and the death of 128 of them, made any difference to the lawfulness of the sinking. Would it have been lawful to attack only British subjects, being 'enemy individuals'?

C. The significance of the neutral U.S. citizens

Oppenheim stated that enemy individuals onboard an attacked or seized enemy vessel but not part of the naval forces may not be directly attacked or killed, 'although they are exposed to all injury indirectly resulting from an attack on or by their vessel'.[56] This must presumably be from a lawful attack. With respect to neutral individuals, Oppenheim did not state an equivalent rule as it may have seemed obvious that neutrals could not be attacked, stating instead that 'Neutrals have a right to demand that their intercourse, and in especial their commerce, with the

---

some passenger ships appears to reflect this order to some extent, United States, *Foreign Relations of the United States*, Washington DC, 1915 Supplement, 463–466.

54 Maud Thompson de Gennes (United States) v Germany, 11 March 1925, 7 RIAA 166, 167.

55 *The Lusitania*, above n 3, 734.

56 Oppenheim, International Law: A Treatise: Volume II: War and Neutrality, above n 35, 251.

enemy shall not be suppressed'.[57] There is nothing in Oppenheim or the exchange of notes or proceedings subsequent to the sinking to suggest that an attack by a belligerent became unlawful only because it affected neutrals indirectly. If it was also unlawful to attack enemy civilians directly, but not unlawful that they suffer indirect injury, then it appears that a similar rule effectively applied to neutrals. The main issue appeared to be that such indirect effects did not amount to a suppression of the rights of neutrals to conduct impartial relations with the enemy.

The main difference with respect to the impact upon the U.S. citizens of the sinking of *Lusitania* was that Germany and the United States maintained diplomatic relations at the time.[58] The sinking was unlawful whether U.S. citizens were affected or not. The fact that they were affected by a deliberate act of Germany which was contrary to its international obligations went to the diplomatic relationship between the two nations. This was a matter of state responsibility for which Germany accepted liability.[59] This was unlikely to occur between Germany and Britain, given the state of war between them.

The impact on neutrals changed the strategic and diplomatic nature of the incident but not its lawfulness. The first U.S. protest note from the Secretary of State to Germany, on 13 May 1915, restated

> the rule that the lives of non-combatants, whether they be of neutral citizenship or citizens of one of the nations at war, cannot lawfully or rightfully be put in jeopardy by the capture or destruction of an unarmed merchantman, and recognize also, as all other nations do, the obligation to take the usual precaution of visit and search to ascertain whether a suspected merchantman is in fact of belligerent nationality or is in fact carrying contraband of war under a neutral flag.[60]

The second U.S. protest note of 9 June 1915 added: 'The fact that more than one hundred American citizens were among those who perished made it the duty of the Government of the United States to speak of these things'.[61] A third note of protest to Germany on 21 July closed with the telling words:

> Repetition by the commanders of German naval vessels of acts in contravention of those rights must be regarded by the Government of the United States, when they affect American citizens, as deliberately unfriendly.[62]

57 Ibid, 379.

58 As shown by the exchange of diplomatic notes already referred to.

59 *de Gennes*, above n 54.

60 United States, *Foreign Relations of the United States*, Washington DC, 1915 Supplement, 393, 394.

61 United States, *Foreign Relations of the United States*, Washington DC, 1915 Supplement, 436, 437.

62 United States, *Foreign Relations of the United States*, Washington DC, 1915 Supplement, 480, 482.

These words make clear the international significance of the deaths of neutral U.S. citizens in the sinking of the *Lusitania*. Their deaths were no more unlawful than those of the British passengers onboard, but the diplomatic consequences of their loss were of greater significance. Continued deliberate unlawful killing of neutral citizens in the First World War would – as would be likely with any war – have profound strategic ramifications.

IV. Contemporary significance

On 17 July 2014, 298 people died when Malaysian Airlines Flight MH 17 crashed as the result of a missile strike over a war zone in eastern Ukraine.[63] None survived.[64] The incident was a matter of international outrage and condemnation, including debate in the UN Security Council.[65] The responses to this incident and the sinking of *Lusitania* have much in common. Although Malaysia had no part in the conflict in Ukraine, the sudden, tragic, and entirely avoidable loss of innocent civilian life in a widely used form of international passenger transport in both cases was truly shocking. Both were forms of gross violence that could have affected anyone, not just those involved in the conflict. It is hard not to see the sinking of *Lusitania* in light of the subsequent conduct of submarine warfare in the First and Second World Wars. The decline of ocean travel in favour of air travel for passengers also places the sinking in another age. It is important, however, to consider how shocking the sinking of *Lusitania* was at the time by equating it to modern experience. This aids an appreciation of whether the law is or should be any different now.

In essence, the relevant law really is not any different now – nor should it be.[66] Two key considerations in the century since the sinking of *Lusitania* are the practice of submarine warfare and the development of the law of naval warfare.

To address the subsequent practice of submarine warfare first, O'Connell assesses both world wars together in his seminal work *The Influence of Law on Sea Power*.[67] He indicates that in both wars, there was some justification for submarines to attack merchant vessels without warning on the grounds that the merchant ships were in convoys, they were armed, or that they always resisted visit and search.[68] This would provide some lawful basis for attack without warning in terms of the exception within the customary international law rule discussed previously. Perhaps more importantly, after both wars there was condemnation of the practice of attack without warning against merchant ships where these

63 Dutch Safety Board, Crash of Malaysia Airlines Flight MH 17, Hrabove, Ukraine, 17 July 2014, 9.

64 Ibid.

65 SC Res 2166, UN SCOR, 7221st mtg, UN Doc S/Res/2166 (21 July 2014).

66 Colombos expressed a similar view in 1967 in C J Colombos, *The International Law of the Sea* (6th ed, McKay, 1967), 788–794.

67 O'Connell, *The Influence of Law on Sea Power*, above n 25.

68 Ibid, 47, and 44–52 generally.

exceptions did not apply.[69] The London Procès-Verbal of 1936, in light of the experience of the First World War, effectively restated the customary international law that existed prior to the First World War. The substantive provisions in their entirety are as follows:

> (1) In their action with regard to merchant ships, submarines must conform to the rules of international law to which surface vessels are subject.
> (2) In particular, except in the case of persistent refusal to stop on being duly summoned, or of active resistance to visit or search, a warship, whether surface vessel or submarine, may not sink or render incapable of navigation a merchant vessel without having first placed passengers, crew and ship's papers in a place of safety. For this purpose the ship's boats are not regarded as a place of safety unless the safety of the passengers and crew is assured, in the existing sea and weather conditions, by the proximity of land, or the presence of another vessel which is in a position to take them on board.[70]

After the Second World War, the International Military Tribunal at Nuremberg, due to the integration of Allied merchant shipping into the naval effort, stated that:

> in the actual circumstances of this case, the Tribunal is not prepared to hold Doenitz guilty for his conduct of submarine warfare against British *armed* merchant ships.[71]

The Tribunal still upheld the validity of the *Procès-Verbal*. It continued:

> However, the proclamation of operational zones and the sinking of neutral merchant vessels which enter those zones presents a different question. This practice was employed in the War of 1914–18 by Germany and adopted in retaliation by Great Britain. The Washington conference of 1922, the London Naval Agreement of 1930, and the Protocol of 1936, were entered into with full knowledge that such zones had been employed in the First

69 Ibid, 43, 50.

70 1936 London Procès-Verbal Relating to the Rules of Submarine Warfare Set Forth in Part IV of the Treaty of London of 22 April 1930 (opened for signature 6 November 1936) UKTS 29 (1936) Cmd 5302 (entered into force 6 November 1936). For a review of the law, and the *Lusitania* sinking, at the commencement of the Second World War see A.H. Charteris, 'Notes on International Law' (1940) 13 *Australian Law Journal* 549.

71 The Trial of German Major War Criminals. Proceedings of the International Military Tribunal sitting at *Nuremberg, Germany*, Part 22 (22 August 1946 to 1 October 1946) 508, NB judgment on Admiral Raeder in the same terms, 511 [emphasis added].

> World War. Yet the Protocol made no exception for operational zones. The order of Doenitz to sink neutral ships without warning when found within these zones was, therefore, in the opinion of the Tribunal, a violation of the Protocol . . . .
>
> The evidence further shows that the rescue provisions were not carried out and that the defendant ordered that they should not be carried out. The argument of the defence is that the security of the submarine is, as the first rule of the sea, paramount to rescue and that the development of aircraft made rescue impossible. This may be so, but the Protocol is explicit. If the commander cannot rescue, then under its terms he cannot sink a merchant vessel and should allow it to pass harmless before his periscope. The orders, then, prove Doenitz is guilty of a violation of the Protocol.[72]

The practice of unrestricted submarine warfare in the Second World War did not change the law but instead led to an affirmation of it when considered after the event. Even if the conduct of all belligerents raised questions as to the extent to which it would be honoured in practice, the judgement of the Tribunal was unequivocal as to the standard against which that conduct should subsequently be assessed.

As to the development of the law of naval warfare, although there has been no new specific treaty, there has been significant development generally in the law of armed conflict, the law of the sea, the law of the air, and human rights law since the Nuremberg judgement. This finds expression to a greater or lesser extent in the *San Remo Manual on International Law Applicable to Armed Conflicts at Sea* ('*San Remo Manual*') which, in the absence of new treaty law, seeks to be a contemporary restatement of the law in question.[73] The *San Remo Manual* essentially amplifies the definition of military objective from Article 52(2) of Additional Protocol I to the Geneva Conventions for the naval warfare context, stating:

> 59 Enemy merchant vessels may only be attacked if they meet the definition of a military objective in paragraph 40.
>
> 60 The following activities may render enemy merchant vessels military objectives:

72 Ibid, 508–509. However, the Tribunal did not assess a sentence against Admiral Doenitz in this respect as:

> In view of all the facts proved and in particular of an order of the British Admiralty announced on the 8th May, 1940, according to which all vessels should be sunk at sight in the Skagerrak, and the answers to interrogatories by Admiral Nimitz stating that unrestricted submarine warfare was carried on in the Pacific Ocean by the United States from the first day that nation entered the war, the sentence of Doenitz is not assessed on the ground of his breaches of the international law of submarine warfare.

73 International Institute of Humanitarian Law, Louise Doswald-Beck (ed) (Cambridge UP, 1995), 5.

(a) engaging in belligerent acts on behalf of the enemy, e.g., laying mines, minesweeping, cutting undersea cables and pipelines, engaging in visit and search of neutral merchant vessels or attacking other merchant vessels;
(b) acting as an auxiliary to an enemy s armed forces, e.g., carrying troops or replenishing warships;
(c) being incorporated into or assisting the enemy s intelligence-gathering system, e.g., engaging in reconnaissance, early warning, surveillance, or command, control and communications missions;
(d) sailing under convoy of enemy warships or military aircraft;
(e) refusing an order to stop or actively resisting visit, search or capture;
(f) being armed to an extent that they could inflict damage to a warship; this excludes light individual weapons for the defence of personnel, e.g., against pirates, and purely deflective systems such as chaff; or
(g) otherwise making an effective contribution to military action, e.g., carrying military materials.

This is essentially the traditional position with the incorporation of the factors taken into account in the Nuremberg judgement. The *San Remo Manual* still would not provide a justification for the attack without warning on *Lusitania* as it specifically makes passenger ships exempt from attack and provides quite strict conditions for the loss of that exemption, as follows:

47 The following classes of enemy vessels are exempt from attack:

(e) passenger vessels when engaged only in carrying civilian passengers;

48 Vessels listed in paragraph 47 are exempt from attack only if they:

(a) are innocently employed in their normal role;
(b) submit to identification and inspection when required; and
(c) do not intentionally hamper the movement of combatants and obey orders to stop or move out of the way when required.

52 If any other class of vessel exempt from attack [that is, exempt vessels other than hospital ships] breaches any of the conditions of its exemption in paragraph 48, it may be attacked only if:

(a) diversion or capture is not feasible;
(b) no other method is available for exercising military control;

(c) the circumstances of non-compliance are sufficiently grave that the vessel has become, or may be reasonably assumed to be, a military objective; and
(d) the collateral casualties or damage will not be disproportionate to the military advantage gained or expected.

Under these rules, it would be difficult to argue that *Lusitania* had become a military objective in that the munitions onboard mainly a relatively small quantity of rifle ammunition – could be sufficient to amount to a grave non-compliance, and there had been no attempt at visit and search. More importantly, it is difficult to see how the military advantage from destroying the ammunition could be proportionate to the potential loss of thousands of lives.

The current British Manual repeats the *San Remo Manual* virtually verbatim.[74] The current German Manual essentially reflects the *San Remo Manual* position, in less detail generally but with the added requirement that passenger ships may only be destroyed in accordance with the law of prize once they are in harbour and the passengers have disembarked.[75] The U.S. Manual states an essentially similar position to the *San Remo Manual* Rule 60 but without reference to the military objective requirements in Rules 47, 52, and 59, noting the United States is not party to Additional Protocol I, and with a specific proviso for submarines requiring compliance with the traditional rule unless:

> The enemy has integrated its merchant shipping into its war-fighting/war-sustaining effort and compliance with the *London Protocol* of 1936 would, under the circumstances of the specific encounter, subject the submarine to imminent danger or would otherwise preclude mission accomplishment.[76]

It is difficult to see how *U20* could have accomplished its mission through visit and search of *Lusitania*, and to do so without subjecting itself to imminent danger from ramming or potential surface gunfire if the commander believed the ship was armed. Even then, given that *Lusitania* was clearly conducting a scheduled passenger service for the general public, it is equally difficult to see that *Lusitania* was sufficiently incorporated into the British war-sustaining effort by her carriage of munitions as to justify an attack without warning. Even under the less restrictive current U.S. position – which is ironic, given that its position in 1915 was more restrictive than Britain or

74 UK Ministry of Defence, *Manual of the Law of Armed Conflict* (Oxford University Press, 2004), 357–360.

75 *Kommandanten-Handbuch – Rechtsgrundlagen für den Einsatz von Seestreitkräften* (German Commanders Handbook: Legal Basis for the Operations of Naval Forces), 177–184, particularly 182.

76 *United States Commander's Handbook on the Law of Naval Operations* (2017, NWP 1–14M) para 8.7.1.

Germany's – the sinking of *Lusitania* is at least likely to be unlawful. Notably, this is also the position in the commentary to the *San Remo Manual*.[77]

V. Conclusion

The sinking of *Lusitania* was as unlawful in 1915 as it would be unlawful if it occurred today. It would not be a permissible act under the international law of armed conflict but rather an unlawful killing under the applicable national or international criminal law. The presence of munitions onboard, whether as little as stated by Britain or as much as initially stated by Germany, did not justify an attack on her without warning. Nor, too, did any of the ways in which *Lusitania* was part of the British war effort – such as being under Admiralty sailing directions and being listed as an auxiliary – justify the attack without warning. These factors point to steps which the UK – and to some extent the United States, in respect of the export of munitions – could have taken to reduce the risk to passenger ships such as *Lusitania*. Even so, that is with the benefit of hindsight. At the time, the sinking of *Lusitania* appears to have been as unexpected and shocking as the downing of Malaysian Airlines Flight MH 17 in 2014. The deaths of neutral U.S. citizens in the sinking did not make it any more unlawful. The diplomatic and strategic consequences of their deliberate and unlawful killing, however, illustrate the significance of the rule against attacking merchant ships without warning, both then and now. Subsequent practice of unrestricted submarine warfare in both world wars has not diminished this significance, although it may have elaborated upon the rule to some extent. That is, the exception to the rule is slightly wider in that attack without warning can now be justified by the incorporation of merchant shipping into the war effort. The definition of military objective now assists in understanding this wider exception to the rule and, had it applied in 1915, the sinking of *Lusitania* would still have been unlawful.

77 124 and 141. See also Chris Griggs, 'Legal Constraints on Maritime Operations Affecting Merchant Shipping', (2005) 19 *Maritime Law Association of Australian and New Zealand Journal* 148, 151–154. For a rejection of the existing rules on submarine warfare and an argument for codification of exclusion zones instead see Jane Gilliland, 'Submarines and Targets: Suggestions for New Codified Rules of Submarine Warfare' (1985) 73 *Georgetown Law Journal* 975.

14

THE *ADMIRAL GRAF SPEE* IN MONTEVIDEO

James Farrant

I. Introduction

On 13 December 1939, the German pocket battleship (Panzerschiff) *Admiral Graf Spee* limped into the neutral Uruguayan harbour of Montevideo following a tenacious day-long engagement with three light cruisers of the Royal Navy: the Battle of the River Plate. The Second World War had begun only three months earlier. The battle was the first significant naval surface engagement of the conflict, was of significant press interest, and was considered a resounding early victory for the British. After the battle, four days of diplomatic wrangling, deception, and not a little 'lawfare' captivated the world as Great Britain and Germany sought to bend the stricken warship's reluctant neutral hosts to their will. *Graf Spee*, having been denied permission to effect major repairs by the Uruguayan government, was eventually compelled to sail. Her commanding officer, Capt. Hans Wilhelm Langsdorff, detonated charges within and scuttled the warship in the Plate Estuary to avoid her internment in Montevideo, and the consequent risk of falling into enemy hands. The case raises several issues of neutrality law which are of enduring interest to a maritime lawyer. These issues will become clear as the facts are stated, and each will be assessed in turn afterwards.

II. Background

Graf Spee sailed clandestinely from Germany for the South Atlantic in August 1939. The auxiliary vessel *Altmark* sailed in support. Their combined mission was, in the event Great Britain declared war in response to the forthcoming invasion of Poland, to interdict and sink as much enemy merchant shipping as possible, but to avoid a direct engagement with the Royal Navy. As fast and well-armed as *Graf Spee* was, her presence at large in the South Atlantic tied up Royal Navy

DOI: 10.4324/9781003307013-18

resources and had a disruptive effect on British merchant shipping schedules. She was more effective the longer she avoided contact with enemy warships. Following this strategy, by December 1939, *Graf Spee* had sunk approximately 50,000 tonnes of British merchant shipping. In each case, Langsdorff had removed the crews to safety before sinking the captured vessel. The majority of the captured crew were transferred to *Altmark*, but some remained on board *Graf Spee*. But by 26 November 1939, Langsdorff had seemingly lost patience with his order to keep clear of enemy warships. On that day, he fatefully recorded that he would not shy away from an engagement with any British units he encountered. This change of approach was at best a broad interpretation of his orders from Berlin and at worst a direct contravention of them. In any event, it was to prove Langsdorff's undoing.

On 7 December, *Graf Spee* encountered and stopped the steamship *Streonshalh*, which would turn out to be her last prize. The boarding party discovered a copy of the *Buenos Aires Herald* which suggested that several British merchant ships were likely to be in the River Plate area, only a few days' westerly steaming from the site of *Streonshalh*'s capture. Langsdorff headed west. Meanwhile, Commodore Harwood, flying his flag in *HMS Ajax*, and in company with *HMNZS Achilles* and *HMS Exeter*, also reasoned that the raider might come to the Plate Estuary. He considered that even with his three much smaller ships and smaller-calibre weaponry, he could get the better of the Panzerschiff by attacking from two sides, dividing her fire and effecting superior gunnery. Thus, when the two sides met in the early hours of 13 December, neither backed away from the fight.

Harwood's plan was a success. His three cruisers inflicted sufficient damage upon *Graf Spee* to persuade Langsdorff to run for a neutral harbour. Montevideo was the nearest and most accessible. *Ajax* and *Achilles* pursued *Graf Spee*, *Exeter* being so heavily damaged that she had broken off from the engagement and was limping towards the Falkland Islands for repairs. *Achilles* pursued *Graf Spee* into neutral Uruguayan territorial waters, and shots were exchanged. Harwood ordered *Achilles* to break off when it became clear that Langsdorff was entering harbour. *Graf Spee* dropped anchor in Montevideo late that evening. The Uruguayan authorities immediately granted her permission to remain for 48 hours: the same time they had given to *Achilles* when she had docked in Montevideo some weeks previously.[1] Langsdorff ordered that his prisoners be released (Lt. Herzberg released them with the now immortal words 'for you, the war is over'[2]) and arranged for his dead crew members to be taken ashore for burial. He also transferred some of his serious medical cases ashore.

Graf Spee had sustained holes in her outer plating, some significant in size and close to the waterline; cracks in her stern; an incapacitated galley, laundry, and

1 Richard Woodman, *The Battle of the River Plate: A Grand Delusion* (Naval Institute Press, 2008), 122.

2 The words were also ironically inaccurate. Many of the merchant seaman prisoners went on to serve in other merchant ships during the war, while Herzberg would see out the war in internment in Buenos Aires.

bakery; damage to the auxiliary drinking water boiler; and damage to the ship's gunnery range-finding equipment.[3] Langsdorff asked to stay for 14 days to effect repairs. He reasoned that a longer stay would enable him to be in better shape to fight the waiting British ships once out of the harbour. He was convinced that Harwood's squadron had been reinforced by *HMS Ark Royal* and *HMS Renown*. The British, having initially pressed for *Graf Spee* to be compelled to sail immediately, then also started to haggle for a delay. The truth was that, while *HMS Cumberland* had taken the place of the battered *Exeter*, *Ark Royal* and *Renown* were still some days sailing away.[4] The Uruguayan Foreign Minister proved unyielding to either side's demands. For a time, the British enforced their position by exploiting a provision of the 1907 Hague Convention XIII Concerning the Rights and Duties of Neutral Powers in Naval War (Hague XIII)[5] which forbade a belligerent warship to sail from a neutral port within 24 hours of an enemy merchant ship (Article 16). They began periodically sailing their own merchant vessels from Montevideo to prevent *Graf Spee* sailing, even if she wished to (which, of course, she did not).[6]

The Uruguayan naval officers sent to assess the damage determined that only 72 hours were required to render the vessel seaworthy. They extended *Graf Spee*'s permission to remain and ordered her to sail by 20:00 on 17 December. If she did not, Uruguayan authorities would intern her and her officers and crew under Hague XIII, Article 24. The German response was to repair as much as possible, in anticipation of an attempt to break out and sail back to Germany, or to make it across the Plate Estuary to Buenos Aires. During this period, the British made use of radio infrastructure ashore in Montevideo to keep Harwood's waiting squadron informed of developments, and to speed up signal traffic between the squadron and London.[7] The Germans remained convinced that a strong British force was amassing in the Estuary and concluded any form of breakout was impossible. The British reinforced this belief by 'leaking' some false logistic plans over non-secure phone lines to persuade the listening Germans that either *Ark Royal* or *Renown* would shortly be calling at Buenos Aires for fuel. German High Command was also convinced that the pro-British Uruguayans would allow *Graf Spee* to fall into British hands if she were interned in Montevideo. Berlin therefore reluctantly agreed to

3 See generally Great Britain Admiralty, The Battle of the River Plate: An Account of Events Before, During and After the Action Up to the Self-destruction of the Admiral Graf Spee (H.M.S.O., 1940); U.S. Office of Naval Operations Intelligence Division, The Battle of the River Plate (U.S. G.P.O., 1940); Uruguayan Ministry of Foreign Affairs, The Documents Relating to the Sinking of the Admiral Graf Spee and the Internment of the Merchant Vessel Tacoma (Hutchinson & Co., 1940) [henceforth 'Uruguay Report'].

4 Sir Eugen Millington-Drake, *The Drama of the Graf Spee and the Battle of the River Plate: A Documentary Anthology 1914–1964* (Peter Davis, 1964), 294.

5 36 Stat. 2415

6 Woodman, above n 1, 126–130; Eric J Grove, *The Price of Disobedience: The Battle of the River Plate Reconsidered* (Naval Institute Press, 2000), 101–114.

7 Woodman, The Battle of the River Plate: A Grand Delusion, above n 1, 123; Grove, *The Price of Disobedience: The Battle of the River Plate Reconsidered*, above n 6, 101.

Langsdorff's suggestion to leave the harbour and sink *Graf Spee* just outside Uruguayan territorial waters.

Thus, on 17 December, all repair work ceased, and *Graf Spee* weighed anchor and proceeded out of the harbour. This endeavour was supported by a German-owned steamship, *Tacoma*. *Tacoma* assisted in transferring *Graf Spee*'s crew to waiting tugs and launches to take them to Buenos Aires, where it was thought that Argentina might allow for them to be repatriated to Germany. Uruguayan authorities discovered the ruse at the last minute. They nonetheless permitted the crew to go to Buenos Aires but then interned *Tacoma* for acting as a German auxiliary in Uruguayan waters.[8] German aspirations of Argentina were not met – Argentina complied with her neutral duty to intern the crew for the remainder of the war. Langsdorff, apparently wracked with guilt at the loss of life in his young crew following his decision to engage the British cruisers, committed suicide in the Immigrants' Hotel in Buenos Aires soon after his arrival.

III. Analysis and outcomes

A. Applicable law

Germany was a party to Hague XIII. Uruguay and the United Kingdom had signed but not ratified Hague XIII, and there was never any dispute that the Convention's provisions bound all states involved. Uruguay was a party to the 1928 Havana Convention on Maritime Neutrality. Neither Great Britain nor Germany was, however, so this Convention was not applicable *inter partes*. Uruguay was a party to the 1939 Pan-American Declaration of Neutrality.[9]

B. Neutral security zone

The Pan-American Declaration of Neutrality, made at Panama on 3 October 1939, included the declaration of a neutral security zone, which extended 300–1,000 miles into the Atlantic Ocean, and ran along almost the entire eastern seaboard of the United States and other American republics (excluding Canada). The Declaration purported to prohibit any belligerent hostile acts within it. Nonetheless, the Battle of the River Plate took place within the zone, and the American Republics issued a joint protest to the belligerent states as a result. Great Britain responded that it was not bound by the zone as it was not a party to the Panama Declaration. Germany objected to the zone on the basis that it was un-neutral, and enormously favourable in its effect to Great Britain because it provided security for merchant shipping bound from the Americas for the

8 See generally Uruguay Report, above n 3.

9 See Declaration of Panama, reproduced at *American Journal of International Law 34*, (1940) Supp. 17.

British Isles.[10] Germany's assessment was correct: indeed, that is why U.S. President Franklin D. Roosevelt had agitated for the zone's establishment.[11] Nonetheless, it seems clear that the zone was without any legal effect without the consent of the belligerent states. Contemporaneous academic assessment of the zone reflected that reality.[12] The conduct of the battle within the zone was, therefore, not unlawful.

As far as the author is aware, no state has purported to rely on a neutrality zone of this nature since. The concept was not included in the *San Remo Manual*, even though the concept of the *belligerent* maritime zone was recognised and seems now to be well established.[13] However, many states maintain that security zones of one form or another could be an effective way of exercising their inherent right of self-defence including, perhaps, when protecting or enforcing their neutrality.[14]

C. Use of Uruguayan territorial waters

In 1939, Uruguay's claim to territorial seas which enclosed the half of the Plate Estuary nearest to it was not recognised by other states outside of the South American continent. The British recognised only a 3-mile territorial sea. On either view, *Achilles* entered Uruguayan territorial waters while shadowing *Graf Spee* to Montevideo. Indeed, she used the Uruguayan coast to make *Graf Spee*'s range-finding more difficult. The two vessels exchanged fire. Although both sides claimed fire was in self-defence (the British even unconvincingly claimed that *Achilles* acted in defence of an Uruguayan cruise liner), contemporary accounts suggest *Achilles* fired first.[15]

Where neutral states permit (or do not prohibit), belligerents are entitled to exercise 'mere' passage through neutral territorial seas (Hague XIII, Articles 9–10). The presence of *Graf Spee* and *Achilles* in Uruguayan territorial sea was, therefore, not *per se* unlawful; however, the conduct of hostilities in neutral territorial sea is strictly forbidden (Hague XIII, Article 2). Notwithstanding, the use of force in

10 The American republics' protest, and responses from the belligerents can be found at Payson S. Wild Jr, *International Law Situations* (1939) (hereinafter 'Payson S. Wild Jr') at 69–78.

11 Great Britain's response to the protest was accordingly less forthright than the German. See D.P. O'Connell, *The Influence of Law on Sea Power* (Manchester University Press, 1975), 28. Some have even suggested the zone was suggested to President Roosevelt by Winston Churchill: see Willi Frischauer and Robert Jackson, *The Altmark Affair* (The Macmillan Company, 1955), 32.

12 Payson S. Wild Jr, *International Law Situations*, above n 10, 78–80.

13 See Louise Doswald-Beck (ed), *San Remo Manual on International Law Applicable to Armed Conflicts at Sea* (Cambridge University Press, 1994) [105–108], and James Farrant, 'Modern Maritime Neutrality Law' (2014) 90 *International Law Studies*, 270–278.

14 See United Kingdom Ministry of Defence, *Manual of the Law of Armed Conflict* (Oxford University Press, 2004) [13.77.1] [henceforth 'UK Manual']; German Navy, Bundessprachenamt – Referat SM 3 Auftragsnummer 2002U-01441, *Kommandanten-Handbuch – Rechtsgrundlagen für den Einsatz von Seestreitkräften*, (2002) [115] [henceforth 'German Commander's Handbook').

15 Contemporaneous eyewitness accounts reported in Millington-Drake, *The Drama of the* Graf Spee *and the Battle of the River Plate: A Documentary Anthology 1914–1964*, above n 4, 243–248.

self-defence by belligerent forces while lawfully present in neutral territorial sea is permitted. While this is probably uncontroversial, the scope of measures which are acceptable in self-defence in those circumstances is unclear. The distinguished drafters of the *San Remo Manual* attempted to define that scope but acknowledged limited success.[16] It is probably now impossible to determine with certainty the legitimacy of either side's claim to be acting in self-defence. While *Achilles* being first to fire is not – as a matter of law – fatal to the British case, it does not assist it.

D. The 24-hour rule

Moving from the battle to *Graf Spee*'s arrival in Montevideo, there are several long-standing rules of customary maritime neutrality law which govern belligerent use of neutral ports, and many of these were codified in Hague XIII. The first is a time limit, generally referred to as the 24-hour rule. But the Convention (Article 12) is clear that the 24-hour rule is a default provision only, and that neutral states are free to determine their own time limit so long as they apply it impartially between the belligerents. Here no issue arises. Uruguay had settled on a 48-hour time limit, and she applied it equitably to Great Britain and Germany.

In contemporary practice, the validity of the 24-hour rule has been doubted in the UK Manual, which observes bluntly that it 'is no longer applicable'.[17] The UK Manual asserts a minority view, and other prominent state manuals maintain the rule's continuing validity.[18] According to one of the UK Manual's authors in a later work, the UK's position is more nuanced than the Manual suggests: instead, it reflects a geographic limitation. If the UK is involved in an armed conflict in the Mediterranean, for example, the 24-hour rule would not operate to prevent a UK warship on separate tasking in, say, the Caribbean from staying in a neutral port longer than 24 hours. There would be no causal link between the length of that stay and the sustainability of the British war effort in the Mediterranean, so the rule is not required.[19] Whether the UK Manual is taken at face value or at the later qualified position, it is not a position adopted by other states and cannot be said to reflect customary law. It seems more likely that the 24-hour rule still binds all neutral states, wherever they are in relation to the conflict. Indeed, the *Graf Spee* incident serves to illustrate the difficulty with any geographic restriction. In hostilities between Great Britain and Germany, which arguably had yet to become a 'world' war, would Uruguay have been exempt from the operation of the rule? Or would the fact of actual nearby hostilities (the Battle of the River Plate) serve to render Uruguay bound? Even as a matter of *lex ferenda*, a geographic qualification to the 24-hour rule (or any other rule of maritime neutrality) lacks appeal.

16 See *San Remo Manual*, above n 13, 106–107 [30.1–30.3]; see also Farrant, 'Modern Maritime Neutrality Law', above n 13, 215–219.

17 UK Manual, above n 14, [13.4]

18 See, for example, German Commander's Handbook, above n 14, [233].

19 Steven Haines, 'The United Kingdom's Manual of the Law of Armed Conflict and the San Remo Manual: Maritime Rules Compared' (2006) 36 *Israel Yearbook on Human Rights* 89, 103–104.

E. Keeping prisoners

Langsdorff was clear that it was his legal duty to release his British prisoners on arrival into a neutral port. As far as the author is aware, none have sought to challenge the German captain's conclusion, even though there is no explicit rule to this effect in Hague XIII. The British Minister in Montevideo, Sir Eugen Millington-Drake, considered that Hague XIII, Articles 21–22, contained such a duty, but strictly speaking, the text of these articles is addressed only to the crew of prize vessels where the vessels themselves are brought into a neutral harbour.[20] Notwithstanding Articles 21–22, the keeping of prisoners is also an arguable breach of the rule against 'basing operations' in neutral ports or waters (Hague XIII, Article 5). Indeed, the British would later partially rely on this position in their objection to the *Altmark*'s behaviour in Norwegian territorial seas.[21]

F. Conducting repairs

Belligerent warships may conduct repairs which are 'absolutely necessary to render them seaworthy and may not add in any way to their fighting force' (Hague XIII, Article 17). The neutral state has the authority to declare which repairs are absolutely necessary. Uruguayan inspectors assessed which damage was related to the ship's seaworthiness and gave only such time as they determined necessary for those repairs. German arguments that the vessel was not seaworthy were somewhat undermined by the fact that she had steamed some 300 miles from the site of the engagement to Montevideo in her unrepaired state. Nonetheless, to be genuinely seaworthy, a ship with a crew the size of *Graf Spee*'s must surely have operating galleys and an intact hull, and there can be little dispute with the Uruguayan position in allowing those repairs. However, it is abundantly clear that repairs – clandestine or otherwise – were made by the crew to *Graf Spee*'s armaments while she was in harbour, and this was in breach of Article 17.[22]

More difficult is the question of whether repair to damage sustained in battle (rather than due to stress of weather, for example) is permitted at all in neutral harbours. Hague XIII, Article 17, is silent on this point, not referring to the cause of damage, but the 1928 Havana Convention[23] forbids battle damage repair, including seaworthiness repairs, altogether (Article 9). Several states' neutrality declarations made in 1939, including those of the United States, Denmark, Finland, Iceland,

20 Millington-Drake, *The Drama of the Graf Spee and the Battle of the River Plate: A Documentary Anthology 1914–1964*, above n 4, 251.

21 See, in this volume, Chapter 15 on the *Altmark* incident and belligerent use of neutral territorial waters.

22 Grove, *The Price of Disobedience: The Battle of the River Plate Reconsidered*, above n 6, 103; A B Campbell, The Battle of the Plate (Herbert Jenkins Ltd, 1940), 156.

23 Convention on Maritime Neutrality, Havana, 20 February 1928, 135 LNTS 187

Norway, and Sweden, all expressly prohibited battle damage repair in their ports.[24] The 1939 Harvard Draft Convention on Maritime and Aerial Neutrality, an academic project to update the 1909 Declaration of London, also took the view that all battle damage repair should be forbidden.[25]

On the other hand, and perhaps surprisingly, no side in the *Graf Spee* incident sought to argue that battle damage repair was unlawful *per se*.[26] Preeminent modern state law of armed conflict manuals make no mention of a prohibition on battle damage repair. Simply put, the law is not clear. As a matter of *lex ferenda*, the present author has argued previously that the law should forbid battle damage repairs, because it should not be permissible for a neutral state to facilitate repairs to damage intentionally and lawfully wrought by one belligerent upon another.[27] In those circumstances Hague XIII, Article 24, would require the internment of unseaworthy belligerent warships in neutral ports, along with their crews. It is to the internment requirement more generally that our attention must now turn.

G. The neutral duty to intern

A neutral state may intern a belligerent warship which stays longer than its entitlement in a neutral port and prevent it 'from taking the sea altogether' (Hague XIII, Article 24). This provision seemed to be interpreted by all of the protagonists as a *duty* to intern as soon as entitlement is exceeded, though some have argued separately that the neutral state has a discretion as to whether or not to intern in these circumstances.[28] Either way, Uruguay was making preparations to intern *Graf Spee* had she not sailed before the deadline. Moreover, Great Britain was making contingency plans to enforce what they regarded as Uruguay's duty, if she had proved unwilling or unable to do so.[29]

Recent litigation in the sphere of *belligerent* states' rights to intern (or detain) enemy combatants and non-combatants may have read-across effect on the *neutral*

24 'Official Documents: Denmark-Finland-Iceland-Norway-Sweden: Declaration Regarding Similar Rules of Neutrality' (1938) 32(S4) *American Journal of International Law* 141. On the other hand, the Uruguayan Foreign Minister, Dr Guani, cited several occasions when neutral States had permitted battle damage repair during the First World War – see Lord Strabolgi, *The Battle of the River Plate* (London, Hutchinson & Co., 1973), 71–73.

25 Philip C Jessup, 'Rights and Duties of Neutral States in Naval and Aerial War' (1939) 33 *American Journal of International Law*, supp 167, art 34.

26 Sir Eugen Millington-Drake acknowledged the ambiguity in art 17 in his representations to the Uruguayan Government – see Lord Strabolgi, *The Battle of the River Plate*, above n 23, 68.

27 Farrant, 'Modern Maritime Neutrality Law', above n 13, 236.

28 Contrasting the explicit provision in Hague V, Article 11, with the vaguer Hague XIII, Article 24 can sustain the argument that the neutral state has only a discretion to intern in the maritime context. See Marco Sassoli, 'Internment', in Rüdiger Wolfrum (ed) *Max Plank Encyclopaedia of Public International Law* (Oxford University Press) [21]. For the opposing view that the obligation to intern extends to maritime forces, see, for example, L Oppenheim, *International Law: A Treatise* (London Longmans, Green and co., first published 1905–6, 1921 ed), 471–473.

29 Grove, *The Price of Disobedience: The Battle of the River Plate Reconsidered*, above n 6, 118.

state's right (or duty) to intern. This litigation has arisen in the context of U.S.-led operations in Iraq and Afghanistan in the early 21st century. Some cases have focussed on whether detainees have access to domestic law remedies or review mechanisms to challenge the decision to detain them. In the United States, *Hamdi v Rumsfeld* and *Boumediene v Bush* affirmed that the law of war allows belligerent states to detain enemy individuals who participate in the conflict or who otherwise represent a sufficient security threat. However, these cases also found that such detainees have access to the writ of *habeas corpus*, through which to challenge the legality of their detention.[30] The principles applied in these cases would surely also apply in the context of neutral internment. An internee in a neutral state might challenge internment on the grounds, for example, that the armed conflict which gave rise to the neutral state's right or duty to intern has ceased.

A more vexed question has been the relationship between states' detention powers under the law of armed conflict and sometimes seemingly incompatible human rights obligations. This has especially been the case for states party to the European Convention on Human Rights (ECHR).[31] This is because, unusually among human rights instruments, the ECHR frames the right to freedom from arbitrary deprivation of liberty by setting out an apparently exhaustive list of six grounds under which it is acceptable for signatory states to detain. The list contains no reference to detention powers under the Geneva or Hague Conventions (ECHR, Article 5[1][a]–[f]). By comparison, the 1966 International Covenant on Civil and Political Rights (ICCPR)[32] merely provides that detention must be 'in accordance with such procedures as are established in law' (ICCPR, Article 9).

Tribunals applying the ECHR have accordingly found it much harder to reconcile law of armed conflict powers of detention with individuals' rights guaranteed in that Convention. A narrow approach adopted in the European Court of Human Rights in *Al Jedda v United Kingdom* (2011) 53 BHRR 23 has since been mitigated by a more pragmatic approach to this question in the subsequent case of *Hassan v United Kingdom* (2014) 38 BHRC 358. In *Hassan*, the Court essentially concluded that the list in Article 5 was not, after all, exhaustive, and should not be read to prohibit ECHR states detaining under Geneva Convention III, Article 21 (the power to detain prisoners of war).[33]

Read narrowly, *Hassan* could be interpreted as applying strictly to prisoners of war. Read more broadly, it could be authority that ECHR states remain permitted to detain under pre-existing international law authorities, whether based in treaty or customary rules, which the ECHR was never intended to disturb. This

30 *Hamdi v. Rumsfeld*, 542 U.S. 507 (2004); see Lewis and Margulies, 'Interpretations of IHL in Tribunals of the United States' in D Jinks et al, *Applying International Human Rights Law in Judicial and Quasi-Judicial Bodies*, Springer (2014), pages 415–449.

31 European Convention for the Protection of Human Rights and Fundamental Freedoms (1950) 213 UNTS 221

32 999 UNTS 171

33 *Hassan v United Kingdom* (2014) 38 BHRC 358 at para 104–105.

broader approach (to what is essentially a conflict of laws question) is also reflected in ICJ cases which have considered the interplay between states' law of armed conflict rights and human rights law obligations.[34] This broad approach is the better view. The UK Supreme Court adopted it in *Al-Waheed v Ministry of Defence* [2017] UKSC 2, using it to conclude that UN Security Council resolutions could grant ECHR states the power to detain, despite Article 5(1)(a)–(f) making no explicit reference to such an authority.[35] The broad approach does not allow for the evasion of ECHR duties altogether. Both the European Court and the UK Supreme Court went on to apply procedural safeguards found within Article 5 to detentions effected under Security Council resolution authority, albeit in a manner contextualised to that authority.[36]

It remains to be seen whether the European Court of Human Rights will sanction this broad approach to its ruling in *Hassan*. For the time being, though, it may be prayed in aid in support of the position that the neutral power (or duty) to intern has survived the subsequent advent of codified human rights law obligations, even in the context of ECHR, arguably the most prescriptive of international human rights law instruments. This is significant, since the authority to prevent belligerent personnel returning to their home state, or otherwise to rejoin the hostilities, is an important means by which neutral states can preserve their neutrality. Nonetheless, no power to detain or intern should operate without legal scrutiny, and the cases discussed here demonstrate a range of mechanisms by which courts can exercise an element of judicial supervision over what might otherwise have the potential to be an unchecked authority to deprive individuals of their liberty.

H. Radio communications from neutral territory

Under the 'basing operations' rule, belligerents may not, in neutral territory, 'erect wireless telegraphy stations or any apparatus for the purpose of communicating with the belligerent forces on land or sea' (Hague XIII, Article 5). The British might have responded that they did not 'erect' the radio station in Montevideo they used to communicate with Harwood and augment his communications with HQ at home.[37] This technical defence does not seem to be within the spirit of the Convention, however, and it seems likely that Britain's use of radio from Montevideo was an oft-overlooked breach of Uruguayan neutrality.

34 See, e.g., *Legality of the Threat or Use of Nuclear Weapons*, Advisory Opinion, [1996] ICJ Rep 226 at paragraph 25, and *Legal Consequences of the Construction of a Wall in the Occupied Territory*, Advisory Opinion, [2004] ICJ Rep 136, at paragraph 106.

35 See, e.g., paragraph 68 *per* Lord Sumption.

36 See *Al-Waheed at* paragraphs 68 *et seq*, *per* Lord Sumption.

37 It was a U.S. journalist who did: Millington-Drake, *The Drama of the Graf Spee and the Battle of the River Plate: A Documentary Anthology 1914–1964*, above n 4, 337.

I. The merchant ship sailing rule

Once Great Britain had determined that a delay in *Graf Spee*'s departure suited her better than insisting on an immediate sailing, she employed the device of ordering her flagged merchant vessels already present in Montevideo to sail periodically from the harbour. In doing so, she was relying on Hague XIII, Article 16, which provides that '[a] belligerent war-ship may not leave a neutral port or roadstead until twenty-four hours after the departure of a merchant ship flying the flag of its adversary'. If the German High Command had wished to sail *Graf Spee*, then on the face of it this would have prevented them from doing so. The British used this device three times before Uruguay lost her patience and refused to allow any more sailings. Germany, wrapped up in her own campaign to allow *Graf Spee* to stay, did not protest. In the final analysis, it did not affect the outcome of the case. Still, it represents an interesting example of a belligerent state using a rule designed for the protection of its merchant vessels to achieve an entirely different operational effect: the confinement of enemy forces.

IV. Conclusion

Graf Spee is of as much enduring interest to naval lawyers as to naval historians. As the preceding analysis shows, the case has something to say on many of the long-established rules of maritime neutrality. The incident does much to support subsequent scholarship and national law of armed conflict manuals which continue to assert the law of maritime neutrality, largely as it was framed in The Hague Conventions of 1907, themselves largely codifying pre-existing customs. As a result, the rules would (and should) be similarly applied if the same facts arose tomorrow. There are two important reservations to this general assessment.

First, should the repair of damage sustained in battle be permissible at all in a neutral port? The British did not argue that the law contained such a prohibition, in circumstances where such a rule would have substantially advantaged her, and at a time when there was a growing consensus in favour of such a rule. Perhaps Great Britain considered, at the time, that she may also need to make use of neutral ports for battle damage repair. The state of the law remains uncertain.

The second was not of concern in 1939; human rights law had not, as such, been invented. The impact of human rights law on the internment duty inherent in neutrality law is yet to be specifically litigated. This chapter has commended the pragmatic approach to this conflict of laws question demonstrated in *Hassan* and *Al-Waheed*, and notes its eminent potential for read-across into the neutrality law context. At the time of writing, few security experts would demur from the view that serious state-on-state conflict is more likely now than at any time since the end of the Cold War. In that context, neutrality obligations – and robust means to comply with them – become an increasingly important means by which states can signal clearly that they wish to avoid being embroiled in such a conflict. There are clear public policy reasons for their preservation.

15

THE *ALTMARK* INCIDENT

James Farrant

I. Introduction

On 16 February 1940, after a long hunt, British forces finally located the German supply ship *Altmark* off the coast of Norway. They had been searching for her since freed prisoners from *Graf Spee* had given valuable intelligence about her role in support of the ill-fated Panzerschiff. In a controversial raid which took place in Norwegian internal waters, *HMS Cossack* sent boarders to liberate the 299 prisoners *Altmark* had carried since her last rendezvous with *Graf Spee* in the South Atlantic. Both Norway and Germany would protest that the British action was a breach of Norwegian neutrality and unlawful. The UK, on the other hand, claimed that *Altmark*'s use of the Norwegian waters to evade capture was but one example of German abuse of Norwegian neutrality, which the UK was entitled to remedy. The case highlights several fault-lines in maritime neutrality law, many of which persist into the modern law and therefore deserve scrutiny.

II. Background

Altmark's mission was to act as a support ship to the *Admiral Graf Spee*, whose fate was the subject of the preceding Chapter 14. The two vessels assembled in the South Atlantic and Capt. Langsdorff, of *Graf Spee*, made it plain to his opposite number in *Altmark*, Capt. Heinrich Dau, that one of *Altmark*'s tasks was to act as a holding ship for prisoners from British merchant ships sunk by *Graf Spee*. As the number of prisoners grew following *Graf Spee*'s successes, Dau became increasingly concerned that his small ship's company would not be able to contain the prisoners if they attempted to break out. Langsdorff agreed and transferred a small armed security party to help guard them.

DOI: 10.4324/9781003307013-19

Dau was also concerned that his ship was ill-suited to hold prisoners for an indeterminate period, and in conditions considered tolerable. Nonetheless, several cargo decks were converted and made more accommodating by the addition of some soft furnishings from the captured merchant ships. Sanitary arrangements were rudimentary, to say the least, and consisted of barrels which were emptied daily by the prisoners, who arranged themselves into watches for these and other domestic purposes. Officers were accommodated separately and were not required to work. All prisoners were, in small groups, given short spells during the day to exercise and get fresh air on the upper deck, under the supervision of *Graf Spee*'s guards. Although conditions were far from ideal, and despite his reputation to the contrary, Dau seemed committed to making life tolerable, even if not comfortable, for his human cargo. He was a strict disciplinarian, punishing crew members and prisoners alike with spells in solitary confinement if they were caught smoking. Many of the prisoners seemed to regard this as more a change of scene than a punishment – living in close quarters with so many others for so long meant being in solitary confinement could be a chance to get some uninterrupted sleep and to read.

Once news of *Graf Spee*'s sinking reached *Altmark*, Dau determined that he would have to make his way back to Germany. He and his officers were wholly aware of the risks in this endeavour – the Royal Navy was looking for them. Dau sailed in circles in the South Atlantic for a time, in the hope the British would either lose interest or be convinced by a German intelligence ruse that she was already back in Germany. Then he allowed his engineers to re-fit the engines at sea. Finally, after briefly flirting with an idea to mount an attack on Cape Town, South Africa, before heading for Germany (Dau was disabused of this plan by his officers), he turned north for home. He evaded detection by the Royal Navy, even when passing through the gap between Iceland and the Faroe Islands – which the UK claimed was blockaded. He crossed the North Sea and decided he would use the cover of Norwegian territorial waters before making the hazardous crossing of the Skagerrak and into Kiel harbour. Dau had determined that a run south through the North Sea was sure to end in disaster, either at the hands of a British patrol, a British (or German) mine, or even a German submarine which might mistake *Altmark* for an enemy tanker.

Altmark had disguised herself as numerous ships on her journey north in case of interception. However, before entry into Norwegian territorial waters, Dau once again displayed the name '*Altmark*' and had her repainted battleship grey. *Altmark* entered Norwegian territorial waters north of the Halten Lighthouse, itself just north of Trondheim, on the evening of 13 February 1940. A Norwegian port official out of Trondheim visited her on 14 February. Dau asked for a Norwegian pilot to guide him down the coast, perhaps to add legitimacy to his voyage. The Norwegians told him he could not have a pilot until Kristiansund, some way south, unless he wished to enter Trondheim. Dau knew a port entry would undoubtedly compel him to release his prisoners, so he carried on south. *Altmark* was revisited on 14 February by the Norwegian ship *Trygg*. The inspecting officer confined himself to the ship's papers, and no further search was carried out. *Trygg*'s commanding officer told Dau that he could not have a certified pilot until Alesund (further south again than Kristiansund) but did provide one of his officers to assist with navigating down the coast. *Trygg* followed in *Altmark*'s wake.

Meanwhile, the prisoners were doing their best to attract the Norwegians' attention, by banging on the superstructure and blowing SOS signals on their whistles. Dau responded by turning on loud machinery on the upper deck and spraying the prisoners with water to silence them. Contemporary accounts suggest the din was enormous; long after the event, Norwegian officers sent to inspect *Altmark* admitted to having heard the prisoners' protestations. Nonetheless, for the time being, at least, Norway feigned ignorance of the prisoners' presence, even though Rear Admiral Tank-Nielsen, the Norwegian naval officer in command of the coastal district, was well aware of *Altmark's* role in the South Atlantic from having read about it in newspapers. The Admiral's intention seemed to be to make a show of enforcing Norwegian neutrality (by repeated 'inspections' and refusing to allow *Altmark* to sail through the Bergen Defended Area unescorted, or at night) but simultaneously to be rid of her before the British realised what was happening.[1] *Altmark* would be visited, although not searched, a further three times by Norwegian authorities before she was eventually intercepted by the British. Dau complained to the Norwegians, and by wireless to the German High Command and the German representative in Norway, that he was unduly harassed for a ship on government service.[2]

British interception came on 16 February 1940. *Altmark* was still under escort by the Norwegian Navy: by this time the escort had grown to three ships. She was detected and identified by an Royal Air Force reconnaissance flight, which seems to have entered Norwegian airspace to allow the pilots to make an identification.[3] HM ships *Arethusa*, *Intrepid*, *Ivanhoe*, and *Cossack* were in the area on a purported ice recce. They were diverted at speed to the *Altmark's* location, where they signalled her to exit Norwegian territorial waters. She refused, and the ships attempted to intercept her physically. They were ridden off by the Norwegian escort vessels, and *Altmark* turned not west, but east, into the Jøssingfjord, a dead-end inlet within Norwegian internal waters. Later in the day, and under cover of darkness, *HMS Cossack* entered the fjord and Capt. Vian, *Cossack*'s captain, told the senior Norwegian captain that he believed *Altmark* to be carrying prisoners. He said his orders were, in the first instance, to seek Norwegian consent for a joint operation to escort *Altmark* to Bergen and release them or to release them forcibly himself. The Norwegians would not consent to a joint operation, but similarly presented

1 Daniel Patrick O'Connell, *The Influence of Law on Sea Power* (Manchester University Press, 1975), 41.

2 Willi Frischauer and Robert Jackson, *The Altmark Affair* (Macmillan, 1955), 200; Richard Wiggan, *Hunt the Altmark* (Hale, 1982), 101.

3 See account given by one of the Hudson aircraft pilots in Lord Strabolgi, *The Battle of the River Plate* (Hutchinson & Co., 1973), 138. The pilot claims he stayed out of Norwegian airspace, but the detail of his narrative suggests he did not.

no further obstacle to the execution of Vian's alternative mission. Dau attempted to resist Vian's boarding and tried to ram *Cossack*; nonetheless, Vian's boarding party successfully boarded *Altmark* by leaping between the two ships. After a short scuffle in which shots were fired (including from escaped *Graf Spee* seamen who had run across the ice in the fjord to take shots at the British from the cover of the shore), the British gained control of *Altmark*. The prisoners were released and transferred to *Cossack*, which departed for Edinburgh. Dau and his crew were left on board the now aground *Altmark*.

III. Analysis and outcomes

A. Applicable law

Norway and Germany were parties to 1907 Hague Convention XIII Concerning the Rights and Duties of Neutral Powers in Naval War (Hague XIII). The UK had signed but not ratified the Convention. There was never any dispute among the parties that Hague XIII represented applicable law. Norway was a party to the 1938 Denmark-Finland-Iceland-Norway-Sweden Declaration Regarding Similar Rules of Neutrality, which set out those states' shared interpretations of maritime neutrality rules as they intended to apply them in a European war, which in 1938 was looking increasingly likely.[4] These primarily reflected Hague XIII, but also made provision for the signatory states to, for example, declare closed ports or defended areas along their coasts where additional constraints would be placed upon belligerent warships.[5] The Declaration was applicable in Norwegian internal waters and territorial seas.

B. Status of the Altmark

There is no doubt that, as a matter of law, *Altmark* met the definition of an auxiliary.[6] According to customary law, this rendered her subject to the same rights and obligations in neutral territorial waters as warships.[7] On initial confrontation with the Norwegian Navy, Dau purported to be a commercial tanker, the implication being that he was treatable as a merchant ship. However, it must have occurred to him subsequently that he would be subject to none of the immunities that benefit a vessel on government service – such as immunity from visit and search by the neutral coastal state. Thereafter, Dau declared himself a government vessel.

4 'Official Documents: Denmark-Finland-Iceland-Norway-Sweden: Declaration Regarding Similar Rules of Neutrality' (1938) 32(S4) *American Journal of International Law* 141.

5 See *Norwegian Regulations*, art 2(1), 154.

6 Louise Doswald-Beck, *San Remo Manual on International Law Applicable to Armed Conflicts at Sea* (Cambridge University Press, 1995) [13(h)].

7 See C.H.M. Waldock, 'The Release of the Altmark's Prisoners' (1947) 24 *British Yearbook of International Law*, 218 for evidence that this was accepted as law in 1940.

Auxiliaries remain subject to the same rules in neutral territorial seas as warships, but they do not enjoy all the same rights and privileges as warships during an armed conflict. For example, by Article 12 of the 1913 Oxford Manual, a vessel which is not a warship is permitted to use force only in self-defence. If Dau's plan to attack Cape Town had been realised, it would have been in clear breach of this obligation.

C. Status of the Altmark*'s prisoners*

Two issues about the status of *Altmark*'s prisoners arise. The first is whether the prisoners were lawfully captured; the second is, if they were lawfully captured, were they prisoners of war? The first issue was most forcefully raised by Lord Strabolgi, both at the time of the incident in the House of Lords, and subsequently in his book.[8] He argued consistently that the prisoners were unlawfully detained because the ships from which they were taken should have been subject to prize proceedings before they could have been sunk or their crews detained. However, as a matter of international law, and indeed English domestic prize law, this view was (and remains) incorrect. First, international law has long recognised that in circumstances when military necessity dictates, enemy prizes may be destroyed rather than taken to a belligerent's home port for prize proceedings.[9] Second, where such action is taken, the 1936 Procès-Verbal to the London Protocol requires that a merchant ship's crew and passengers be placed in a position of safety beforehand. The Protocol explicitly observes that lifeboats are not to be considered a place of safety unless, in the circumstances, safety can be assured (such as by proximity to land).[10] The only way, in practice, for this to be achieved is to take them prisoner. Consequently, there can be no doubt that the prisoners captured by *Graf Spee* and transferred to *Altmark* were lawful captives.

The second issue is more complicated.[11] After 1949, the 1949 Geneva Convention relating to the Treatment of Prisoners of War (Geneva Convention III) settled the matter that merchant seamen were henceforth to be considered prisoners of war. Article 4A(5) provides that they shall be prisoners of war unless they benefit from more favourable treatment under any other rule. This is a reference to 1907 Hague Convention XI Relative to Certain Restrictions with Regard to the Exercise of the Right of Capture in Naval War (Hague XI), Article 6, which provides that

> the captain, officers, and members of the crew, when nationals of the enemy State, are not made prisoners of war, on condition that they make a formal

8 Lord Strabolgi, *The Battle of the River Plate*, above n 3, 151.

9 See *The Felicity* (1819) 2 Dodson 386, per Lord Stowell.

10 *1936 Procès-Verbal to the London Protocol*, art 2. While specifically addressed to submarines, it is plain that the rule reflects law which applies also to surface warships.

11 For Langsdorff's and Dau's divergent views on the issue, see Willi Frischauer and Robert Jackson, *The Altmark Affair* (Macmillan, 1955), 52–53 and 75–76.

> promise in writing, not to undertake, while hostilities last, any service connected with the operations of the war.[12]

Altmark's prisoners were never allowed to make such an undertaking to secure their release. Even if they had, there could surely be no objection to such persons being retained in the capturing warship (or an auxiliary) until military circumstances permitted their release. There is no evidence of any intention, even had *Altmark* reached Germany, to elicit an undertaking to release the seamen: Dau's intent, and the prisoners' independently reached assumption, was that they would be delivered to a German prisoner-of-war (POW) camp. The International Committee of the Red Cross' Commentary to Article 4A(5) of Geneva Convention III indicates that even by the First World War, Hague XI was roundly ignored: by the Second World War, this was *a fortiori* the case.[13] It is accordingly difficult to say which classification of *Altmark's* prisoners was correct in 1940, although both sides (onboard, at least) seemed to prefer the view that they were POWs.

D. **Altmark***'s presence in Norwegian territorial waters*

As the preceding *Graf Spee* chapter shows, where neutral states permit (or do not prohibit), belligerent warships and auxiliaries may exercise mere passage through neutral territorial seas.[14] Norwegian neutrality rules were consistent with this position. *Altmark*'s entry, and presence, in Norwegian territorial waters was therefore not unlawful. However, mere passage is a narrow right and must be exercised only for navigational purposes. It must be read in conjunction with three other duties upon belligerents in neutral territorial seas. First, belligerents are forbidden from 'basing operations' in neutral waters.[15] Second, belligerents may not use neutral territorial waters as a sanctuary from their enemy. Third, mere passage is subject to the 24-hour rule which, except in certain circumstances, limits belligerent presence in the territorial sea to less than 24 hours.[16] Each will be examined in turn.

E. Basing operations

Captain Dau indeed appeared to believe that if he were discovered carrying prisoners in Norwegian territorial waters, he would be compelled to release them: that

12 Both Germany and the UK had signed and ratified Hague XI, so its application criteria were met in the Second World War (Hague XI, art 9).

13 See *1949 Geneva Convention (III) relating to the Treatment of Prisoners of War*, opened for signature 12 August 1949, 75 UNTS 135 (entered into force 21 October 1950) art 4; General Provisions.

14 *1907 Hague Convention (XIII) concerning the Rights and Duties of Neutral Powers in Naval War*, signed 18 October 1907, 205 CTS 395 (entered into force 26 January 1910) arts 9 and 10 (Hague Convention XIII).

15 Hague Convention XIII, art 5.

16 Ibid, art 12.

is why he worked so hard to conceal the fact. It was also initially the British position that the mere fact of *Altmark's* carriage of prisoners was sufficient to justify the British incursion into Norwegian waters.[17] However, this position was refined over the course of the incident. To the present author, it seems that the fact of carrying prisoners was something of a red herring. Dau's misunderstanding may be forgiven on the basis that he had no legal advice available. On the British side, the misunderstanding seems to have been based on an erroneous belief that *Altmark* had been permitted to enter Bergen harbour and this would have meant that her prisoners should have been released (Hague XIII, Articles 21–22).[18] Professor O'Connell has stated that the UK was frankly unconcerned with the law until after the fact, when the law was used by the British purely retrospectively to offer the best justification available. On reflection, the 'basing operations' argument appeared to the British to carry little weight, correctly in the view of this author.[19] For the unreliability of it, one need only observe that Hague XIII, Article 10, explicitly permits mere passage to 'prizes belonging to belligerents': it would be absurd if belligerents were entitled to move prizes through neutral territorial seas, but not prisoners taken from prizes. Consequently, the Norwegian failure to discover the prisoners, or even to look for them, cannot be criticised.[20]

F. Seeking sanctuary

The prohibition on seeking sanctuary is a rule of customary law not expressly reflected in Hague XIII. However, the drafters of the *San Remo Manual* considered in 1994 that several of Hague XIII's provisions had the combined effect of producing such a general rule.[21] Captain Dau's express intent in entering Norwegian territorial waters was to evade capture and detection by the British. Did this intention rob his passage of otherwise lawful character? The British Prime Minister Neville Chamberlain asserted in Parliament that it did.[22] One nearly contemporaneous scholar reflected that there was no rule which prohibited mere passage, assuming it was navigationally justifiable, even notwithstanding the captain's purpose in evading capture.[23] Only use of neutral waters outside the confines of mere passage would breach the belligerent vessel's obligations to the neutral state. On this analysis, so long as Dau was exercising passage lawfully, which arguably he was all the while he was making progress south towards Germany, the lawfulness of his

17 Royal Institute of International Affairs, 'The '*Altmark*' Incident' (1940) 17(4) *Bulletin of International News* 225, 225, 231.

18 The discovery of the truth no doubt influenced the shift in British rhetoric on the law. See generally FO 371/28983, *Correspondence re "Altmark" Incident*, available at the National Archives, Kew.

19 O'Connell, *The Influence of Law on Sea Power*, above n 1, 40–41.

20 Norway made this point in response to the British protest; see Royal Institute of International Affairs, above n 18, 227–279. For an alternate view see Waldock, above n 8, 222–226.

21 *San Remo Manual*, above n 6, 97 [17.1].

22 Royal Institute of International Affairs, above n 18, 231.

23 Waldock, 'The Release of the Altmark's Prisoners', above n 7, 232.

presence in territorial waters might not be impugned on the basis of the sanctuary principle.[24] Against this, the British argued that mere passage could not be lawful if it were not 'innocent', and *Altmark*'s passage was not innocent because she was carrying prisoners and at the same time seeking to evade capture.[25] The boundaries of what is and is not 'innocent' in the context of mere passage are, however, poorly defined. The difficulty with the British position in this respect was summed up in a letter, dated 27 February 1940, from a Foreign Office official to an official in the Admiralty, concluding as follows:

> As a matter of strict law, we would doubtless always maintain that HM Ships were entitled in certain circumstances to enter neutral territorial waters, or even ports, with prisoners, but it seems obvious that we must do our best to avoid this particular contingency arising in existing circumstances, or we shall lay ourselves open to very telling charges of hypocrisy and should have to rely on somewhat fine distinctions which would not appeal to the man in the street. Any argument as to what constitutes 'innocent passage' with prisoners and what constitutes 'innocent passage' without prisoners will be hailed as a quibble of the most blatant kind, and I would suggest a confidential instruction might be given to commanders to watch their step in this particular connexion.[26]

Accordingly, the scope of the rule, whether expressed as a prohibition on seeking sanctuary, or an insistence that mere passage be 'innocent', is unclear and, when applied to the facts of the *Altmark*, it does not allow for a firm conclusion as to the lawfulness or otherwise of her presence in Norwegian waters.

G. The 24-hour rule

Hague XIII, Article 12, provides that 'belligerent war-ships are not permitted to remain in the ports, road steads, or territorial waters of [a neutral] Power for more than twenty-four hours, except in cases covered by the present Convention'. Norwegian neutrality regulations (Article 4) reflected this rule 'except on account of damage or stranding', exceptions which did not apply to *Altmark*. Other specific exceptions 'covered by' Hague XIII were also reflected in Norway's neutrality regulations. For example, belligerent warships were forbidden from sailing from Norwegian ports within 24 hours of the departure of a merchant vessel flying its enemy's flag.[27] On the face of it, then, *Altmark*, which entered Norwegian territorial waters on 13 February and was still there demonstrating no intention to depart

24 Royal Institute of International Affairs, above n 17, 228.

25 R W Tucker, 'The Law of Neutrality at Sea' (1955) 50 *International Law Studies* 239 n 87a.

26 Letter from C E Steel (Foreign Office) to Mr C G Jarrett (Admiralty), dated 27 February 1940, FO 371/28983, National Archives, Kew.

27 Hague Convention XIII, art 16; Norway's neutrality rules, Article 4(4).

on 16 February, was in breach of the 24-hour rule as it was contained in Hague XIII and Norway's neutrality rules. She should, therefore, have been interned by the Norwegian authorities.[28]

The attractive clarity of this position is regrettably undermined by persisting doubt about the relationship between the 24-hour rule and the passage provisions in Hague XIII, Articles 9–10. Is 'mere passage' an exception to the 24-hour rule 'covered by' Hague XIII, or must passage rights be exercised subject to the 24-hour rule? The specific inclusion of 'territorial waters' in the text of Article 12 suggests that passage is subject to the rule. Later works, including the *San Remo Manual* and the Helsinki Principles, have also concluded that mere passage is, or should be, subject to the 24-hour rule, but add the rider that where the length of passage is such that it could not ordinarily be completed within 24 hours, a longer period is allowed.[29] Dau intended to transit from above Trondheim to the Skaggerak, a passage which would usually take more than 24 hours. Based on these two authorities, Dau's passage was lawful under Hague XIII, regardless of his plain intent to evade capture in doing so. If this view is correct, the British should have waited until Dau exited Norwegian waters to cross the Skaggerak before acting. However, it should be added that if interpreted in this way, the 24-hour rule does not really act to limit passage in neutral waters at all: the exception somewhat eclipses the rule.

The upshot of this analysis is that *Altmark's* extended presence in Norwegian territorial seas cannot categorically be asserted to have been unlawful. Professor O'Connell argues this was of little concern to the UK at the time. It is certainly true that contemporaneous accounts of the *Graf Spee* affair demonstrate much more sophisticated reliance on the law in the representations by HM government than do those of the *Altmark*. Many of the initial British assertions in the latter case – that the prisoners were unlawfully captured or that their mere presence on board rendered *Altmark's* passage through neutral waters unlawful – do not survive scrutiny. Professor O'Connell's point is neatly illustrated by the following passage, taken from a letter from Foreign Secretary Lord Halifax to His Majesty's Ambassador to Norway on 17 February 1940:

> I did not, however, labour the legal side of all this. I was no lawyer, and the legal considerations anyhow seemed to me to be of secondary importance. What I felt matters was that 300 or 400 British subjects had been kept for weeks and months in conditions which no decent-minded person would have kept a dog or a sheep. Her Majesty's Government felt that the least the Norwegian Government could have done would have been to have found some pretext to detain the *Altmark* at Bergen, and in any case to have looked

28 Hague Convention XIII, art 24.

29 *San Remo Manual*, above n 6, [21]; International Law Association, *Helsinki Principles on the Law of Maritime Neutrality*, 1998 section 2.2, in Dietrich Schindler and Jiri Toman (eds), *The Laws of Armed Conflicts* (Brill, 2004), p1425, 1427.

> for and taken off any sick among the British prisoners. It was the fact that they had not even done this of which we felt so well entitled to complain.[30]

The way the letter is phrased supports the view that, even as late as 17 February, the British still believed *Altmark* had entered Bergen.

H. British authority to enforce Norwegian neutrality

If *Altmark's* presence in Norwegian waters was unlawful, then the UK would have had to show that Norway was 'unwilling or unable' to enforce its position as a neutral vis-à-vis *Altmark* before using force to rectify the breach. Militarily, the naval resources committed to the *Altmark* incident do not suggest Norwegian inability. At the political level, however, Norway was undoubtedly unwilling to provoke invasion by antagonising Germany. As it happened, Norwegian fears in this respect would be realised within a month. The British would later argue that Norway had routinely turned a blind eye to German submarines operating in Norwegian territorial waters and that *Altmark* was just another example of Norway's favourable treatment of Germany.[31] The British government would never explicitly say that these repeated infringements of Norway's neutrality allowed it to take reprisal action, or that it was on this basis that *Altmark's* prisoners were liberated. However, this hypothetical argument has received favourable treatment by other scholars.[32] Of course, such an argument would entail an admission that the liberation was otherwise an illegal act. If the reprisal argument failed, this would leave the British government with no choice but to accept that its actions were unlawful, which could have been diplomatically disastrous. The risk in such a position may explain the British reluctance to adopt it, although belligerent reprisal would be used throughout the war by the British to justify other conduct – for example, the long-distance Atlantic blockade against Germany.[33]

I. British use of Norwegian territorial and internal waters

If the reprisal argument is put aside, then the British use of Norwegian waters (both territorial and internal) must be assessed under the specific rules of maritime neutrality. Two elements of the British operation – aircraft reconnaissance, and the first attempt to board *Altmark* – were carried out in Norwegian territorial waters. The second, successful, boarding by *HMS Cossack* was carried out in Norwegian internal waters.

30 Letter, Lord Halifax (Foreign Secretary) to His Majesty's Ambassador to Norway, 17 February 1940, FO 371/28983, National Archives, Kew.

31 Lord Strabolgi, *The Battle of the River Plate*, above n 8, 136.

32 Tucker, 'The Law of Neutrality at Sea', above n 25, 221–222.

33 See generally Tucker, 'The Law of Neutrality at Sea', above n 25.

While belligerent vessels have certain passage rights in territorial waters, belligerent aircraft have none. Neutral airspace is inviolable.[34] If the British reconnaissance planes entered Norwegian airspace (which includes airspace above Norwegian territorial seas), as the pilot of one of them hinted afterwards, then this was *prima facie* an unlawful incursion.

As regards the first attempt to board *Altmark* by *Arethusa*, *Intrepid*, and *Ivanhoe*, these vessels did have a right of mere passage in Norwegian territorial waters but acted in breach of it by attempting to board an enemy vessel. This amounted to the conduct of hostilities in neutral waters, clearly prohibited by Hague XIII, Article 2. However, the 'unwilling or unable' rule discussed previously permits proportionate and necessary actions to rectify a breach of neutrality regulations by an enemy. If *Altmark*'s presence in Norwegian territorial waters on 16 February was unlawful, then the present author believes that an operation limited to liberating those prisoners would have been a proportionate response.

Altmark entered Norwegian internal waters when she entered the Jøssingfjord. The various government statements largely ignored the fact the Jøssingfjord was in Norwegian internal, not territorial, waters.[35] Arguably, though, this was a critical fact. Here, *Altmark* had no right of passage whatsoever and was plainly in breach of Norwegian neutrality regulations. Dau's decision to enter the Jøssingfjord is curious because he had seen once already the Norwegian warships come to his rescue by riding off the first British attempt to draw close enough to board him. This should have led him to stick to his plan.[36] He would be reasonably safe all the while he was in Norwegian care, and a British attempt to board in the Skaggerak was likely to end in disaster, especially due to its proximity to Germany and German naval and air assets. The British would have been unlikely to sink him because of the number of British lives that would have been imperilled. Sticking to his plan, even notwithstanding his discovery by the British, remained Dau's best chance of success. Instead, he concluded that he would be safer in internal waters, perhaps because it would have seemed a more egregious breach of Norwegian neutrality by the British to rescue their prisoners here rather than in the territorial sea. In the present author's view, however, the reverse was true. By now, he was using a dead-end inlet in internal waters to attempt to evade capture by the enemy and was in flagrant excess of passage rights. Once he entered internal waters, the law required him to release his prisoners. By rights, the Norwegian authorities, in the form of the Norwegian warships present, should have compelled him to do so or threatened him with internment. They did not, arguably justifying the British

34 Hague Regulations on Aerial Warfare, art 40. See also Program on Humanitarian Policy and Conflict Research, Commentary on the *HPCR Manual on International Law Applicable to Air and Missile Warfare* (2009) 312.

35 See generally Royal Institute of International Affairs, above n 17.

36 The German government's protest attributed the decision to one of necessity in self-defence, but the proven robustness of Dau's Norwegian escort undermines this position. See Royal Institute of International Affairs, above n 17, 230.

intervention. This argument may have sat ill in the mouth of the UK, whose harassment it was that had driven Dau to seek refuge in internal waters. That may be why it was never raised in official British government pronouncements.

IV. Conclusion

The *Altmark* incident affords a fruitful discussion of the rules on belligerent passage in neutral waters, even if it provides relatively few firm answers. O'Connell uses this case and that of the *Graf Spee* to illustrate the capacity and the limitations of the law's ability to influence the exercise of sea power. He is certainly correct that the UK's approach to legal justification in each case was markedly different. British activity in Norwegian territorial waters possibly exceeded what maritime neutrality law permitted, although this author believes that the vagaries in the rules make both sides arguable. In part at least, British behaviour was driven by a factual error: the British believed, at the material time, that *Altmark* had entered Bergen. If the facts were as the British had thought them to be, then their justification for forcing the prisoners' release would have been all the stronger, as the *Graf Spee* chapter makes clear.

There are arguments in support of the lawfulness of the British operation in the Jøssingfjord, even though they were not advanced by Britain at the time. The reprisal argument could well have justified the British action, as Tucker demonstrated long ago.[37] Moreover, Dau's decision to enter Norwegian internal waters was ill-advised, and would have been an important fact supporting the British legal case if they were inclined to rely on it. While he may or may not have been in breach of his passage rights in the territorial sea, he had no right to enter internal waters, even as an act of self-preservation. It was open to Norway to take remedial action in respect of that breach: Norwegian failure to do so, or to communicate an intention to do so, could have been used by the British to ground a legal case for the prisoners' release. Ultimately, the diplomatic dispute went unresolved: Germany invaded Norway in March 1941, Norway and the UK became allies, and each lost its appetite to labour the point any further.

37 Tucker, 'The Law of Neutrality at Sea', above n 25, 221 n 57.

16

THE SINKING OF *ARA GENERAL BELGRANO*

David Letts

I. Introduction

The Falkland/Malvinas Islands[1] are a small group of islands situated in the South Atlantic Ocean approximately 350 nm east of the Argentine mainland. An ongoing dispute over the sovereignty of the islands has existed between Argentina and the United Kingdom of Great Britain and Northern Ireland[2] for nearly two centuries. Various attempts have been made to resolve the sovereignty dispute over the islands, including action by the United Nations General Assembly in 1965, when UNGA Resolution 2065 called upon both the UK and Argentina to ' . . . proceed without delay with . . . negotiations . . . with a view to finding a peaceful solution to the problem'.[3] Although negotiations between the UK and Argentina did commence in 1966 and continued on occasion until February 1982, they were not successful in resolving the question of sovereignty over the islands.

Against this backdrop, the ruling Argentine military junta decided in early 1982 to forcibly assert its sovereignty claims over the Falkland Islands by deploying

1 The islands are referred to as the Falkland Islands by the United Kingdom and Las Islas Malvinas by Argentina. For ease of reference, this chapter will refer to the islands as the Falkland Islands, but in doing so, no inferences regarding sovereignty claims over the islands is intended or should be inferred.

2 The official name of the political union formed by England, Scotland, Wales and Northern Ireland. For an explanation of the difference in terminology between 'United Kingdom', 'Great Britain' and 'British Isles', see Ordnance Survey, *The difference between UK, Great Britain and the British Isles* (3 August 2011) Ordnance Survey <www.ordnancesurvey.co.uk/blog/2011/08/whats-the-difference-between-uk-britain-and-british-isles/>. Notwithstanding these differences, on occasion in this chapter the terms 'the UK' or 'Britain/British' are used interchangeably to refer to the same entity.

3 *Question of the Falkland Islands (Malvinas)*, GA Res 2065 (XX), UN Doc A/RES/2065 (16 December 1965) available at <https://documents-dds-ny.un.org/doc/RESOLUTION/GEN/NR0/218/28/IMG/NR021828.pdf?OpenElement>.

DOI: 10.4324/9781003307013-20

Argentine military forces to overthrow the British authorities in the islands. On 2 April 1982, an international armed conflict broke out between the UK and Argentina when Argentine military forces landed on the Falkland Islands and took control of the islands by forcing the governor of the Falkland Islands to surrender.[4] The armed conflict continued until British forces retook the islands following a naval, air, and land campaign which concluded with the formal surrender of Argentine forces on the Falkland Islands on 14 June 1982.[5]

At the time of the armed conflict, the UK and Argentina were both experiencing internal political and economic disruption, which was having an impact on the political stability and leadership in each country.[6] The government led by Margaret Thatcher in the UK was attempting to introduce wide-ranging economic reform to the British economy amid widespread resistance among significant elements of the population. One outcome of these reforms was that the Royal Navy was in a fragile economic and materiel state, with budget pressures resulting in decisions being made to reduce the size and capability of the Royal Navy – including the sale of the light aircraft carrier *HMS Invincible* to Australia.[7] Argentina was experiencing similar difficulties as the country was being led by an unpopular military junta

4 The precise nature of the conflict between the United Kingdom and Argentina has been the subject of varied opinion. See, e.g., Marina Mancini, 'The Effects of a State of War or Armed Conflict' in Marc Weller (ed), *The Oxford Handbook of the Use of Force in International Law* (Oxford University Press, 2015), 1001; she opines that '(D)uring the Falklands conflict, both the UK and Argentina established maritime exclusion zones, though neither of them recognized the state of war': at 1001. See also William Fenrick, 'The Exclusion Zone Device in the Law of Naval Warfare' (1986), 24 *Canadian Yearbook of International Law* 91; he refers to the war being a 'limited conflict' as distinct from a 'general war': at 115. Others adopt a more circumspect approach without directly addressing the nature of the conflict. See, e.g., Stephen Haines 'War at Sea: Nineteenth-century laws for twenty-first century wars?' (2016) 98(2) *International Review of the Red Cross Volume* 419; he simply notes that the 'Falklands/Malvinas War (April – June 1982) was fundamentally a maritime campaign involving classic sea-control and sea-denial operations coupled with power projection through amphibious assault': at 427. The approach taken in this chapter is that an international armed conflict existed once Argentine forces landed on the Falkland Islands, and as a matter of law, military action could have occurred between the two belligerents anywhere in each other's territory, including maritime zones, as well as other maritime and land areas that were beyond the sovereignty of neutral states.

5 For a timeline of the Falklands/Malvinas war, see: 'The Falklands War: Timeline' (14 June 2016) *The Telegraph* <www.telegraph.co.uk/news/2016/06/14/the-falklands-war-timeline/>.

6 See Simon Jenkins, 'How Margaret Thatcher's Falklands gamble paid off', *The Guardian* (online), 9 April 2013 <www.theguardian.com/politics/2013/apr/09/margaret-thatcher-falklands-gamble>.

7 The sale of HMS Invincible to Australia was proposed as part of the cuts to British Defence spending that were identified in the 1981 UK Defence White Paper: <https://publications.parliament.uk/pa/cm199798/cmselect/cmdfence/138/13804.htm>. After the Argentine forces landed in the Falkland Islands the sale of HMS *Invincible* was placed 'on hold' at the request of the United Kingdom government so that HMS *Invincible* could take part in the Falklands campaign. Ultimately, the proposal to sell HMS *Invincible* to Australia did not proceed following an exchange of letters on this topic between the Australian and UK Prime Ministers that can be found at <www.margaretthatcher.org/document/123346>. See also 'Navy chief a lone voice in push for new carrier', *The Canberra Times* (online), 1 January 2012 <www.canberratimes.com.au/act-news/navy-chief-a-lone-voice-in-push-for-new-carrier-20120101-1tjaq.html>.

which was overseeing an economy that was in chaos, with unemployment and inflation reaching record levels.[8]

Immediately after Argentine forces landed on the Falkland Islands on 2 April 1982, the UK broke off diplomatic relations with Argentina and announced that a naval task force would be assembled to take back the islands – by armed force if necessary.[9] The main elements of the task force sailed from major naval bases in the UK on 5 April 1982. Contemporaneously, the British government began to declare several maritime and air exclusion 'zones' (discussed later in this chapter) in areas in which British air and naval forces were located (or anticipated being located as the operation proceeded), including the area immediately surrounding the Falkland Islands. Argentina reciprocated these declarations.[10]

During the period between the landing of Argentine forces and the arrival of the British task force in the vicinity of the Falkland Islands, considerable efforts were made to attempt to resolve the conflict peacefully. These efforts included the 'shuttle diplomacy' of U.S. Secretary of State Alexander Haig as he tried to negotiate a settlement, as well as the passing of a UN Security Council resolution dealing with the situation.[11] Ultimately, these efforts were unsuccessful.

In terms of the build-up which led to battles between the British and Argentine forces, the period from 25 April through 1 May is crucial, as during this time, British forces successfully retook South Georgia[12] and the British naval task force arrived in the vicinity of the Falkland Islands. On 1 May 1982, Argentine aircraft launched an attack against the British naval task force and British aircraft launched their first raids on the Port Stanley (Falkland) airfield. On 2 May 1982, the British submarine *HMS Conqueror* successfully attacked and sank the Argentine cruiser *ARA Belgrano*, and nearly 400 sailors lost their lives.

Almost immediately afterwards, elements of controversy began to emerge regarding the circumstances surrounding the sinking of *Belgrano*, including questions regarding the location of the vessel in terms of the maritime exclusion zones which had been declared by the British around the Falkland Islands. This chapter will examine the key legal issues that accompanied the sinking of *Belgrano* on 2 May 1982.

8 For a brief description of the prevailing political situation in Argentina at the time, see generally 'Dirty War (Argentine History)', in *Encyclopaedia Britannica* (online) <www.britannica.com/event/Dirty-War>.

9 Margaret Thatcher, 'Speech to House of Commons: Falkland Islands', (Speech delivered at House of Commons, London, 3 April 1982). Audio of Thatcher's speech is available at: *HC S: [Falkland Islands] [Audio]*, Margaret Thatcher Foundation <www.margaretthatcher.org/document/110946>.

10 See Sandesh Sivakumaran, 'Exclusion Zones in the Law of Armed Conflict at Sea: Evolution in Law and Practice' (2016) 92 *International Law Studies* 154–181.

11 United Nations Security Council Resolution (UNSCR) 502 of 3 April 1982 was released immediately after the Argentine forces landed in the islands and, inter alia, it called for the immediate withdrawal of these forces. A subsequent resolution was passed (UNSCR 505 of 26 May 1982) well after the British landing operations had commenced.

12 South Georgia (and the South Sandwich Islands) is a small British Overseas Territory in the South Atlantic Ocean approximately 840 nm from the Falkland Islands.

A. History of the islands and the sovereignty dispute

To properly understand the facts leading up to the sinking of *Belgrano*, it is necessary to contextualise the sovereignty dispute over the islands which had existed between the UK and Argentina since 1833.

Reports of initial discovery and settlement of the Falkland Islands are conflicting, but it appears certain that at various times in the 1700s and early 1800s the islands were visited, and possibly inhabited, by the British, Spanish, and French for differing periods.[13] Before this time, the islands were uninhabited. Despite the existence of different views between the British and Argentines regarding the precise nature of occupancy, it is common ground that at the time of Argentine independence from Spain in 1816, the islands had been occupied by Spain from 1767–1811. During the 1820s, Argentina exercised some control over the islands through the appointment of governors, the regulation of fishing activities in the vicinity of the islands, granting of land concessions, and the establishment of small settlements.[14] The UK disputed the legality of the Argentine possession of the islands in the 1820s, and in 1833, after a visit by Capt. Onslow of the British Royal Navy, the Argentine military commander and his garrison were, according to the British, persuaded to leave the island peacefully.[15] Argentina has consistently and vigorously disputed this version of events.[16] Ownership, at least in a *de facto* sense, has rested with British authorities ever since, apart from the period 2 April through 14 June 1982 when Argentine forces were located in the Falkland Islands.

Notwithstanding, during the period from 1833 until the present time, there have been persistent calls from Argentina for sovereignty over the Falkland Islands to be handed to Argentina. Additionally, during the 1960s, the UN General Assembly passed two resolutions which had a bearing on the sovereignty of the islands. The first of these was UNGA Resolution 1514 (1960), which granted the right of self-determination to all peoples of non–self-governing Territories.[17] The second was UNGA Resolution 2065 (1965), which called upon the UK and Argentina to

13 The official position of the Falkland Islands government regarding the history of the islands is contained on its website: Falkland Islands Government, *Our History, Falkland Islands Government* <*www.falklands.gov.fk/our-people/our-history/*> *(henceforth 'Falkland History'); see also Joseph Mauro, 'The Falkland Islands War: Diplomatic Failure in April 1982' (Spring 2008) History Matters*, 17–39 <http://historymatters.appstate.edu/sites/historymatters.appstate.edu/files/falklandislandswar_000.pdf>.

14 Ibid.

15 Falkland Islands Government, *Our History*, above n 13.

16 See, e.g., letter from Cristina Fernández de Kirchner, President of the Argentine Republic, to Prime Minister David Cameron, 3 January 2013 <www.theguardian.com/uk/2013/jan/02/cristina-fernandez-kirchner-letter-cameron>, and the Press Release in response from the Falkland Islands Government: Falkland Islands Government, 'Reaction to open letter from President Fernández de Kirchner' (Press Release, 3 January 2013) <www.falklands.gov.fk/reaction-to-open-letter-from-president-fernandez-de-kirchner/>.

17 *Declaration on the granting of Independence to colonial countries and peoples*, GA Res 1514 (XV), UN Doc A/RES/1514 (14 December 1960). Note: the Falkland Islands had been listed as a non–self-governing Territory by the UN since the late 1940s.

peacefully resolve the sovereignty dispute over the islands.[18] Ultimately, however, neither of these UN resolutions made any significant headway towards resolving the sovereignty dispute between the UK and Argentina.

This brief outline of the historical context in which the April–June 1982 armed conflict between the two states unfolded, which ultimately led to the sinking of *ARA Belgrano*, is necessary to properly appreciate the circumstances that surrounded the sinking of the vessel on 2 May 1982. Having outlined this context, consideration of the situation that was unfolding in late April 1982 will now occur.

II. Background

A. ARA Belgrano

ARA Belgrano (ex-*USS Phoenix*) was a Brooklyn-class light cruiser that served in the Argentine Navy from 1951 after being purchased from the United States.[19] The ship entered service with the U.S. Navy in 1938, escaped unscathed following the Japanese attack on Pearl Harbor in 1941, and mainly saw service in the Pacific war theatre for the remainder of the Second World War. The ship had a displacement of approximately 10,000 tonnes and carried 6-inch (150 mm) guns as its heaviest armament. After purchase by Argentina, missiles were added to the ship's armament. At the time *Belgrano* was sunk, the ship was carrying a crew of nearly 1,100 officers and sailors.

B. HMS *Conqueror*

HMS Conqueror was a *Churchill*-class nuclear-powered submarine in service with the Royal Navy from 1971 until the boat was decommissioned in 1990. The submarine was 285 feet long and had a crew of 120 officers and sailors.[20] The submarine's sonar and its six torpedo tubes were all located in the bow of the boat.[21] At the time of the engagement with *Belgrano*, *HMS Conqueror* was carrying both Mark 8 and Mark 24 (Tigerfish) torpedoes.[22]

C. Military situation before the sinking

It was briefly noted earlier in this chapter that in the period immediately before the sinking of *Belgrano*, elements of British forces had successfully retaken South

18 *Question of the Falkland Islands (Malvinas)*, GA Res 2065 (XX), UN Doc A/RES/2065 (16 December 1965).

19 '*USS Phoenix (Cl-46)*', HistoryOfWar.org: Military History Encyclopedia on the Web, <www.historyofwar.org/articles/weapons_USS_Phoenix_CL46.html>.

20 Stuart Prebble, *Secrets of the Conqueror* (Faber and Faber Limited, 2012), 18, 37–41.

21 Ibid, 38.

22 Ibid, 110–111.

Georgia Island from the Argentine troops who had occupied that island since 3 April 1982. The significance of this action was that it clearly signalled the UK's intent to use the military forces that had been deployed to the South Atlantic, if necessary, to re-assert UK sovereignty over the Falkland Islands. Accordingly, there could be no doubt that military action to deal with potential threats to the British task force, such as the threat posed by the Argentine Navy, would be undertaken.

D. The declaration of 'zones'

One of the features of the conflict between Argentina and the UK was the declaration of a large number of maritime operational zones by both sides to the conflict. The sequence of declarations commenced with the UK's declaration of a 200-nm maritime exclusion zone (MEZ) around the Falkland Islands on 7 April 1982.[23] The character of this zone was altered on 30 April 1982 with the declaration by the British that there was now a total exclusion zone (TEZ) around the Islands.[24] The existence, and legal effect, of this zone became one of the central issues in the aftermath of the *Belgrano* sinking, due to claims and confusion regarding precisely where that vessel was located and heading at the time of the attack.

Two other zones declared by the UK were the 23 April 1982 declaration of a 'bubble' around the UK task force as it steamed south towards the Falkland Islands, and finally an extension of the TEZ to 12 nm from the Argentine mainland on 7 May 1982.

Zones established by Argentina were mainly in response to those declared by the UK. On 8 April 1982, Argentina declared a 200-nm exclusion zone around Las Islas Malvinas which reciprocated the zone declared by the UK the previous day. On 28 April 1982, Argentina declared a 200-nm exclusion zone extending from its coastline which was targeted at any British ships or aircraft that were found in that area. The final zone declared by the two belligerents during the conflict occurred on 11 May 1982, when Argentina declared the entire South Atlantic Ocean was a 'war zone'.

It is not necessary to thoroughly examine the range of zones which were declared by each of the two parties to the armed conflict in this chapter, but some further comment regarding the British TEZ around the Falkland Islands is needed as this was the zone which directly affected the operation which resulted in *Belgrano* being sunk. The stated purpose of the TEZ was to ensure that 'Argentine occupying forces will then be totally isolated – cut off by sea and air'[25], which

23 For a detailed analysis of these zones, see Sivakumaran, above n 10, and Richard Jaques (ed), *Maritime Operational Zones* (United States Naval War College, 2006), 4–8–4–13. <https://usnwc.edu/getattachment/Departments---Colleges/International-Law/Maritime-Operational-Zones/2013-Zones-Manual-(1).pdf.aspx>.

24 Jaques (ed), *Maritime Operational Zones*, above n 23, 4–8–4–11.

25 Margaret Thatcher, 'Address to House of Commons: Falkland Islands', (Address delivered at House of Commons, London, 29 April 1982) <https://api.parliament.uk/historic-hansard/commons/1982/apr/29/falkland-islands>.

would clearly assist the British forces with their plans to retake the islands by force (if necessary). In referring to the TEZ during a debate in the House of Commons, Prime Minister Thatcher advised[26] that the zone applied to:

> all ships and aircraft, whether military or civil, operating in support of the illegal occupation of the Falkland Islands. A complete blockade will be placed on all traffic supporting the occupation forces of Argentina. Maritime and aviation authorities have been informed of the imposition of the zone, in accordance with our international obligations.

The explanation of the purpose of the TEZ provided by Prime Minister Thatcher had one important impact in terms of the conduct of the Argentine Navy, as it may have created an expectation that ships and aircraft would only be attacked if they were found within the TEZ. While this 'expectation' may have existed, there is no legal basis for such a contention under the applicable *jus in bello* (i.e., the law of naval warfare). Provided it is accepted that there was an international armed conflict underway between the UK and Argentina, then the sinking of *Belgrano* was lawful as an enemy warship may be attacked merely because of its nature/status as a warship anywhere in the world outside of neutral states and neutral territorial seas.[27]

E. The attack

In late April 1982, the British task force was approaching the Falkland Islands from the northeast in preparation for the landings that would be needed to attempt to retake the Falkland Islands from the Argentine forces that were now stationed there. At the same time, the Argentine Navy also had major force elements at sea with the Argentine carrier, *ARA Veinticinco de Mayo*, and its escorts located to the north of the Falkland Islands while the cruiser *ARA General Belgrano* and its escorts were sailing in an area to the south.[28]

The commander of the task force, Rear Admiral 'Sandy' Woodward, was concerned about the threat posed to his ships by both *Veinticinco de Mayo* and its aircraft and *Belgrano*. Fortunately for Woodward, on 2 May, 1982 the submarine *Conqueror* was in contact with *Belgrano* and in a position to attack the cruiser – if permission to do so was obtained from his higher headquarters in London. Woodward did not have operational control of the submarine, and the extant rules of engagement (ROE) did not permit attacking the cruiser.

26 Ibid.

27 See Louise Doswald-Beck (ed), *San Remo Manual on International Law Applicable to Armed Conflicts at Sea* (Cambridge University Press, 1995), 114–117 for discussion of the applicability of targeting rules in the naval environment.

28 Admiral Sandy Woodward, *One Hundred Days: The Memoirs of the Falklands Battle Group Commander*, (Harper Collins), pp 146–148.

Woodward has described how he sought to issue an order to *Conqueror* to sink *Belgrano* as a means of communicating to his superiors in London that there was some urgency in seeking a change to the ROE that had been issued to the submarine so that an immediate attack could be launched while the submarine remained in contact with the cruiser.[29] This order was intercepted in the UK before it could be relayed to the *Conqueror*. However, the intent of the order was understood by Woodward's superiors, and after a hastily convened meeting between senior Royal Navy officers and the Prime Minister, the ROE issued to *Conqueror* were changed and the order given to sink the *Belgrano*.[30]

After receiving the order to sink *Belgrano* from headquarters in the UK, *Conqueror*'s commanding officer, Cmdr. Chris Wreford-Brown, decided to get into a firing position on the bow of the cruiser at a range of 1,400–1,800 yards on the opposite side from the two escorts that were accompanying the cruiser. It took approximately 30 minutes for the submarine to get itself into a firing position, and once this had been achieved, three Mark 8 torpedoes were fired at the cruiser. Two torpedoes reached their intended target and Cmdr. Wreford-Brown saw the result of one of the torpedoes striking *Belgrano* through the submarine's periscope. After confirming that the attack against *Belgrano* had been successfully carried out, Cmdr. Wreford-Brown's immediate priority was to ensure the safety of his submarine by clearing the area as quickly as possible.[31]

The effect of the torpedo strikes onboard *Belgrano* was immediate, with loss of power and a consequential loss of any real ability to prevent the sinking of the vessel. Capt. Hector Bonzo, *Belgrano*'s commanding officer, soon realised that it was necessary to abandon the ship and seek to save as many of his crew as possible. The order to abandon ship was duly given, and *Belgrano* sank a short while afterwards late in the day on 2 May.[32]

III. Analysis and outcomes

A. Means and methods of warfare

The method of warfare used to attack *Belgrano* was to order an attack by submarine against the cruiser. There is no doubt that using a submarine to launch an attack against a surface ship is a legitimate method of warfare,[33] so attention should now be turned to the means of warfare (i.e. the weapon used in the attack) to see if any issue arises.

29 Ibid, pp 154–156; Prebble, *Secrets of the Conqueror*, above n 20 p 109.

30 Woodward, *One Hundred Days*, above n 28, pp 149–163 where a description of the immediate sequence of events that led to the sinking of the *Belgrano* is provided; reference to the change in ROE being approved is provided at p 158.

31 Ibid, pp 162.

32 Woodward, *One Hundred Days*, above n 28, p 162; Prebble, *Secrets of the Conqueror*, above n 20, p 117.

33 See *San Remo Manual*, above n 27, 121–122.

The means of warfare used to attack *Belgrano* were Mark 8 Mod 4 torpedoes. The Mark 8 torpedo had been initially developed in the First World War and subsequently modified over the succeeding years. The basic legal requirement governing the use of torpedoes in international armed conflict is laid out in Hague Convention VIII of 1907, which requires that torpedoes must 'become harmless when they have missed their mark'.[34] Meeting this requirement was not seriously an issue in the waters of the South Atlantic Ocean on 1 May, as the only vessels in the immediate vicinity of the attack were *Belgrano* and its escorts. Accordingly, the three Mark 8 torpedoes fired by *Conqueror*, with two of them being assessed as having hit the cruiser and the third thought to have hit one of *Belgrano*'s accompanying escorts without exploding,[35] do not present any problem in terms of the legality of the means of warfare deployed in the attack against *Belgrano*.

Another consideration that might be contemplated is whether an issue of proportionality arises in relation to the sinking. From a *jus in bello* perspective, proportionality will usually be quite irrelevant in the context of sinking an enemy warship during an international armed conflict, as there is little doubt that sinking such a vessel will provide a definite military advantage and the prospect of any civilian casualties is low. Indeed, in the case of the *Belgrano* sinking, it would be difficult to establish any breach of *jus in bello* proportionality, given that the location of the engagement meant that the potential effect on civilians was non-existent. With only military objects and combatants targeted, there was not anything excessive in terms of how the attack was conducted.[36]

If the question of proportionality is viewed from a *jus ad bellum* perspective, the conventional approach would be to assess the legal validity of the decision to apply the strategic level of force in self-defence by sending the naval task force to the South Atlantic at all. There is considerable support for the view that the response from the UK to the Argentine occupation of the islands was appropriate, and if that view is accepted, then there was not a breach of *jus ad bellum* proportionality as a result of the overall military response to the Argentine military action.

B. The use of zones

A brief description of how zones were declared and used during the conflict was provided earlier in this chapter. The question that now needs to be posed is: what was the legal effect of these declarations and their use? First, there is no doubt that the declaration of a maritime exclusion zone during armed conflict cannot be interpreted as the establishment of any type of 'kill box' or 'free-fire zone' where the mere

34 *Convention (VIII) Relative to the Laying of Automatic Submarine Contact Mines*, 36 Stat. 2332, The Hague, 18 October 1907 (Hague Convention VIII); see also *San Remo Manual*, above n 27, 168 [79.1–79.2].

35 Prebble, *Secrets of the Conqueror*, above n 20, 116.

36 AP1 art 51 (5)(b); also, Geoffrey S. Corn, 'Self-defense Targeting: Blurring the Line between the Jus ad Bellum and the Jus in Bello', 88 *International Law Studies* 57.

presence of a vessel would be sufficient to render an attack against that vessel lawful. The legality of attacking a target either inside or outside the zone is governed by the same rules of international humanitarian law – in this case, the law of naval warfare – that would apply in any armed conflict. Further, terminology applied in making the zone declaration must be considered in context, and in this regard, the use of the phrase 'liable to be attacked' when the UK declared the TEZ does not amount to any certainty that a vessel that entered the TEZ without permission would be attacked.[37] Analysis of the manner in which Argentina declared the entire South Atlantic a 'war zone' with any UK-flagged vessel navigating 'towards the area of operations' being considered hostile and subject to action being taken 'accordingly', could, on one view, lead to the conclusion that this declaration was not consistent with the law of armed conflict.[38] However, it is also possible to view the Argentine declaration as being something less than an outright breach of the law in the same manner as that which was contemplated for the UK's declaration. In any event, and perhaps because of the remote location of the conflict, the opportunity for Argentina to implement its declaration through military action did not arise during the conflict.

While the declaration of zones by both the UK and Argentina provided considerable disquiet among the international community, it appears that the former Soviet Union was the only neutral state that lodged a formal protest concerning these zones.[39] Finally, while the declaration of a zone may serve as a means of attempting to limit or restrict the area in which operations are being conducted, it does not prevent lawful military action occurring outside the zone, as the sinking of *Belgrano* clearly demonstrates.

C. The Second Geneva Convention

One of the requirements placed on parties to an international armed conflict that occurs at sea is provided by Article 18 of the Second Geneva Convention:[40]

> After each engagement, Parties to the conflict shall, without delay, take all possible measures to search for and collect the shipwrecked, wounded and sick, to protect them against pillage and ill-treatment, to ensure their adequate care, and to search for the dead and prevent their being despoiled.

Several considerations must be taken into account to determine if the parties to the conflict have complied with the requirements of Article 18. First, it should be

37 See Jaques, *Maritime Operational Zones*, above n 23, 4–11.

38 Ibid.

39 Howard S. Levie, 'Means and Methods of Combat at Sea' (1988) 14 *Syracuse Journal of International Law and Commerce* 227–234.

40 Geneva Convention for the Amelioration of the Condition of Wounded, Sick and Shipwrecked Members of Armed Forces at Sea (Second Geneva Convention), 12 August 1949, 75 UNTS 85 (entered into force 21 Oct 1950).

noted that the obligation is placed on 'the Parties to the conflict', which means that both the UK and Argentina had an obligation to search and collect those sailors who had been wounded, shipwrecked, or killed by the sinking of *Belgrano*. While it is very clear that Argentina complied with this obligation, it is not clear whether the UK took any steps towards meeting its obligations.

It was noted earlier in this chapter that *Conqueror* did not remain in the vicinity of the sinking as the commanding officer's priority, quite reasonably, was to ensure the safety of his vessel. However, the legal obligation is not placed on an individual commanding officer – it is placed on 'the Parties', so the relevant question to be asked is whether the UK did whatever could reasonably be done to discharge its obligation under Article 18 'after [the] engagement'.

Perhaps the answer to this question lies in an appreciation of the limitations that are placed on the submarine commander, as well as the task force commander, after the successful attack and the application of those limitations to the circumstances that prevailed in the South Atlantic in 1982. At the time *Belgrano* was sunk, the British task force was hundreds of miles away from the area where the attack by *Conqueror* took place. Knowledge of the sinking took a little while to occur, and even with that knowledge, the ability of the task force commander to provide any meaningful assistance in recovering those affected by the sinking was extremely limited. Accordingly, it can be reasonably concluded that from a practical point of view, there was very little that the UK, as a party to the conflict, could do to assist with recovering any of *Belgrano*'s crew members.[41]

D. Changes to the rules of engagement

The fact that the rules of engagement issued to *Conqueror* were amended to permit the sinking of *Belgrano* does not provide any substantial legal issues. Seeking a change of rules of engagement to reflect a change in the tactical situation is a reasonably common occurrence during an armed conflict, and the change that was authorised to permit *HMS Conqueror* to sink *Belgrano* was certainly permitted under the law of naval warfare.

IV. Legal proceedings

There were several calls for legal action to be initiated following the sinking of *Belgrano*. In Britain, concerns were raised that the sinking of the vessel had occurred at a time when there was still the possibility that a peaceful resolution to the dispute between the UK and Argentina was possible. The leading figure who raised these

41 Further information regarding the obligation placed on Parties under art 18 of the Second Geneva Convention can be found in the International Committee of the Red Cross (ICRC) Commentary of 2017 available at: *Commentary of 2017 Article 18 Search for casualties after an engagement*, International Committee of the Red Cross <https://ihl-databases.icrc.org/applic/ihl/ihl.nsf/Comment.xsp?action=openDocument&documentId=EF5D4375E2D6EB80C1258115003C1D4A>.

concerns was the Labour MP Tam Dalyell, who accused the Prime Minister of authorising the attack at a time when *Belgrano* did not pose any threat so that any prospect of avoiding military action to retake the Falkland Islands would be lost. The matter was pursued in the public domain, and in the House of Commons, for a considerable period after the war ended, with a satisfactory resolution of the accusations against Mrs Thatcher never fully achieved.[42]

A different attempt to initiate legal proceedings occurred in the year 2000, when relatives of two sailors who were killed when *Belgrano* sank attempted to bring a claim for compensation against Britain before the European Court of Human Rights on the basis that the right to life of Argentine conscripts serving in *Belgrano* had been violated. The European Court of Human Rights rejected the claim as it found it inadmissible due to time limitations on lodging a claim that was stipulated under the European Convention on Human Rights.[43]

V. Enduring significance and conclusion

Accordingly, although a variety of legal proceedings were contemplated or commenced following the sinking, none of them reached a court or tribunal for final adjudication on the merits of the matter. Claims that the sinking occurred in dubious legal circumstances therefore remain, although the position adopted in this chapter is that the decision to attack *Belgrano* was permitted under the law of armed conflict and it was conducted lawfully. Nevertheless, there is ongoing interest and comment regarding various aspects of the sinking of *Belgrano* due to the divergence of opinion regarding the legality of the action which remains contentious.[44]

42 See, e.g., the opposing views on this matter provided in The Guardian as part of Tam Dalyell's obituary: Brian Wilson, Tam Dalyell obituary' (27 January 2017) *The Guardian* <www.theguardian.com/politics/2017/jan/26/tam-dalyell-obituary>, and cf: the views in Sir Lawrence Freedman, *The Official History of the Falklands Campaign* (Routledge, 2005), 240; and reported in Francis Elliott, '"Belgrano" ordered to attack British ships on day before sinking, secret report reveals' (28 December 2003) *The Independent* <www.independent.co.uk/news/uk/politics/>. belgrano-ordered-to-attack-british-ships-on-day-before-sinking-secret-report-reveals-84183.html>. See also 'UK sued over Belgrano sinking' (29 June 2000) *BBC News* <http://news.bbc.co.uk/1/hi/uk/812146.stm>. Here it is claimed that 'the Argentine Defence Ministry, in a report in 1994, concluded that the Belgrano's fate was "a legal act of war"'. However, this claim is disputed in a number of web-based forums, including 'The Belgrano Inquiry': *Thirty years on: an Argentine view*, The Belgrano Inquiry <http://belgranoinquiry.com/may-2nd-2012-mr-moro-replies>.

43 Luis Diamantina Romero de Ibanez and Roberto Guillermo Rojas v United Kingdom, Application No 58692/00. See Press Release at: Registrar, European Court of Human Rights, 'Luis Diamantina Romero de Ibanez and Roberto Guillermo Rojas v. UK inadmisible' (Press Release, 19 July 2000) <http://hudoc.echr.coe.int/eng-press?i=003-67974-68442>.

44 See *EJIL Talk*, where questions regarding proportionality from both *jus ad bellum* and *jus in bello* perspectives have been raised: Kieran Tinkler, 'Understanding the Use of Zones and the Concept of Proportionality: Enduring Lessons from the Falklands War' on European Journal of International Law', *EJIL: Talk!* (13 December 2017) <www.ejiltalk.org/understanding-the-use-of-zones-and-the-concept-of-proportionality-enduring-lessons-from-the-falklands-war/>.

17

THE *MAVI MARMARA* INCIDENT

Douglas Guilfoyle

I. Introduction

As is well known, Israel became the occupying power of the Palestinian territories known as the West Bank and the Gaza Strip in 1967. These territories are now widely, though not universally, acknowledged as forming the territory of the state of Palestine.[1] Israel remains in occupation of the West Bank, but began a staged military withdrawal from the Gaza Strip in 1994 as part of the peace negotiations of 1993–1995 between Israel and the Palestinian Authority which resulted in the agreements called the 'Oslo Accords'.[2] However, in Palestinian Authority elections in 2006, the militant armed group Hamas won enough seats in the Legislative Council to form a government. A protracted struggle between Hamas and the previously dominant Fatah faction followed and resulted in 2007 in a situation whereby Fatah governs the West Bank and Hamas the Gaza Strip.[3] Given Hamas' 'extremely belligerent stance towards Israel', Israeli declarations of Hamas as a 'terrorist organisation' and Gaza as 'hostile territory' followed in 2007.[4] In

1 See UN Doc A/RES/67/19 (4 December 2012) according to Palestine the status of a non-member observer State, adopted by a recorded vote of 138 in favour to nine against, with 41 abstentions and five absent. On the voting record, see: UN Press Release GA/11317 (29 November 2012), <www.un.org/press/en/2012/ga11317.doc.htm>.

2 See generally: 'Report of the international fact-finding mission to investigate violations of international law, including international humanitarian and human rights law, resulting from the Israeli attacks on the flotilla of ships carrying humanitarian assistance', Human Rights Council, 27 September 2010, UN Doc. A/HRC/15/21, para. 26 ('FFM Report').

3 'Profile: Hamas Palestinian movement', *BBC News*, 11 July 2004, <www.bbc.com/news/world-middle-east-13331522>.

4 Russell Buchan, 'The Mavi Marmara Incident and the Application of International Humanitarian Law by Quasi-Judicial Bodies' in D. Jinks et al. (eds), *Applying International Humanitarian Law in*

DOI: 10.4324/9781003307013-21

particular, and as a result of increased rocket attacks upon Israel from within the Gaza Strip, Israel implemented from 2007 onwards a series of restrictions on the 'passage of goods, the supply of oil and electricity and the movement of persons to and from the Gaza Strip'.[5] (The intensity of these restrictions has varied over time.) In 2009, these measures were supplemented by a maritime blockade of the Gaza Strip, originally imposed in the context of 'Operation Cast Lead' (a major Israeli offensive within Gaza against Hamas). Israel has published details of its blockade giving notice that the maritime area off the coast of Gaza 'is closed to all maritime traffic',[6] and has justified it as a measure permitted under the law of armed conflict (LOAC).[7]

II. Background[8]

At 04:30 on 31 May 2010, the Israeli Defence Force (IDF) boarded a flotilla of six vessels on the high seas bound for the Gaza Strip in order to enforce Israel's blockade of that territory.[9] The largest of these vessels was the *Mavi Marmara*, flagged to Comoros.[10] It carried a cargo of humanitarian supplies and activists from a number of organisations of diverse nationalities (though many were Turkish). The stated aim of the flotilla was both to deliver aid and to breach Israel's naval blockade.[11] Israel made it clear that unless the vessels diverted to Ashdod and submitted their cargoes to inspection and distribution through Israeli channels, they would be boarded.[12]

The IDF boarding of the *Mavi Marmara* involved first the use of stun grenades and subsequently live fire. The other five flotilla vessels were intercepted without loss of life; aboard the *Mavi Marmara*, clashes between IDF soldiers and activists resulted in nine civilian deaths. The principal difference between the boarding of the *Mavi Marmara* and other flotilla vessels is that the others were boarded by boat.

Judicial and Quasi-Judicial Bodies (TMC Asser Press, 2014), 480 (quoting the 'Statement of Israel's Foreign Minister Regarding Israel's Policy towards Hamas and its Terrorism', 1 October 2007).

5 The Public Commission to Examine the Maritime Incident of 31 May 2010, 'Report: Part One' (23 January 2011), p. 30 ('Turkel Commission Report'), <www.gov.il/BlobFolder/generalpage/downloads_eng1/en/ENG_turkel_eng_a.pdf>.

6 Ministry of Transport and Road Safety (Israel) 'Blockade of Gaza Strip' (Notice to Mariners 1/2009), <http://asp.mot.gov.il/en/shipping/notice2mariners/547-no12009>.

7 See Israel Ministry of Foreign Affairs, 'The Gaza flotilla and the maritime blockade of Gaza: Legal background' (31 May 2010), <http://mfa.gov.il/MFA/AboutIsrael/State/Law/Pages/Gaza_flotilla_maritime_blockade_Gaza-Legal_background_31-May-2010.aspx>.

8 This section draws extensively on D Guilfoyle, 'The *Mavi Marmara* Incident and Naval Blockade in Armed Conflict' (2010) 81 *British Yearbook of International Law* 171.

9 FFM Report, above n 2, para 112.

10 Ibid, para 67.

11 UNSC Verbatim Record (31 May 2010) UN Doc S/PV.6325, 2.

12 Ibid.

When two efforts at boarding the *Mavi Marmara* by boat failed due to resistance from those aboard, a helicopter was used.[13]

While the precise facts are contested, it would appear that the IDF inserted soldiers one at a time by a single fast rope from helicopter onto the *Mavi Marmara* upper deck, where they met resistance from approximately 15 protestors and encountered an increasingly volatile situation.[14] The aim of such a boarding is usually to place a sufficient number of troops on deck sufficiently quickly to assert and maintain immediate control. Several of the first few soldiers inserted were instead captured by protestors and appear to have been injured.

Within minutes, two groups of soldiers had been deployed by helicopter and assembled on the ship's roof before descending to take control of the vessel.[15] Subsequent live fire used by the IDF killed nine civilians and left many others wounded. Both sides have publicly claimed they acted in self-defence after first being attacked by the other. Despite some claims to the contrary, the IDF soldiers in the boarding party were armed only with riot control weapons and personal protection sidearms in the form of 9 mm pistols (the calibre of the latter is significant in that the lower exit velocity of such bullets makes them less lethal).[16] IDF claims that they were met immediately with active and violent resistance on boarding the *Mavi Marmara* have eyewitness support.[17]

The Turkish autopsy reports on the nine protestors killed concluded 'five of the victims were shot either in the back of the head or in the back'.[18] These reports and other medical records were examined by an independent pathology expert retained by the UN Human Rights Council inquiry into the incident (discussed in what follows), who concluded in respect of several of the killings that persons were fatally shot in the head at point-blank range or from above and at a distance; in some cases, the injuries are consistent with the deceased having already been shot once and then being shot again in the head once already prone on the deck.[19] The IDF conducted an internal inquiry into the incident and each fatality. While the results of that inquiry were not made public, it suggested such force would only be used in self-defence (for example, if a protestor was bending over a fallen soldier to attack with an iron bar or axe).[20]

13 'Videos [and] Timeline of Flotilla Incident as Presented by Eiland Team of Experts', Israel Defense Forces Blog, 15 July 2010, <http://idfspokesperson.com/2010/07/15/videos-timeline-offlotilla-incident-as-presented-by-eiland-team-of-experts-english-version-13-july-2010/>.

14 Sabrina Tavernise and Ethan Bronner, 'Days of Planning Led to Flotilla's Hour of Chaos', *New York Times* (4 June 2010), <www.nytimes.com/2010/06/05/world/europe/05reconstruct.html?pagewanted=all>

15 Israel Defense Forces, 'Videos [and] Timeline of Flotilla Incident', above n 13.

16 FFM Report, above n 2, paras 112–118.

17 Tavernise and Bronner, 'Days of Planning', above n 14.

18 R Booth, 'Gaza flotilla activists were shot in head at close range' *The Guardian* (London 4 June 2010) <www.guardian.co.uk/world/2010/jun/04/gaza-flotilla-activists-autopsy-results>.

19 FFM Report, above n 2, table at 30–31.

20 'Israel Navy probe of Gaza flotilla raid finds "planning and intel flaws"', *Haaretz* (Tel Aviv 20 June 2010), <www.haaretz.com/news/diplomacy-defense/israel-navy-probe-of-gaza-flotillaraid-finds-planning-and-intel-flaws-1.297216>.

The *Mavi Marmara*, once captured, was diverted to Ashdod, where those aboard were detained incommunicado and denied consular access.[21] The civilian deaths sparked an angry response, with Turkish official statements describing the interception as a 'gross violation of international law'.[22]

III. The processes of inquiry

No national or international court has had the opportunity to rule authoritatively on the legality of (or law applicable to) the *Mavi Marmara* incident. Instead, there have been a series of national and international enquiries into the incident, namely:

- the report of the fact-finding mission established by the Human Rights Council released on 27 September 2010;
- the first report of the 'Israeli Public Commission to Examine the Maritime Incident of 31 May 2010' (commonly known as the 'Turkel Commission' after its chairman) published on 23 January 2011;
- the Turkish National Commission of Inquiry Report of 11 February 2011;
- the report of the UN Secretary-General's 'Panel of Inquiry on the 31 May 2010 Flotilla Incident' (often called the 'Palmer Report' after its chairman), convened to assess the two national reports, published in July 2011;[23] and, most recently,
- the report of the Office of the Prosecutor (OTP) of the International Criminal Court of 6 November 2014, outlining the OTP's assessment as to whether the incident warranted investigation by the Court.

Each of these inquiries have been subjected to varying degrees of criticism and often reach different views regarding questions of both fact and applicable law. The origins and methodology of each will be briefly treated here, before the relevant legal questions are discussed in the next section.

The UN Human Rights Council voted on 23 June 2010 'to dispatch an independent international fact-finding mission [FFM] to investigate violations of international law, including international humanitarian law and human rights law, resulting from the Israeli attacks on the flotilla of ships carrying humanitarian

21 P McGeough, 'There was a lot of blood in the stairwells and then the sound of ammunition hitting metal changed again', *Sydney Morning Herald* (5 June 2010), <www.smh.com.au/world/there-was-a-lot-of-blood-in-the-stairwells-and-then-the-sound-of-ammunition-hitting-metal-changed-again-20100604-xknm.html>.

22 Ministry of Foreign Affairs (Turkey) 'Press Release Regarding the Use of Force by the Israeli Defense Forces Against the Humanitarian Aid Flotilla to Gaza' (31 May 2010), <www.mfa.gov.tr/no_-115_-31-may-2010_ – press-release-regarding-the – use-of-force-by-the-israeli-defenseforces-against-the-humanitarian-aid-fleet-to-gaza.en.mfa>.

23 Report of the Secretary-General's Panel of Inquiry on the 31 May 2010 Flotilla Incident (September 2011) <www.un.org/unispal/document/auto-insert-205969/> ('Palmer Report').

assistance'.[24] The FFM itself noted that this language suggested pre-judgement of the occurrence of 'violations' and 'attacks', but considered its task to be one of independently investigating the facts and concluding whether the applicable law had been violated.[25] The FFM, appointed on 23 July 2010, consisted of three members: it was chaired by Judge Karl T. Hudson-Phillips, QC (a retired judge of the International Criminal Court and former Attorney General of Trinidad and Tobago) and also included Sir Desmond de Silva QC (a UK national and former Chief Prosecutor of the Special Court for Sierra Leone) and Ms Mary Shanthi Dairiam (a Malaysian national and former member of the Committee on the Elimination of Discrimination against Women and a human rights advocate). Their report was based on more than 100 interviews with flotilla members and passengers aboard the *Mavi Marmara*, an inspection of the vessel itself, and the report of an independent pathologist who examined the bodies of those passengers killed. It had no access to Israeli officials but was able to rely on transcripts of evidence being given at the time before the Turkel Commission. It found the blockade to be illegal by reason of being part of a collective punishment of the population of Gaza and considered that Israel committed numerous breaches of the Fourth Geneva Convention and international human rights in its conduct of the interception and subsequent treatment of the detained protestors. While it conducted a surprisingly thorough fact-finding exercise in only two months, the FFM Report has been criticised for the brevity of its legal reasoning and assumptions on often complex and contested issues.[26] Equally, the brevity (or lack) of supporting reasoning by the FFM for contentious conclusions such as 'The Mission considers that one of the principal motives behind the imposition of the blockade was a desire to punish the people of the Gaza Strip for having elected Hamas'[27] does not lend the report an impartial tone. Such flaws have been seen as undermining the credibility of its fact-finding.[28] Less fair is criticism directed at the report on the basis that it originated in the Human Rights Council, a body with a noted history of criticism of (or even hostility towards) Israel. This significantly underestimates the independence of the FFM members and their working methods.[29] The FFM Report undeniably contains the most precise account of the injuries sustained by the nine dead protestors, including the credible finding of an independent pathologist that several protestors were shot from above or in the back, in some cases when already on the deck.[30]

24 UN Doc A/HRC/RES/14/1 (23 June 2010), para 8.

25 FFM Report, above n2, paras 4–5 and 272.

26 Yuval Shany, 'Know Your Rights! The Flotilla Report and International Law Governing Naval Blockades', *EJIL: Talk!*, 12 October 2010 <www.ejiltalk.org/know-your-rightsthe-flotilla-report-and-international-law-governing-naval-blockades/>.

27 FFM Report, above n 2, para 54.

28 Shany, 'Know Your Rights!', above n 26.

29 Anyone sufficiently eminent to be appointed to such a body, particularly if they are a QC, is likely to have a fairly healthy ego and a professional reputation to maintain.

30 See FFM Report, above n 2, table at 29–30.

The Turkel Commission was chaired by Justice Jacob Turkel (a retired judge of the Israeli Supreme Court) and included four other members with legal, diplomatic, or military backgrounds (one of whom was the late Shabtai Rosenne). It also included two international observers (from the UK and Canada). Its mandate was, in part, to evaluate whether the maritime closure of the Gaza Strip and the measures taken to enforce it on 31 May 2010 were 'compatible with international law' and to assess 'the actions undertaken by the organizers of the flotilla and those who participated in it and their identities'.[31] While flotilla participants were invited to appear before the Commission, none did, restricting its pool of witnesses to Israeli officials. The Turkel Commission report is comprehensive, especially on questions of law, and it certainly 'attempts to adopt an objective tone'.[32] Nonetheless, it notably concludes that the blockade was legal and that the interception was, at least in large part, legally conducted.

The Turkish National Commission of Inquiry was prepared by (unnamed) senior officials from a number of government departments including the Office of the Prime Minister and the Ministry of Foreign Affairs. It has, regrettably, the most tendentious tone of any of the relevant reports. It concludes the blockade was entirely unlawful and that the Israeli interception of the *Mavi Marmara* was both unlawful per se and involved excessive force.

The four-person UN Secretary-General's Panel of Inquiry was probably the most palpably balanced body set up to inquire into the incident, in that it included both Israeli and Turkish members and two independent members: Sir Geoffrey Palmer QC (its chair), a lawyer and former Prime Minister of New Zealand, and Alvaro Uribe (its vice-chair), a lawyer and former President of Colombia. Its report was, however, complicated by two factors. The first is the dissent of the Turkish member from the final report and the partial dissent of the Israeli member. The main report is thus the work of the chair and vice-chair. Second, it had only a limited mandate to enquire into the facts and make recommendations to avoid similar future incidents. Despite having no mandate to review questions of law, it nonetheless appended an annex (authored by the chair and vice-chair) discussing the applicable law, and the body of the report is replete with legal analysis and conclusions of law. Overall, the report expressly found the Israeli blockade of Gaza to be legal and a 'legitimate security measure' but condemned Israel's use of force in boarding the *Mavi Marmara* as 'excessive and unreasonable' and the deaths of civilians which followed as 'unacceptable' and lacking any 'satisfactory explanation'.[33]

31 E Sanders, 'Israelis are conflicted about probe', *Los Angeles Times* (15 June 2010) 3; J Ferziger and A Odenheimer, 'Israel Adds Two Members to Inquiry into Gaza Flotilla', *Businessweek* (25 July 2010) <www.businessweek.com/news/2010-07-25/israel-adds-two-members-to-inquiry-intogaza-flotilla.html>.

32 James Farrant, 'The Gaza Flotilla Incident and the Modern Law of Blockade' (2013) 66 *Naval War College Review* 81–82.

33 Palmer Report, above n 23, p. 4.

It further found that there was 'significant mistreatment' of detained passengers.[34] On the other hand, it considered the conduct of the flotilla 'reckless' and carrying a needless risk of escalation.[35] While the report found that the majority of the protestors had only peaceful intentions, some nonetheless engaged in 'significant, organised and violent resistance' to the Israeli boarding.[36] It also found that serious questions remained regarding the true intentions of some of the flotilla organisers.

Finally, the report of the OTP of the International Criminal Court concluded that although there was a *prima facie* case that war crimes had been committed, and while it had jurisdiction over events occurring aboard the flagged vessel of a member state (Cormoros), these events were not of themselves of sufficient gravity to warrant further investigation by the Court.[37]

In the view of this author, the Turkel Report and the Palmer Report are the most useful to scholars in terms of the breadth of issues considered and the quality of their legal analysis. (Though I note I have reservations about aspects of the reasoning in both.)

IV. Analysis and outcomes

Broadly speaking, each of these reports had a number of significant common issues to address (with perhaps the exception of the OTP Report which had a more limited set of questions to address under the ICC Statute.) These included:

1 whether the doctrine of blockade remains available in the 21st century;
2 presuming it does, whether is it applicable only in international armed conflicts (IAC) or also non-international armed conflicts (NIAC);[38]
3 if blockade is only available in an IAC, whether the conflict between Israel and Hamas is an IAC and if so on what reasoned legal basis;
4 presuming blockade to be available, whether the present blockade was unlawful on grounds that it inflicted disproportionate civilian damage (and how was such damage to be assessed); and

34 Ibid, p. 23, para. 40.
35 Ibid, p. 48, para. 95.
36 Ibid, p. 57, para. 124.
37 Office of the Prosecutor (International Criminal Court), 'Situation on Registered Vessels of Comoros, Greece and Cambodia: Article 53(1) Report', 6 November 2014. On the torturous procedural history of efforts to compel the OTP to open a formal investigation: Jeremie Bracka, 'Third Time Lucky? ICC Appeals Chamber Directs Prosecutor to Consider Mavi Marmara Incident for a Third Time', *Opinio Juris*, 29 October 2019, <http://opiniojuris.org/2019/10/29/third-time-lucky-icc-appeals-chamber-directs-prosecutor-to-consider-mavi-marmara-incident-for-a-third-time/>.
38 On the controversy see: Wolff Heintschel von Heinegg, 'Blockades and Interdictions' in Marc Weller (ed) *The Oxford Handbook of the Use of Force in International Law* (Oxford University Press, 2015), 930–933; Andrew Clapham, 'Booty, Bounty, Blockade, and Prize: Time to Reevaluate the Law' (2021) *97 International Law Studies* 1200, 1241–1243; and Martin Fink, 'Naval Blockade and the Humanitarian Crisis in Yemen' (2017) 64 *Netherlands International Law Review* 291, 296–297.

5 what the applicable legal standards were governing the boarding of *Mavi Marmara* and the subsequent treatment of those detained, including questions of human rights.

These are complex issues which can only be treated briefly here. However, all the inquiry processes appeared to start from the proposition that blockade is an available tool of naval warfare and that the *San Remo Manual* contains – broadly – an authoritative and widely accepted codification of the law applicable in an IAC.

More contentious were the second and third questions: whether blockade is available in a NIAC and whether the conflict between Israel and Hamas can be qualified as such. Most of the reports, in effect, dodged this question by concluding that the relevant conflict was an IAC. For example:

- the FFM Report concluded that Israel remains in occupation of the Gaza Strip (despite its withdrawal of military forces from the territory) by virtue of its significant control over conditions within the Gaza Strip and its capacity to project force there. On the basis that occupation is part of the law of IAC, it concluded that IAC was the governing law of the conflict (the 'occupation thesis');
- the Turkel Report found the law of IAC applicable (at least in part) on the basis that the conflict crossed the borders of Israel and therefore had a necessarily international character (the 'transboundary thesis');
- the Palmer Report concluded that the conflict bore 'all the trappings of an international armed conflict' on the basis that one must not let legal debate 'obscure the realities' that the armed violence involved 'goes beyond purely domestic matters.'[39] This seems, at best, to be a variant on the transboundary thesis (at worst, it is an assertion that an *a priori* political characterisation of the facts should determine the applicable law).

All of these approaches have been criticised on the basis that the essence of an international armed conflict is that it is one between states and, in contradistinction, a non-international armed conflict is one between a state and a non-state armed group (or between such groups) where a threshold of 'protracted armed violence' is crossed.[40] On this approach, the occupation thesis and the transboundary thesis simply miss the point. Of course, matters are not quite so neat. The generally accepted definition of a NIAC found in Additional Protocol II to the Geneva Conventions requires inter alia that such a conflict 'take place in the territory of a High Contracting Party'.[41] This necessarily suggests that the

39 Palmer Report, above n 23, p. 41, para. 73.

40 See generally: Guilfoyle, '*Mavi Marmara*', above n 8, 185–188; *Hamdan v Rumsfeld*, 548 US 557, 630 (2006).

41 Protocol Additional to the Geneva Conventions of 12 August 1949, and relating to the Protection of Victims of Non-International Armed Conflicts (Protocol II), 8 June 1977, 1125 UNTS 609.

transboundary thesis may be correct; although equally one could suggest that the provision does not expressly require the conflict occur in the Contracting Party's *own* territory.[42]

In any event, all the international inquiries concluded the relevant conflict was an IAC and thus strictly did not need to address the availability of blockade in a NIAC. Nonetheless, the Turkel Commission and the Palmer report both touched on the issue and suggested that the use of blockade in NIACs is lawful. Supporting state practice is hard to come by, however, with most arguments that blockade is available in a NIAC having to rely largely on the U.S. Prize Cases (which were founded on the 19th-century doctrine of recognition of belligerency) and also having to explain away the general assertion by states during the Spanish Civil War that blockade was unlawful in a NIAC.[43] The best evidence that blockade might be available (or at least tolerated) in a NIAC is the Israeli blockade of Lebanon during its conflict with Hezbollah in 2006 which went generally unprotested. (Of course, if one accepts the transboundary thesis, then this was an IAC and is not relevant evidence as to the law applicable in NIACs).

The more difficult question was whether the blockade was unlawful for causing disproportionate civilian damage. Of course, such damage must be judged against legitimate military objectives. In 2009, there were 692 rocket attacks against Israel, killing approximately six people and wounding hundreds of others.[44] Preventing rockets and weapons systems from entering the Gaza Strip was clearly an important and legitimate military objective.[45] However, there is no doubt that the closure regime imposed by Israel against the Gaza Strip and especially its limitations upon food supplies has caused – and was causing in early 2010 – acute civilian distress. Indeed, so bad were conditions on the ground that the International Committee of the Red Cross and Red Crescent set aside its usual policy of strict neutrality to denounce the closure regime as a form of collective punishment.[46] However, by far the greatest humanitarian impact was caused by the closure of land crossings for the simple reason that Gaza had no functioning deep-water port. In this context, each report had to make a choice: the legality of the closure regime could be judged as a whole, including the maritime blockade as a component which would stand or fall with the rest; or one could assess the maritime blockade in isolation and judge it on the basis only of any civilian damage directly attributable to it. Two views were generally taken in the reports and the literature:

42 Noam Lubell, Extraterritorial Use of Force against Non-State Actors (OUP, Oxford 2010), 102.

43 Guilfoyle, '*Mavi Marmara*', above n 8, 192–193.

44 Ibid, 188–189.

45 Eyal Benvenisti, 'The International Law of Prolonged Sieges and Blockades: Gaza as a Case Study' (2021) 97 *International Law Studies* 969–983.

46 International Committee of the Red Cross, 'Gaza closure: not another year!' (News release 10 June 2010), <www.icrc.org/web/eng/siteeng0.nsf/htmlall/palestine-update-140610>.

- as the maritime blockade functioned to perfect the goals of the land blockade (the denial of arms to Hamas), the two were linked at the tactical level and therefore were to be judged together; or
- the maritime blockade was sufficiently distinct from the land border closures to be judged separately.

The overwhelming consensus of the reports and literature was that the closure regime constituted an integral whole. It is especially noteworthy that this was the view taken by the Turkel Commission, which concluded that the blockade did not exist 'in a vacuum', but was linked to the land border crossing policy at both strategic and tactical levels.[47] On this line of analysis, if the civilian damage inflicted by the regime as a whole was disproportionate, then the blockade was also illegal as a component part of that regime. Once this methodological step is taken, a conclusion of illegality by reason of disproportionate damage would seem inevitable. The Turkel Commission concluded otherwise on the wholly unconvincing basis that while 61% of households in Gaza might be food insecure,[48] food insecurity does not by itself mean there was not enough food in the Gaza Strip – but rather that there was 'an inability of the population to purchase this food'.[49] The argument falls somewhere between tendentiously legalistic and callous. On any overall assessment, most commentators have concluded that reducing a population to a subsistence diet and crippling its economy through a protracted siege is neither a necessary nor proportionate response to rocket attacks.[50] While those attacks are clearly despicable and criminal, by the standards of armed conflict, they have proven themselves vastly more effective as a means of inflicting terror rather than widespread civilian or military casualties. Further, Drew has put a coherent argument that blockade as it presently exists in customary international law will, in its application, almost invariably violate the modern IHL principle of distinction as it is an inherently 'indiscriminate method of warfare'.[51]

The Palmer Report, in judging the blockade as a separate measure to the general closure regime, concluded its additional impact on the humanitarian situation was 'slight'. It therefore found it not to be disproportionate. It held the naval blockade to be a separate measure because: (a) it was imposed later in time; (b) while the intensity of border controls between Israel and the Gaza Strip have fluctuated over time the naval blockade has remained absolute; and (c) the blockade targeted only the importation of weapons and related goods.[52] The tactical/strategic con-

47 Turkel Commission Report, above n 5, para 63.

48 UN Food and Agriculture Organization, 'Consolidated Appeals 2010: West Bank and Gaza Strip' (2010), <www.fao.org/emergencies/tce-appfund/tce-appeals/consolidated-appeals-2010/wbgs10/en/4> (defining food insecurity as: 'secure access to sufficient amounts of safe and nutritious food for normal growth and development and an active and healthy life').

49 Turkel Commission Report, above n 5, para 76.

50 For example, Benevenisti, 'The International Law of Prolonged Sieges and Blockades', above n 45, 984.

51 Philip Drew, *The Law of Maritime Blockade: Past, Present, and Future* (Oxford University Press, 2017), 2 and Chapter 7.

52 Palmer Report, above n 23, Annex I, para. 70.

cerns addressed by the Turkel Commission did not feature in the Palmer Report's analysis.

A final complexity was introduced by the question of what were the applicable legal standards in the conduct of the boarding, and once the vessel was under effective Israeli control. Generally, this has been treated in the reports and literature as two separate questions. The topic inevitably introduces the debate over the relationship between the law of armed conflict (LOAC) and the law of human rights. Briefly put, the commonly accepted view is now that during an armed conflict, LOAC does not automatically displace human rights as *lex specialis*, rather:

> some rights may be exclusively matters of international humanitarian law; others may be exclusively matters of human rights law; yet others may be matters of both these branches of international law.[53]

In that third case, international humanitarian law and human rights law may be mutually informing or fall to be reconciled through systemic interpretation. The obvious example is that where international humanitarian law gives rise to a right to detain an individual, then human rights law may inform the conditions under which detention should occur.[54] It is unsurprising that, by analogy, it was found by all reports that a 'policing' paradigm applied to the boarding and 'capture' of the *Mavi Marmara*, an act permitted under LOAC when a vessel attempts to run a blockade.[55] That is, general international law requires when boarding a ship at sea in a 'policing' action:

> that the use of force must be avoided as far as possible and, where . . . unavoidable, it must not go beyond what is reasonable and necessary in the circumstances. Considerations of humanity must apply . . . . It is only after the appropriate actions fail that the pursuing may, as a last resort, use force . . . . Even then . . . all efforts should be made to ensure that life is not endangered.[56]

Generally, where force is used, it should be used in a series of escalating steps.[57] This approach was not found to have been applied by Israeli forces aboard the *Mavi Marmara*. The Palmer and Turkel reports concurred that the operation was poorly planned, and – at a minimum – clearer warnings and 'more controlled and isolated use of force' could have prevented escalation and when resistance was encountered

53 *Legal Consequences of the Construction of a Wall in the Occupied Palestinian Territories*, Advisory Opinion [2004] ICJ Rep 136, para 106.

54 Palmer Report, above n 23, Annex I, para 63.

55 Turkel Commission Report, above n 5, para. 179 and see also para. 135.

56 *M/V Saiga (No. 2)* (Saint Vincent and the Grenadines v. Guinea) ITLOS Case No 2, para 155 see Chapter 11.

57 Compare Turkel Commission Report, above n 5, paras. 178–179 and the useful formulation at para. 189.

withdrawal and reassessment would have been appropriate.[58] The overwhelming international reaction was that the operation had clearly involved excessive and unreasonable force and unacceptable civilian deaths.[59]

This, however, does not exhaust the potentially applicable law. Three other sets of rules may apply:

- first, those individual Israeli soldiers who were attacked by protestors would retain the right of self-defence (including defence of others);
- second, if the *Mavi Marmara* as a whole could be considered to be 'clearly resisting capture', it would render itself a legitimate military target capable of being directly attacked;[60] and
- third, if individual protestors became direct participants in hostilities, they could be targeted with lethal force as unlawful combatants.

The law permitting the reasonable use of force in individual self-defence will not be further discussed here. The reports are divided as to whether the *Mavi Marmara* became a lawful object of attack, but even if it did, such action remains subject to the duty to 'take all feasible precautions . . . to avoid or minimize collateral [civilian] casualties or damage'.[61] Unilaterally sinking a vessel carrying hundreds of protestors would clearly remain unlawful. Finally, while it is possible that some of the violent protestors supported Hamas, the test for when a civilian becomes a direct participant in hostilities under the ICRC guidance requires: first, that a 'threshold of harm' must be crossed, such as an act threatening death or injury; second, that a causal link must exist between the civilian's act and that harm; and third, that the act must be done 'in support of a party to the conflict' (belligerent nexus).[62] However, in the context of boarding a vessel at sea far from the theatre of conflict, it may be difficult to conclude at the time that a protestor violently resisting a boarding party is necessarily doing so to support a party to a conflict.[63] In cases of doubt, the person must be treated as a civilian immune from direct targeting under the laws of war (though such a person could still have force used against them in self-defence or under the 'policing paradigm'.)

Returning to the core human rights question: once the vessel was 'captured' and under Israeli control, what standards applied? The FFM Report applied, almost exclusively, human rights law. The Turkel Report applied, almost exclusively,

58 Palmer Report, above n 23, pp. 53–54, paras 113–116; and Turkel Commission Report, above n 5, p 273.

59 Palmer Report, above n 23, p. 4.

60 Louise Doswald-Beck (ed), *San Remo Manual on International Law Applicable to Armed Conflicts at Sea*, (IIHL/Cambridge, 1995), para 98.

61 Ibid, para 46(c).

62 Nils Melzer, *Interpretative Guidance on the Notion of Direct Participation in Hostilities under International Humanitarian Law* (International Committee of the Red Cross, Geneva, 2009), 46.

63 Ex post facto the Turkel Commission had no difficulty concluding some protestors were direct participants in hostilities: Turkel Commission Report, above n 5, paras 196–198.

international humanitarian law. The better approach, it is submitted, is that of the Palmer Report. It suggested, by reference to decisions of various human rights committees and the European Court of Human Rights case *Medvedyev v France*, that once state forces have taken effective control of an interdicted vessel, their human rights obligations will, in principle, apply aboard the vessel.[64] This is undeniably the current trend in human rights jurisprudence and can now be treated as well-established law under the European Convention on Human Rights at the least.[65] In any event, certain core standards would apply under either international humanitarian law or human rights law including but not limited to: the prohibitions on murder, torture, and humiliating or degrading treatment, as well as the requirement of according detained persons certain due process rights.[66] The Palmer Report considered there was consistent and credible evidence from witnesses of significant mistreatment of detained persons after the *Mavi Marmara* was captured, including physical assaults and humiliating treatment.[67]

IV. Significance

Of great significance for the law of naval operations is that several national and international inquiries have concluded that the law of blockade is available in modern IACs and each commenced from the proposition that the *San Remo Manual* contains the most authoritative attempted codification of the applicable law. The position in non-international armed conflicts is less certain. The 20th-century state practice is at best equivocal (with the general denial of blockade in the Spanish Civil War being the hardest episode to ignore), and the relevant 21st-century practice is limited to the general absence of protest when Israel blockaded Lebanon in the course of its conflict with Hezbollah in 2006.

There also appears to be a general consensus that, going beyond the ordinary principles of distinction and proportionality, a policing paradigm applies to the use of force in any operation to capture a blockade-running vessel. There would also appear to be a strong trend in the jurisprudence – given that human rights law and international humanitarian law are not inherently incompatible – suggesting human rights standards will be found to apply aboard a captured vessel once it is under the control of boarding forces. Practically, when planning such a boarding or capture operation to enforce a blockade, it will therefore be necessary to use force in an escalatory fashion and – should conditions permit – to withdraw and reassess the options if a boarding is resisted. While a civilian vessel resisting capture

64 Ibid, Annex I, paras 66–69.

65 See *Hirsi Jamaa and Others v Italy* App no 27765/09 (ECtHR 23 February 2012), applying much the same principle to maritime migrant rescue/interdiction operations. For further discussion, see: Benvenisti, 'The International Law of Prolonged Sieges and Blockades', above n 45, 986–989.

66 Palmer Report, above n 23, Legal Annex, para 65. Farrant, 'The Gaza Flotilla Incident and the Modern Law of Blockade', above n 32, 93.

67 Palmer Report, above n 23, pp. 62–66, para 138–144.

obviously becomes a military target open to attack, the principle of proportionality remains applicable and the consequence may be that only limited force can be justified in any event. Finally, from an operational standpoint, it should always be borne in mind that enforcement of a blockade will almost inevitably affect neutrals – with attendant political consequences – should anything go wrong. The response to the *Mavi Marmara* incident also strongly suggests that civilian deaths aboard a neutral vessel may attract significant international attention, condemnation, and enquiry.

INDEX

Note: page numbers followed by 'n' indicate a note on the corresponding page.